# VALUES FOR SURVIVAL

*BOOKS BY LEWIS MUMFORD*

To my dear son

GEDDES

*Long before his work was done*
*He was the father, I the son.*

Geddes Mumford was born in Brooklyn, New York, on
5 July 1925. He served in the United States Army as
Private First Class, and became First Scout, Second
Platoon, Company L, 363 Infantry, 91 Division. In
the opening drive on the Gothic line in Italy he was
killed while making contact with the enemy on night
patrol. He died alone, on Mount Altuzzo, probably on
13 September 1944.

*This book consists of variations on a single theme: What must modern man do to be saved? While these papers were written separately without any thought of ultimate publication, the germ of the book itself was planted in a letter that came from my son before he went into combat. From Africa he wrote:*

*"While I think of it, I might mention the subject of the overseas soldier's reaction to the war. . . . Our existence depends upon our being hard and tough in every phase of our life and therefore we are. However, we were not raised to that type of life and we are inclined to seek relief in thoughts of home. As far as I can see, it's a reaction to a life which, by its definition, is too narrow to permit reasoning on the forces which so vitally affect it. I seriously doubt that anything can be done about this situation while the war is still in progress. Battle leaves little time for thought and if the subject were broached now the soldier would only make an incomplete survey of the case. He would probably think only 'Why should I fight?' and go no further. To my knowledge it will have to wait until after the war. Then, with further education, the returned soldier will be able to look back and see 'why he fought.' It will be up to the people who did not go, to give this education and they will have to approach the subject in a completely objective manner to succeed. . . . The completion of this task, not the peace treaties and the pacts concerning government, will really end the war."*

*I promised my son to compose a book that would, if possible, aid in this task; and I hope that the present volume will serve that purpose, not merely making the past more intelligible, but casting a wide cone of light over the future. This future is doubtless a different one from that which the smug and the unawakened comfortably look forward to; but I trust my words will make sense to the returned fighting man, and to all those civilians in every land who have in any way shared his privations, his miseries, his dangers, or his sacrifices. If mankind survives the present catastrophe, it will be because the war itself has summoned up the deepest reserves of our nature and has put them to work. Unconditional surrender will be a mocking symbol of victory unless it leads to the unconditional redemption of man: the victor no less than the vanquished.*—L. M.

# CONTENTS

BOOK ONE:

# ESSAYS ON POLITICS

I prefer liberty with danger
to peace with slavery.
JEAN-JACQUES ROUSSEAU

. . . Where danger lies
Salvation also grows.
FRIEDRICH HÖLDERLIN

# CALL TO ARMS

[This appeal was first published in The New Republic for 18 May 1938: it was written four months before the appeasement at Munich. Since the only importance of this essay now is as historic record, I have made no attempt to expunge its errors and misjudgments. Perhaps the most serious error was that of accepting the current judgment of the effect of the Treaty of Versailles upon Germany; but needless to say it was not for this reason that my plea for action remained unanswered. Because of editorial restrictions, my original article appeared in a shorter and less adequate version. In reprinting it, I have taken the liberty to restore the omitted pages, which are indicated by brackets.]

## 1. THE DANGER OF OPTIMISM

An atmosphere of foggy unreality hangs over current discussions of peace. Most of the proposals to keep war from coming to America are noble and high-minded and humane; but they have one serious defect: the world on which they are based no longer exists. The proposals are dated 1938; but the premises remain those of 1928.

This failure to keep up with events may prove almost as fatal as the events themselves. For we are now confronted with a worldwide political phenomenon, fascism, whose deeply malignant character and cancerous spread have changed every problem of civilized political existence. Peace-loving people are still trying to make themselves believe that fascism is not what it seems and that fascists do not mean to do the things they actually do. Such people even hope, by some show of affability, by some economic bribe, to transform the very nature of the evil that threatens to engulf us all. Surely, these people say to themselves, turning away from the latest fascist barbarity in the morning paper, the world cannot be so bad as that; or if it is for the moment, it cannot long remain so.

But the world *is* as bad as that: what is more, the skies threaten to become much blacker before the clouds lift again. Those who persist in closing their eyes to the vicious forces that are now deliberately attacking our civilization are the victims of unprofitable hopes and palsied wishes. Hating war, they are preparing themselves and their countrymen to endure something far more hideous than war: the "peace" perpetrated by fascism. I accuse my colleagues and friends on The New Republic of maintaining this state of wishful apathy. In the very last paragraph of its supplement on National Defense, The New Republic dared dismiss the threat of fascism and assure the reader that it cannot long "seriously menace the world."

Those words might indeed have been pardonable ten years ago: today they indicate self-deception or misjudgment of the gravest kind. Such optimism, such reckless optimism, is far more appalling when it comes from the mouths of the editors of an important liberal weekly than is the most strident war-mongering by professional militarists. And to my mind, The New Republic's attitude carries with it greater danger, for the ultimate treason of the intellectual is to place his credulous wishes above fact and truth, merely because the facts are repugnant, or because the situation they point to cannot be changed without heroic exertion. To be prepared to deal with fascism, it is better to overestimate the extent of our military needs than to underestimate the political necessity of having to fight.

## 2. THE POTENCY OF THE PATHOLOGICAL

The most serious mistake a civilized man can make today is to assume that the fundamental values of life have not been altered in the fascist countries. Yet large groups of people still refuse to believe that nations which use the electric motor and the radio can, by a purely ideological transformation, become inimical to the larger scheme of our society. Too thinly rational to understand the nature of irrationality, our advocates of "co-operation" hope to bring the fascist states back into the normal channels of human intercourse. As Reinhold Niebuhr has well put it, such minds are incredulous of the existence of radical evil: they imagine that they are dealing with differences of degree. But they are wrong: they are dealing with a difference in kind. Fascism is a codified and co-ordinated barbarism. To the extent that fascism has become self-conscious, in both Italy and Germany, it has systematized its delusions, erected its perversities into a standard of values and set up a series of barbarian alternatives to the ideals of our civilization: ideals first expressed in Judea and Greece, widened for mankind by Christianity and reinforced through large drafts upon other civilizations by the spirit of humanistic science.

The mission of fascism, of which its leaders openly boast, is not to fulfill the promise of the modern world but to destroy it. Those who hope to find some common ground with fascism through a policy of "appeasement" or who would ward off the terrors of war by a policy of meek passivity and fearful isolation do not reckon with the strength of the irrational forces they have to face. Fascism's victories have not been based upon the superiority of fascist arms or military leadership—both are extremely doubtful: the fascist principle is to bully and blackmail the indecisive, to fight only the weak, and to conquer with exemplary savagery the helpless. Its strength lies in its capacity for demoralization.

To seek to get along with fascism on the democratic principle of live and let live is to open the way for a more complete fascist conquest. Whatever strength fascism has lies precisely in its pathological condition: its predisposition to suspicion and hatred, its violent paranoia, its readiness to exalt the maimed ego through collective sadism and murder. Every form of dishonesty, torture, and violence is justified by the fascist if it promotes the advantage of the state; every form has already been used by the German Nazis and the Italian Fascists and the Japanese militarists. The bestial torture of political victims in concentration camps, the piratical sinking of defenseless cargo boats, the pitiless bombing and strafing of innocent civilians are merely the objective symbols of this philosophy of government. It is not a new philosophy: what is new to the modern world is that it is now unchallenged and unchecked.

These collective pathologies of course have their long history in the nations they afflict: that in Germany goes back centuries before the Treaty of Versailles—at least as far as the Thirty Years' War—and Borgese has shown in "Goliath" that the roots of Italian fascism are even older. But when an unbalanced person threatens immediate physical violence, it is more pressing to put him under control than to understand his symptoms. If we are to do justice to the Japanese, the Italians and the Germans, we must first rob the fascist governments of their immediate capacity to work incurable mischief. Unlike democratic polities, fascist states have no place for moral correctives within their system: their barbarism is unchallengeable, their pathology is now incurable from within. What a large proportion of Italians and Germans may still think or feel in their private capacities no longer counts; they have no means of expression; within a generation most of the values they embody will have been extirpated by the school and the military camp.

## 3. THE THREAT TO FASCISM

[Fascism indeed faces a serious threat from within. It is continually threatened by the humanness of humanity. It is threatened by the tendency of normal men and women to temper their newly acquired barbarism by ancient sentiments of pity and generosity; by their tendency to modify irrationality by common sense, by respect for truth, by the acceptance of objective testimony and rational thought. Fascism is threatened further by the tendency to modify absolute claims to despotic authority by the simple co-operation of men working intimately in groups, in the factory, the office, the household, the neighborhood, the city; finally, it is insidiously undermined by the underlying irreverent sense of humor with which lowly humanity revenges itself upon the pretensions of the great and powerful. Ignazio Silone, in his superb Fontamara stories, has pictured these latent human tendencies. But left to themselves, these reactions are all innocuous. Fascism knows how to combat them. When propaganda is insufficient, the concentration camp finishes the job.

Being on the defensive against the normal manifestations of humanity and the normal give-and-take processes of civilization, fascism meets the forces that threaten it in two ways. Internally, it erects a wall around its own country: seeking economic self-sufficiency in times of war, it imposes restrictions upon the peacetime inter-regional exchanges of surpluses, which would weaken this autarchic economy. It limits the movements of its subjects; it seals their mouths; it stops up their ears; it halts those processes of communication and intercourse that are the very life-blood of civilization. Externally, to guard against the insidious example of freedom and democracy, fascism wages a pitiless campaign against non-fascist states: it seizes every opportunity to disorganize the political life of democratic countries, to menace their external security, to encourage those groups in the country that seek to imitate fascism: it takes advantage of the very opportunities for discussion and free initiative that democracy offers to undermine democracy.

Plainly, fascism cannot afford to risk the challenge of democracy. For its own security, it must now widen the base of fascism and attack, piecemeal if possible, the more rational and humane system of life that still prevails in countries that have not submitted to the totalitarian yoke. This barbarism is not passive: it is militant: its first purpose is the systematic extermination of democracy. The present success of fascism in carrying through this policy, not merely within Germany and Italy, but in neighboring countries, radically changes the nature of the problem that confronts the American people. There is now no conceivable limit to fascist aggression until the world is made over into the fascist image. For the only security of fascism against the ever-rising forces of civilization is to reduce mankind as a whole to its own state of barbarism. In the face of this situation, a policy of passive defense, of watchful waiting, is a policy of submission.


4. THE CHALLENGE OF THE AMERICAN HERITAGE

We Americans live under the oldest written constitution in the world. We have a tradition of freedom, braced by the long experience of the frontier, with its free land and its sturdy opportunities for the self-reliant man. This tradition is sanctified by daily habits of life that include every rank of American, no matter what his economic station, no matter what his religious or political opinions.

Despite occasional waves of irrationality, which existed even before the days of the Know-Nothings or the Ku Klux Klan, the dislike of servility and authoritarianism is deeply engrained: free speech, free government, free choice may on occasion be threatened by local reactionary minorities, but they are still precious to the common American who runs the farms and the factories of this country. This tradition is embedded in the protestantism and rationalism that formed the foundation of the original American ideology.

Every writer, every political leader who has left his impression on the American mind, has upheld this tradition: it is in Hawthorne as much as in Whitman; it is in plantation Jefferson as much as in frontier Jackson; it is in Melville as much as in John Dewey.

This American tradition carries with it the promise of a high civilization. It has fostered great human figures, the sweet austere humanity of an Emerson, the shrewd tender wisdom of a Lincoln: it is a tradition that is opposed to any fixed and final status, in knowledge, in belief, in doctrine, other than the belief that men themselves have individually and collectively the responsibility of guiding their own destiny, and working out their own salvation. Such a tradition is favorable to co-operative endeavors in art and science and government: for its disciplines must, in the nature of things, be self-imposed, and its synthesis must remain an open one, always subject to the correction of new truths, to the challenge of a higher morality. Our government has succeeded by the pragmatic test: it has brought into a working communion vast millions of people, coming from diverse countries, bearing the most disparate national traditions: it has taught them to live in amity, and beneath all their national and regional and economic differences, to remember their common humanity.

Whatever the defects of American political life, whatever the blots on our system of law or our grossly imperfect economic organization, we still preserve in grand outlines the traditions of a free people. Such a system of government may temporarily lend itself to misrule or class exploitation; it may blunder and explore blind alleys: but it holds within itself the perpetual possibility of correcting its errors, of improving its methods, of recovering its human goals. Even now, though we are far from having distributed economic abundance, our fundamental traditions still keep alive the elementary sense of human self-respect. Every true American honors these traditions and knows they give shape to his character and are a source of his personal strength.

What we Americans need to be reminded of now is something different, though it springs out of this pride in our heritage; and that is, our way of life is if need be likewise worth dying for, so that our children and our children's children may continue to enjoy this heritage. In a world now being over-run by barbarians who are deeply and systematically inimical to our democracy, the choice offered us as a people is not a choice between peace and war: it is a choice between defending our institutions or of submitting to a servile and barbarous tradition that is repugnant to all that we hold dear. The risks of death are already upon us: the risk of physical death, the far worse risk of moral death. Fascism has declared war on our institutions. We have a few months, at most a few years, to decide what the answer of free men must be.]

## 5. THE HARD CHOICE BEFORE US

What is needed to prevent the flames of fascist ideology from searing the world is to start a backfire. We must be ready to meet the irrational demands and claims of the fascists with the only means their philosophy recognizes as valid: superior military strength, backed by a more concentrated moral purpose on behalf of the values of civilization. To think that civilization can be saved on cheaper terms is an error.

In the long run, fascism cannot compete with democracy or afford to risk its counter-challenge. Hence there is no conceivable limit to fascist aggression against democracy until the whole world is made over into fascism's own maniacal image. Reason may still emerge from this irrational world; civilization may still be rescued from those who wantonly practice decivilization. But these things will come to pass, not by vaguely wishing for them or by "trusting to time"; they will come only if we meet fascism with decisive force and fresh initiative—with a plan and a program that embody the long hopes of humanity.*

Do not imagine that fascism will sweep over the world without touching America. Every country contains morbid elements that will gladly harbor this disease, just as every individual has weaknesses which may, if uncorrected by

---

* In fighting the second World War the United States concentrated on technical facility and military strength, to the neglect of moral and political purposes. Since the generation that fought it had been stript of its heritage of universal values by its leaders in literature and education, our ideological equipment was so much straw armor. The contrast here between Woodrow Wilson and Franklin D. Roosevelt was markedly in the latter's disfavor. Lacking any well-formed purposes and goals, our people mistakenly thought that the war was over when the fighting had ceased: hence the demoralization that accompanied demobilization need hardly be wondered at.

treatment or happy circumstances, lead him into a prison or an asylum for the insane. Still less must one fancy that the nightmare that now confronts us will disappear if we close our eyes tightly and smile propitiatory smiles—that is the behavior of children. Unfortunately, the present world is not fit for children to live in; fascists delight to drop bombs on their heads. Thousands of men are now in concentration camps who kept on "hoping that time would change things." Time changes nothing; men must act.

## 6. PLAN AGAINST FASCISM

By a curious paralysis of the imagination, only two lines of effort have been canvassed in relation to peace and national security. One is isolationism; the other is interventionism, or collective security. Both policies glare with inadequacies; they are the work, alas! of the blind, the timid, the slothful, and the deceived. Neither program is adequate to defend our way of life against the hostile assault of fascism; on the contrary, both would render the American tradition impotent.

As for collective security, it was ditched by the British in 1932 and by the French in 1935; by now the possibility of a concerted defense against fascism in Europe is gone and Europe is in all probability already lost to civilization. No effort of ours now will undo the mischiefs that have heaped up since the Treaty of Versailles. Had there been a show of justice and magnanimity among the democratic states of Europe before 1932, collective security might have had the approval of an intelligent American; today our main concern must be to save the United States, and not be drawn into the vortex of European barbarism. In the end, this may be Europe's salvation.

Isolationism, on the other hand, is nothing less than a declaration of submission to the forces that threaten our Constitution, our own way of life, our traditional dislike of despotism. As embodied in our Neutrality Act, this policy assumes that what happens to the rest of the world makes no difference to us so long as we keep to ourselves. Such isolationism is dangerous in two ways: it gives the fascists opportunity to extend their conquests—they have already drawn Tory Britain into their orbit—and it gives encouragement to those obscene, irrational forces in the United States that favor fascism. Our isolationism, indeed, does not go far enough: it does not withdraw fascist influence from the United States. What we must isolate is not ourselves but fascism.

What do the facts demand by way of a realistic American policy, boldly carved in the traditions of our country? First, we must affirm our faith in our own institutions by taking a positive stand for them in open opposition to fascism. The instrument of this policy should be a comprehensive Non-Intercourse Act, which would dramatically withdraw all economic and political intercourse, to begin with, from the three militant fascist states—Germany, Italy, Japan.

This policy has excellent historic precedent; but whereas it failed in Jefferson's administration because of our economic insignificance then, its application today would be a different matter. Our refusal to buy Japanese silk and Japanese cheapjack wares, or to sell scrap iron to Japan, would put a crimp in both her economic activities and her war preparations. Similarly, the prohibition of tourist travel in Germany and Italy would rob these countries of important financial aids for their armament. As an economic stroke, such a policy would not of course immediately stay the spread of fascism, but as a moral gesture it would restore to democracy the élan, the self-confidence and, above all, the initiative, which up to now have been the special possession of dictatorial regimes. In advance of war, it would weaken fascism and aid democracy.

But to implement non-intercourse we must take risks. We have no guarantee against fascist piracy even in times of peace; our shipping might have to be placed on a war basis to avoid such typical barbarian attacks. And further to strengthen our hand, we should—in contradiction to our present policy of "neutrality"—build up a navy capable of keeping the sea-lanes open in peace and war for the passage of goods to non-fascist countries.* I make no effort to gloze in pacifist terms the assumptions of this policy; the axiom on which it is based is that *fascism has already declared war*. Fascism is a vicious force that now seriously threatens American democracy, and to defend ourselves and our institutions we must take the initiative, before it has consolidated its power, before it has further undermined our self-confidence, before its successful depredations have increased its capacities for conquest. If that means war, it means war only as an alternative to something far more brutal and disastrous than war—submission to fascism itself.

## 7. THE ADVANTAGES OF DEMOCRATIC MILITANCY

This policy of action against fascism has many tactical advantages. And the first of them is that the time, the place and the weapons used in the battle are primarily of our own choosing. We do not wait for fascism to choose the right

* So-called military experts singled out this proposal as an outstanding howler. In 1938 it seemed to most people as absurd to demand our present two-ocean navy as to suggest that the combined armies of France, England, and Poland might be beaten by the Axis.

moment to strangle us, while the forces friendly to fascism have had an opportunity to rally together in our country and undermine our democratic morale and our will to fight on behalf of civilization against the pathology of barbarism.

Again, this policy is based on our national tradition of self-reliance; it does not involve us in blanket commitments or entangling alliances with Europe; it is Washingtonian and Jeffersonian to the core. So far as this policy of non-intercourse works out favorably to the European democracies, it does so on our own terms: it is based on our needs and is limited by our plans. We do not have to commit ourselves to supporting such disconcerting advocates of democracy as the pro-Hitler Tories of Great Britain or the Stalinist dictatorship in Russia. In short, we act alone. But we act in behalf of those permanent values of civilization that we share with all men of good will, not least those in the fascist countries. Democratic Europe may still find a way to join *us*.

Meanwhile, non-intercourse gives us the opportunity to liquidate the skeleton army that the fascist states have already planted in this country. No adequate policy of national defense can ignore this menace, for it consists, not only of isolated spies and provocateurs, but of thousands of active Nazis and Fascists who, if they are Americanized at all, are citizens only in the narrowest legal sense; every action betrays their foreign allegiance. In addition to these active disseminators of fascism, busily drilling their private armies and spreading their gospels of anti-Semitism and anti-democracy, there is a new set of fascist allies: the Roman Catholic hierarchy. While the great body of Roman Catholics are genuinely loyal to American institutions, despite their authoritarian religion, the Church has chosen to ally itself with democracy's chief enemy, fascism. The Roman Catholic priesthood has even taken over the typical fascist hoax of making war on popular government by playing up the fictitious threat of communism. This is a particularly odious trick in an overwhelmingly un-bolshevik country like ours, where the Church is now threat-ened by nothing but its own folly.*

Non-intercourse would deprive the fascist groups of active external support and direction: it would isolate and curb their activities. At the same time it would give the Catholic hierarchy in America an opportunity to reconsider its suicidal policy of upholding fascism, by nature hostile to Christianity, as against our secular democracy, which has maintained a consistently neutral, tolerant attitude toward all religious creeds. The sooner the Church shows good will to American democracy—even if democracy should numerically veto the Church's political views on child labor or birth control—the easier will it be for loyal Americans to maintain their pre-cious political tradition of religious tolerance.

As a matter of elementary military protection, the national registration and surveillance of all active fascists should be undertaken. Likewise, the disbanding of all private armies, including cadet corps. This would lessen the opportunities for organized disruption and sabotage and it would reserve mili-tary force for the duly constituted arms of the government, sworn to respect and uphold the Constitution and laws of the United States.

* Every upholder of democracy must welcome unreservedly the present Pope's post-victory statements on behalf of the principles of democratic government. But the world has reason to regret that the Vatican made no such encouraging pronouncements when the democracies were in dire peril and the forces of fascism were still gaining strength.

## 8. LIBERTY STILL TASTES SWEET

Until the disintegration of fascism takes place, the United States is probably destined to play the role of Byzantium in the new Dark Ages: a beleaguered island in the rising sea of barbarism that may eventually sweep over us, unless, meeting resistance outside, fascism dissipates its power and suddenly ebbs away.* But such a place cannot be maintained without inner certainty and cohesion as well as external military strength. By retreating cravenly before fascism we shall not reduce the threat of war. All that such a policy can do is to postpone the active stage of the struggle till our own morale is shattered. That is not the way of peace; it is the way of death. Spengler gloatingly predicted this submission of the more humane and domesticated groups before an arrogant Caesarism; it is for us to throw this lie in the fascists' teeth.

Now is the time to make a stand. The hour of hoping for the fascist countries to listen to reason or be upset by inner turmoil is long past. We must answer fascism with a challenge and a plan; above all, with a faith in our American institutions, and in the possibilities of a civilization based, not upon violent tyrannies, but upon the natural co-operations

* This was a serious misjudgment, because, as it turned out, I had measured Britain's actions too exclusively by its appeasing Chamberlains and its complaisant Hoares. Doing so, I underestimated Britain's immense moral reserves. Britain's initiative in declaring war against Nazi Germany in 1939 and her fortitude in standing alone against that power between the retreat at Dunkirk and Germany's attack on Soviet Russia turned the tide. Had Britain followed France that fatal year my predictions would have proved far too optimistic. For if I had under-rated Britain's reserves I had also over-estimated our own. Even had we finally resisted the Axis attack we would, without the three years of preparation Britain's efforts had given us, have faced the Germans with little more than our naked hands to defend us. There the parallel with Byzantium would have ended.

and friendly rivalries of all men of good will. Woe to them who, as Blake said, would forever depress mental and prolong corporeal war! Admittedly, the situation itself is a tragic one: it is part of the nature of tragic choices that they leave no easier alternative. But had I a rostrum to address my countrymen from, I would shout to them, as one would shout to a sleeping man threatened by fire: "Wake up! If you stay a moment longer with your dreams, you are lost. You must act firmly, my countrymen, in the menacing situation into which you are thrown. You are not prepared to deal with this sinister world; its boastful militarisms make you shrink from raising your own arms; you hate the insensateness, the bitter irrationality of war. Every civilized man shares those feelings.

"But if we are to achieve real security, we must not be supine and inert. There is a graver danger than the temporary barbarism of war: namely, the all-devouring and forcefully ingrained and enduring barbarism of the fascist state. To avert this greater danger, we must risk the lesser. To arms! We must rally to our free republican institutions and be prepared to fight for them. Now. . . . *Now!* Tomorrow may mean never; the day after tomorrow may bring on the long brutal reign of fascism's servile ideal of life and its savage, demented notion of human destiny: a world in which the humane and the wise will be in concentration camps and the rest of humanity in a prison whose bars will be so universal that the very fact of their degrading confinement will not be known to them.

"My countrymen, we have at best only a few moments left in which to face our situation intelligently and to carry through the necessary measures to preserve our integrity. Is it worth it? I do not ask that question. This appeal is not addressed to those who do not believe in our American tradition or in the humane ways of civilization; nor is it addressed to those who will not believe that there are worse ignominies to the spirit and worse cruelties to the flesh than killing or being killed. The time for action is now. The place is the United States. The people to do it are the great mass of free, self-governing, liberty-loving Americans. To arms! Gather together your strength and prepare for action. Strike first against fascism; and strike hard. But strike."

# THE CORRUPTION OF LIBERALISM

[This essay, in a shortened version, was first printed in
The New Republic for 29 April 1940, and was then used
in a revised form in Faith for Living, published in September the same year. It was an attempt to meet the superficial arguments against participation in the war by
an examination of the underlying philosophy of life
which had warped the judgment and paralyzed the
actions of a whole generation. Very reluctantly did those
who held this philosophy revise their judgments. Fortunately those engaged in active combat found it possible to swiftly change their minds and acquire a faith
more adequate to the issues of life and death. The coming generation will prove how far this change has gone.]

## 1. THE CONFUSION OF LIBERALISM

As an economic creed, liberalism was undermined by im-
perialism and monopoly before the nineteenth century closed.
But as an active system of ideas, ideal liberalism has been
dissolving before our eyes during the past decade. The liberal
lacks confidence in himself and in his vision of life. He has
shown in every country where the attacks on liberalism have
been forceful that he either does not possess stable convictions, or that he lacks the insight and the courage that would
enable him to defend them. Continually hoping for the best,
the liberal remains unprepared to face the worst; and on the
brink of what may turn out another Dark Ages, he continues
hopefully to scan the horizon for signs of dawn.

The record of liberalism during the last decade has been

20

one of shameful evasion and inept compromise. Liberals have been kind to their enemies and suspicious of their friends; they have stuck to the letter of the law, without being concerned over the fact that their punctilio brought the lawless into power; they have defended the free speech of those who openly vowed to exterminate it; they have helped to preserve freedom for all except those who believe in it.

Liberalism has compromised with despotism because despotism promised economic benefits to the masses—an old device of despotism. In the case of Soviet Russia liberals continued to preserve an embarrassed silence about the notorious plight of freedom and justice in that country because they had esthetic scruples about appearing to align themselves with those forces in America that opposed Russia for purely reactionary reasons. So they preferred to be tacitly on the side of the greater despots, like Stalin and Hitler, in order to be free of any taint of association with minor despots like the Girdlers and the Rands. In international affairs liberalism has likewise graciously lent support to the forces of barbarism, in an effort to give the devil his due. And on the theory that war is the worst of evils, the liberals have tearfully acquiesced in the rule of those who, as Blake said, would "forever depress mental and prolong corporeal war."

Liberalism has been on the side of passivism, in the face of danger; it has been on the side of appeasement, when confronted with aggressive acts of injustice; and finally, in America today, as in England yesterday, liberalism has been on the side of "isolation," when confronted with the imminent threat of a worldwide upsurgence of barbarism. Today liberals, by their unwillingness to admit the consequences of a victory by Hitler and Stalin, are emotionally on the side of "peace"—when peace, so-called, at this moment means capitulation to the forces that will not merely wipe out liberalism, but will overthrow certain precious principles with which one element of liberalism has been indelibly associated: freedom of thought, belief in an objective reason, belief in the dignity of the human personality.

The weakness and confusion and self-betrayal of liberalism during the crisis that has now come to a head, provide one of the most pitiable spectacles that these pitiful times have shown. By some fatal enchantment, liberals still have the illusion that they are living in the hopeful world of the eighteenth century; that world which still seemed intact in 1914, and even seemed on the point of resurrection once more in the falsely bottomed revival that took place after the signing of the Locarno agreement in 1925. Liberals continue to think and act as if the present sinister world would some fine morning pass away like a bad dream, through the mere act of waking up, and that without any change in the direction of their effort the world will again be a fit place for kindly and well disposed people to live in. In 1932, an intelligent German liberal said to me, with respect to the prospects of the Nazis: "We passed through that disease here in the South: now they are getting it in the North. But it is like the measles; a lot of people catch it, but in a little while we will all be immune." In a little while Hitler was in power.

Unable to take the measure of our present catastrophe and unable, because of their inner doubts and contradictions and subtleties to make effective decisions, liberals have lost most of their essential convictions: for ideals remain real only when one continues to realize them. Liberals no longer act as if justice mattered, as if truth mattered, as if right mattered, as if humanity as a whole were any concern of theirs: the truth is they no longer dare to act. During the period of the United Front, liberals accepted the leadership of a small communist minority, fanatical, unscrupulous, deeply contemptuous of essential human values, incredibly stupid in tactics and incredibly arrogant in matters of intellectual belief; they accepted this leadership simply because the Communists, alone among the political groups, had firm convictions and the courage to act on them.

Now that the treachery of the communists has placed them alongside their natural tactical allies, the fascists, many of these liberals have, on practical points at issue, even drifted into a covert defense of Hitlerism. They show far more distrust of the English and French and Finnish peoples, who are resisting the barbarians, than they do of the German and Russian masses who follow, blindly, stupidly, irrationally, without access to any sources of objective fact, the leadership of Hitler and Stalin. These liberals were against Chamberlain when he sought to appease the fascist powers; and they are still against Chamberlain, now that he has reversed his original position. To comfort themselves and keep to their illusions, they concoct imaginary situations in which Stalin suddenly reverses his obvious plans and undermines Hitler—as if anything would be gained for humanity by substituting one impudent dictator for two. Or they conjure up the ghost of a Holy War fought by Chamberlain and Hitler, shoulder to shoulder, against Stalin. In their imaginary world, these liberals are always right; in the real world, they have been consistently wrong. So victimized are some of these liberals by their protective illusions and self-deceptions that it is easy to predict that they will presently swallow without a grimace Hitler's hoax that Nazi Germany is defending the masses against the "capitalist plutocracies" that are seeking to stifle them.

The Romans used to say that the worst results come about through the corruption of what is good; and one may say this about the present state of liberalism. But the defects of liberalism are not due to isolated mistakes of judgment that individual liberals have made; they are due to fatal deficiencies that go to the very roots of liberal philosophy. Unfortunately, liberalism's weaknesses are so debilitating that they not merely undermine its own will-to-survive, but they may also surrender elements in a longer human tradition, on whose maintenance our very civilization depends. If we are to save the permanent human core of liberalism, we must slough off the morbid tissue that now surrounds it.

## 2. PRAGMATIC VERSUS IDEAL LIBERALISM

Liberalism is a very mixed body of doctrine. So it is important that, in discussing its errors, we should detach its essential and enduring values from those which have characterized a particular age, class, or group.

Like democracy, with which it has close historic affiliations, liberalism during the last generation has been subject to a violent assault. This came originally from the Marxian revolutionaries of the Left; but the blows were doubled through the triumphant action of the fascist revolutionaries of the Right. By now these extremes have met in their attack on liberalism, and for all practical purposes, the enemies of liberalism cannot now be separated.

According to the Marxian critics, liberalism arose at the same time as capitalism; and therefore, liberalism is doomed to disappear when capitalism is overthrown. From the Marxian point of view, ideas are but the shadows of existing economic institutions: human liberty depends upon freedom of investment, freedom of trade. One might think, to hear a Marxian critic, that the concept of freedom had never been framed before the Manchester school came into existence, or the condition never enjoyed. In attacking economic liberalism, the anti-liberal groups have made a deliberate side-swipe against certain other fundamental attributes of liberalism: in this they have been helped by the human tendency to identify as the same fact two quite different facts to which people loosely apply the same word.

So the anti-liberals, pretending mainly to attack capitalism, have also attacked the belief in the worth and dignity of the individual personality: they have undermined the notion of *Humanitas*, extending beyond race, creed, class, or other boundaries. So, too, they have sought to wipe out the concept of an impersonal law, built up by slow accretions that reach back into an ancient past, forming a coherent pattern tending toward justice. The anti-liberals have upheld, rather, the one-sided personal rule of a party or a man. In Germany and Spain the basic concept of law has been so completely overthrown that a man may be tried and convicted for a crime that did not exist in law at the time he committed it.

Now the universal elements in liberalism, the moralizing elements, are the real objects of the fascist attacks. These universal elements arose long before modern capitalism: they were part of the larger human tradition, embodied in the folkways of the Jews, in the experimental philosophy of the Greeks, in the secular practices of the Roman Empire, in the sacred doctrines of the Christian Church, in the philosophies of the great post-medieval humanists. The Marxian notion that ideas are always the shadows of the existing economic institutions runs bluntly against facts precisely at this point. For although a culture forms a related and partly integrated whole, a residue is left in each period and place which tends to become part of the general heritage of mankind. This residue is relatively small in amount but infinitely precious; and no single race, class or people can create it or be its sole keeper.

The effort to equate Manchester liberalism with the humanist traditions of personal responsibility, personal freedom and personal expression is sometimes shared by the defenders of capitalistic privilege; that is the gross fallacy of those who try to tie together private capitalism and "the American way." But these notions are false, whether held by the absolutists of private property or by the absolutists who would challenge the regime of private property. The most important principles in liberalism do not cling exclusively to liberalism: what gives them their strength is their universality and their historic continuity. Confucius, Socrates, Plato, Aristotle, testify to them no less than Jefferson and Mill. Liberalism took over this humanist tradition, revamped it, and finally united it to a new body of hopes and beliefs that grew up in the eighteenth century.

This second element in liberalism, which seems to many people as important as the first, rests upon a quite different set of premises. Liberalism in this sense was symbolically a child of Voltaire and Rousseau: the Voltaire who thought that the craft of priests was responsible for the misery of the world, and the Rousseau who thought that man was born naturally good and had been corrupted only by evil institutions. It was likewise a by-product of the inventors and industrialists of the period, who, concentrating upon the improvement of the means of life, thought sincerely that the ends of living would more or less take care of themselves. Was it not obvious that the end of living, for the poor, was to be graduated into the middle classes, and for the middle classes to have the luxuries and privileges of the rich?

This pragmatic liberalism, which I shall here distinguish from the ideal liberalism, was vastly preoccupied with the machinery of life. It was characteristic of this creed to overemphasize the part played by political and mechanical invention, by abstract thought and practical contrivance. And accordingly it minimized the role of instinct, tradition, history; it was unaware of the dark forces of the unconscious; it was suspicious of either the capricious or the incalculable, for the only universe it could rule was a measured one, and the only type of human character it could understand was the utilitarian one. The pragmatic liberal thought that science, which asks all questions, would in time answer all questions: he was at home in problem-solving situations, and ill at ease in realms where his type of intellectual technique was unprofitable.

For the "liberal" only knowledge promoted power; and power—power over other men, power over nature—was the chief goal of knowledge. That there are other modes of insight into human character and into the cosmos, which science does not possess, the liberal did not suspect; he took for granted that the emotional and spiritual life of man needs no other foundation than the rational, utilitarian activities associated with the getting of a living. Hence, finally, liberalism's progressive neglect of the fields of esthetics, ethics, and religion: these matters were left to traditional thinkers, with the confident belief that they would eventually drop out of existence, mere vestiges of the race's childhood. Rousseau was concerned with all three fields; Spencer recognized esthetics and ethics, but treated religion as a superstition; most liberals today have produced no effective thought in any of these fields; and they live, as it were, on the debris of past dogmas and buried formulations. Unconscious, for example, of the sources of their ethical ideas, they pick up more or less what happens to be lying around them, without any effort at consistency or clarity, still less at creativeness: here a scrap left over from childhood, there a fragment of Kant or Bentham, or again a dash of Machiavelli, pacifist Quakers one moment and quaking Nietzscheans the next.

In short, it is not unfair to say that the pragmatic liberal has taken the world of personality, the world of values, feelings, emotions, wishes, purposes, for granted. He assumed either that this world did not exist, or that it was relatively unimportant; at all events, if it did exist, it could be safely left to itself, without cultivation. For him men were essentially good, and only faulty economic and political institutions—defects purely in the mechanism of society—kept them from becoming better. That there might be internal obstacles to external improvement seemed to him absurd. That there was as big a field for imaginative design and rational discipline in the building of a personality as in the building of a skyscraper did not occur to him. Unfortunately, immature personalities, irrational personalities, demoralized personalities are as inevitable as weeds in an uncultivated garden when no deliberate attempt is made to provide a constructive basis for personal development. Craft remained in politics, even when priestcraft was abolished; the demonic will-to-power remained, even when the princes and capitalists were deposed by pious revolutionaries, vowed to establish heaven on earth. Man's physical powers increased without any comparable growth in his moral stature: on the contrary, the growing love of power proved a means of demoralization.

Behind this failure to establish, on a fresh basis, a normative discipline for the personality was a singular optimism—the belief that it was not needed. Did not liberalism imply an emancipation from empty institutional religion, from the saws, precepts, moralizings of the past? Did this not mean that "science," which confessedly despised norms, would eventually supply all the guidance necessary for human conduct? Such was the innocence of the liberal that those who were indifferent to ethical values thought of themselves as realists. They could hardly understand William James when he called emotionality the *sine qua non* of moral perception. But the fact was that the most old-fashioned theologian, with a sense of human guilt and sin and error, was by far the better realist. Though the theologian's view of the external world might be scientifically weak, his view of the internal world, the world of value and personality, included an understanding of constant human phenomena—sin, corruption, evil—on which the liberal closed his eyes.

## 3. THE REALITY OF EVIL

Pragmatic liberalism did not believe in a world where the questions of good and evil were not incidental but of radical importance. Its leaders thought that they would presently abolish the evils inherent in life by popularizing anesthetics and by extending the blessings of the machine and the ballot. They did not believe in the personal life: they believed in as much of it as could be fitted into their practical routine. Esthetic interests, moral discipline, the habits of contemplation and evaluation, all this seemed mere spiritual gymnastics: they preferred more physical exercises. By activity (busy work) pragmatic liberals kept their eyes manfully on the mere surface of living. They did not believe that any sensible man would, except when he made his will, face the more ultimate facts of existence. For them, the appraisal of death was a neurotic symptom; happily, science's steady advances in hygiene and medicine might postpone further and further that unpleasant occasion itself.

This failure to deal with first and last things, to confront, except in a hurried, shamefaced way, the essential facts of life and death, has been responsible for some of the slippery thinking on the subject of war that has characterized liberals recently.* One of them, in private conversation, told me that he could not face a political decision which might lead to war and thereby bring about the death of other human beings. When I objected that the failure to make such a decision in the present international crisis would possibly lead to the less fruitful death of the same human beings six months or six years hence, he confessed that any extra time spared for the private enjoyment of life today seemed that much gained. I do not doubt the honesty of this liberal; but it is obvious that he has ceased to live in a meaningful world. For a meaningful world is one that holds a future that extends beyond the incomplete personal life of the individual; so that a life, sacrificed at the right moment, is a life well spent, while a life, too carefully hoarded, too ignominiously preserved, may be a life utterly wasted.

Is it any wonder, then, that pragmatic liberalism has been incapable of making firm ethical judgments or of implementing them with action? Its color-blindness to moral values is its most serious weakness today; hence it cannot distinguish between barbarism and civilization. Indeed, it is even inclined to pass a more favorable verdict on barbarism when it shows superiority in material organization. Refusing to recognize the crucial problem of evil, those who follow this

* In April, 1940, no "sensible" person thought either France or England was in danger. When I sought to get a group of distinguished writers and public servants to petition Congress to create an army of a million men, after the Norway invasion, even my best friends regarded that number as fantastically high. No one would sign the memorandum. Do not forget the fact that, but for a single vote, Congress would have dropt the Selective Service Act and demobilized the American army just four months before Pearl Harbor—a blunder that would have cost us even more than our fatal lethargy at Pearl Harbor and Manila did. Our fighters paid heavily for these massive exhibitions of wishful thinking and thoughtless wishing.

creed are incapable of coping with the intentions of evil men:
they look in vain for merely intellectual mistakes to account
for the conduct of those who have chosen to flout man's long
efforts to become civilized. Evil for the pragmatic liberal has
no positive dimensions: he conceives it as a mere lack of
something whose presence would be good.* Poverty is an evil,
because it indicates the lack of a good, namely riches. For
this kind of liberal, the most heinous fact about a war is not
the evil intentions and purposes that one or both sides may
disclose: it is mainly the needless waste of material, the unbearable amount of human suffering, the premature deaths.
All this follows more or less from the liberal's assumption
that all men are fundamentally good and that they follow
with equal zest the same rational (economic) goals.

Lacking any true insight into these stubborn facts of human
experience—corruption, evil, irrational desire—liberals also
fail to understand that evil often lies beyond merely rational
treatment, that a mere inquiry into causes, mere reasonable-
ness and sweetness in one's attitude, may not only fail to cure
an evil disposition but may aggravate it. Now, unfortunately,
there are times when attitudes of intellectual humility and
emotional sympathy are entirely inappropriate to the press of
a particular situation. If a neurotic patient is in a dangerous
manic state, one may have to put him in a lukewarm bath before one can reduce him to a relatively tractable condition—
and one must have force enough to put him there and keep
him there, as well as enough self-confidence to act promptly
when the emergency arises.

* He is not, of course, alone in committing this error: it was one of
the curious departures of Augustine—perhaps an unconscious carryover
from his Manichaeism. Orthodox Christianity, wiser than Augustine, regards evil as a positive force, capable of incarnation; marked by the
Devil's presence, not merely by God's absence. This symbolizes a reality
of human experience.

This illustration has wide reference: it applies to all grades of irrational conduct, and it applies, above all, to such conduct when it is accompanied by threats of physical violence, as in the case of the fascist assault against civilization today. There are times when active resistance or coercion is the only safeguard against the conduct of men who mean ill against human society. The alternative to coercion is what the religious call conversion, salvation, grace, on the part of the offender. That, too, is essentially a pre-rational process, not hostile to reason, but proceeding by a short cut into an area that reason cannot directly touch. Liberals tend to minimize the effectiveness of both coercion and conversion, both force and grace; but it is hard to point to any large and significant social change in which both elements did not play a part.

Coercion is, of course, no substitute for intelligent inquiry and no cure in itself for anti-social conduct. But just as there are maladies in the human body which call for surgery rather than diet—though diet, if applied at an early stage, might have been sufficient—so there are moments of crisis in society when anti-social groups or nations that resist the ordinary methods of persuasion and compromise must be dealt with by coercion. In such moments, to hesitate, to temporize, only gives the disease a deeper hold on the organism; and to center one's efforts upon changing the mind of one's opponent, by opposing reason to his irrationality, and to overlook the elementary precaution of depriving him of his weapons for attacking one, is to commit a fatal offense against the very method one seeks to uphold: persuasion.

The issue of slavery in the United States is a case in point; I use it because it parallels the present issue of war and is far enough away to be seen in perspective. No mere prolongation of the controversy, in the face of the South's resistance to reason and its threats of domination, could have brought about a peaceful solution. Lincoln's offers of appeasement parallel Chamberlain's, and proved as ineffective. His policy was shattered because of the new planter class's deliberate intention to maintain and perfect its form of barbarism: human slavery. People sometimes assume that slavery would have been wiped out on this continent anyway, in the course of time, without warfare, even had the South achieved independence. But those who take this view unconsciously rely upon the nineteenth century's shibboleth of progress: for them the prolongation of slavery or its spread is simply "unthinkable."

Before 1925 one might have defended that ingenuous view. But with the rise of fascism one can now see that social movement in a direction contrary to that of world civilization is not in the least unthinkable. Slavery, which had few passionate defenders even in the South in 1800, had many defenders even in the North by 1860: hence one must now interpret it, not as a survival, but as a fresh mutation into barbarism: forerunner of the even grosser forms of barbarism and servility that the totalitarian systems have produced in our own days. But for the active use of overwhelming physical force, this institution might have gotten a permanent grip on the whole American continent. He who still believes otherwise has no insight into current history.

The liberal's notion that reasoning in the spirit of affable compromise is the only truly human way of meeting one's opponent overlooks the important part played by force and grace. And his unctuous notion that evil must not seriously be combated because the person who attempts to oppose it may ultimately have to use physical force, and will become soiled by the act of fighting, is a gospel of despair. This belief is the basis of his defeatist response to fascism; it means in practice turning the world over to the rule of the violent, the brutal and the inhuman, who have no such fine scruples, because the humane are too dainty in their virtue to submit to any possible assault on it. Now the dangers are real: force *does* brutalize the users of it; when blood is spilt, anger rises and reason temporarily disappears. Hence force is not to be used daily in the body politic, like food or exercise; it is only to be used in an emergency, like medicine or the surgeon's knife. Fascism is barbarous, not because it uses force, but because it *prefers* force to rational accommodation: it deliberately turns mental and physical coercion into human nature's daily food and reduces reason to occasional homeopathic doses.

But to surrender in advance, to take no step because one may make a false step, is to pursue an illusory perfection and to achieve an actual paralysis. Force cannot be left behind, no matter how humane and rational our standards of conduct. He who under no circumstances and for no human purpose will resort to force, abandons the possibility of justice and freedom. The German socialists took their legalistic pacifism seriously; they got their reward in the concentration camp. The English Laborites, following the nerveless Tory leadership, took the same position in international affairs; and that led not alone to the betrayal of Czechoslovakia but to the present endangerment of Western civilization itself.

Despite these sinister examples, the same guileless reasoning has been driving our American liberals into a position of queasy non-resistance, on the ground that the only motive that could sanction our immediate opposition to Hitlerism would be our belief that those opposing him now are angels. People who think in these terms are secretly complimenting themselves upon virtues and purities that neither they nor their countrymen possess; they are guilty of that most typical liberal sin, the sin of Phariseeism. It is because we, too, are not without guilt that we may, in the interest of preserving humanity from more abject humiliations, oppose Hitler and Stalin with a clean heart.* To be too virtuous to live is one of the characteristic moral perversions of liberalism in our generation. To be logical, people who act on these principles should hope only for Heaven and the Day of Judgment; they are too spotless for this world.

## 4. EMOTIONAL ANESTHESIA

The essential moral weakness of liberalism, which I have only glanced at here, is coupled with a larger weakness in the liberal philosophy. Along with liberalism's admirable respect for rational science and experimental practice, goes an overvaluation of intellectual activities as such, and an undervaluation of the emotional and affective sides of life. In the liberal theology, emotions and feelings have taken the place of a personal devil.

Now as every good psychologist knows, and as Count Korzybski has ably demonstrated, emotions and feelings, associated with the most involved and remote body processes, are involved in all thought. Reason and emotion are inseparable: their detachment is a practical device of limited use. Thought that is empty of emotion and feeling, that bears no organic relation to life, is just as foreign to effective reason as emotion that is disproportionate to the stimulus or is with-

* At that moment, I must remind the reader, there was active collaboration between the Soviet Government and Germany— not alone in the interchange of goods, but in the world-wide denunciation of the democracies by the communists for resisting Hitler. By a suicidal stupidity, or an equally suicidal cunning, the communists sought to break down democratic morale, and in divided countries like France, where their influence was strong, actually did so.

out rational foundations and references. The body, the unconscious, the pre-rational are all important to sound thought.

But because the liberal has sought no positive discipline for emotion and feeling, there is an open breach between his affective life and his intellectual interests. His first impulse in any situation is to get rid of emotion because it may cause him to go wrong. Unfortunately for his effort to achieve clarity, a purely intellectual judgment, eviscerated of emotional reference, often causes him to go quite as wrong. The calmness and sang-froid of Beneš was perhaps his most serious weakness during the long period before the Munich crisis; ominously, it repeated the self-defeating mood of Bruening, in the days before his removal. Instead of priding himself on not being "carried away by his emotions," the liberal should rather be a little alarmed because he often has no emotions that could, under any conceivable circumstances, carry him away.

This is not a new criticism. Graham Wallas lectured on the subject twenty years ago. He showed that in all valid thinking that referred to human situations it was important to be able to use the emotions, not to put them into cold storage. Liberalism, by and large, has prided itself upon its colorlessness and its emotional neutrality; and this liberal suspicion of passion is partly responsible for the liberal's ineptitude for action. In a friendly world, pragmatic liberalism leads to nothing worse than a tepid and boring life; but in a hostile world, it may easily lead to death. If one meets a poisonous snake in one's path it is important, for a *rational* reaction, to have a prompt emotion of fear; for fear releases the flow of adrenin into the bloodstream, and that will not merely put the organism on the alert but will give it the extra strength either to run away or to attack. Merely to look at the snake abstractedly, without sensing danger and experiencing fear, may lead to the highly irrational step of permitting the snake to draw near without being on guard against the reptile's bite. The liberal's lack of a sense of danger in the present crisis is one of the causes of our rapid disintegration. What is barely an adequate emotional response to the situation he recoils from as outrageous hysteria.

Liberalism under its assumption that men ideally should think without emotion or feeling deprives itself of the capacity to be human. This is one of the gravest features of the present crisis: the cold withdrawal of human feeling by the liberals today is almost as terrible a crime against civilization as the active inhumanity of the fascists.*

Closely allied with the liberal's emotional anesthesia is his incurable optimism: a wrinkled smile left over from the eighteenth century, when, in the first flush of confidence, the possibilities of human advance seemed boundless. This optimism belonged to a constructive and expanding age: in its inception, it was a healthy reaction against the moldering institutions and precedents of the past. But it has become an unfortunate handicap in a period when destructive forces are gaining the upper hand, and when, in the approaching stabilization of population and industry, the malevolence of the human will, on the part of the propertied classes, may at critical moments—as already in Germany and Italy—give unlimited power to those who represent barbarism. Destruction, malice, violence, hold no temptation for the liberal; and in the kindness of his heart, he cannot bring himself to believe that they may seriously influence the conduct of any large part of mankind. The liberals could not understand that the

---

* This sin has been universal. The failure of the United States to lift its immigration barriers temporarily to allow unrestricted entry of bona fide refugees of fascism, places us all in the same category as the British official who sent the Jews on the *Struma* to their doom.

gift of Czechoslovakia to Nazi Germany could not appease Hitler: that one might as well offer the carcass of a dead deer in a butcher store to a hunter who seeks the animal as prey— the meat being valued chiefly as a symbol of his prowess. And that is why the talk of mere economic adjustments that would enable the fascist states to live at peace with the rest of the world is muddled nonsense; it assumes, contrary to fact, that fascism springs out of rational motives and pursues concrete utilitarian ends. The bad arrangements of the peace of Versailles did not by themselves create fascism, nor will the best results of a magnanimous peace conference be able at once to wipe out its destructive impulses and undermine its irrational philosophy. Unfortunately it is not in Ricardo or Marx or Lenin, but in Dante and Shakespeare and Dostoyevsky, that an understanding of the true sources of fascism are to be found. Economic explanations reflected a reality in the nineteenth century; they *disguise* a reality—the claim to barbaric conquest—today.

During the last ten years, the optimism of the liberals has remained unshaken. But what is going on in Asia and Europe today, what is going on under cover in the activities of a Father Coughlin and his associates in America, is going on, in effect, with the liberal's permission, because his philosophy is helpless to understand the nature of the evil and the irrational, or to take effective steps toward resisting the merciless aggression that springs from them. The incurable tendency of the liberal is to believe the best about everybody: to hope when there is no reason to hope, and to exhibit the nicest moral qualms, the most delicate intellectual scruples, in situations that demand that he wade in and coarsely exert his utmost effort. All this springs, as I have said, not from accidental misjudgments about particular events; it springs from an essential defect in the philosophy of pragmatic liberalism.

We now face a world that is on the brink, perhaps of another Dark Age; and because a Dark Age is not included in the liberal chronology, the liberal glibly refuses to accept the evidence of his senses. Like the sundial, he cannot tell time on a cloudy day. So, habitually, the pragmatic liberal brands those whose eyes are open to the human devastation around them as "hysterical," "mystical," "having concealed fascist tendencies," or—taking a leaf from the Stalinists and the Hitlerites—as "war-mongers." *

## 5. THE REDEMPTION OF IDEALS

Now one must remember that liberalism has two sides. There is an ideal liberalism, deeply rooted in the example

---

* A pathological resistance to rational persuasion characterized a great part of the civilized world during this period. Even now that resistance remains: witness the people who still believe that the horrors of the German extermination factories are but the figments of propaganda. The responsibility for this state of mind must be widely distributed: it is the end-product of a general campaign of de-valuation and de-verification in which many supposedly decent people took part. Thus the well-attested record of German atrocities at the beginning and at the end of the first World War was dismissed by an historian like Dr. Charles A. Beard as a "tale for babes." Analysts of propaganda, exposing the rhetorical devices of persuasion, themselves put over one of the biggest propaganda frauds of our time: namely, the conviction that the important part about a statement is not its truth or falsity, but the question whether someone wishes you to believe it. Such analysts held in effect that the mere desire to persuade is a sufficient ground for rejecting a statement: hence any unwelcome truth could be dismissed out of hand as "propaganda" if he who uttered it sought to move the hearer to action. On those terms only indifference and paralysis were guarantees of reputability. As a result, a large part of our fighting men went into the war thinking that there was no essential difference between their own cause and that of the enemy. In a world where no universal principles were valid and where no values were universal, skepticism and relativism, by undermining the reasons for fighting, also vitiated the will to fight. This will-to-disbelieve produced a grave moral debacle. For an acute analysis of this situation see Mr. Harold Nicholson's comments in The Spectator (London) for 28 September 1945.

and experience of humanity: a doctrine that commands the allegiance of all well-disposed men. And there is a transient doctrine of liberalism, the pragmatic side, which grew up in the eighteenth century out of a rather adolescent pride in the scientific conquest of nature and the invention of power machinery: this is the side that emphasizes the utilitarian aspects of life, that concentrates on purely intellectual issues, and that, in its exclusive concern for tolerance and "open-mindedness" is ready to extend its benevolent protection to those who openly oppose the very purposes of civilization. What is important in ideal liberalism are elements like the great Roman notion of *Humanitas,* united in the pursuit of freedom and justice, embracing all races and conditions. This ideal is radically opposed at every point to the autarchy advocated by the fascists; and it is no less opposed to the isolationism, moral and physical and political, advocated by most American liberals—a passive milk-and-water version of the fascist's contemptuous attitude toward the rest of the human race.

Plainly the liberal who proposes to do nothing on behalf of humanity until the lives of individual Americans are actually threatened by a fascist military invasion will have very little left to save. For life is not worth fighting for: bare life is worthless. Justice is worth fighting for, order is worth fighting for, culture—the co-operation and the communion of the peoples of the world—is worth fighting for: these universal principles and values give purpose and direction to human life. At present, the liberals are so completely deflated and debunked, they have unconsciously swallowed so many of the systematic lies and beliefs of barbarism, that they lack the will to struggle for the essential principles of ideal liberalism: justice, freedom, truth. By clinging to the myth of isolationism, they are helping to create that insane national pride and that moral callousness out of which fascism so easily flowers.

What is the result? Pragmatic liberalism has flatly betrayed ideal liberalism. The values that belong to the latter have been compromised away, vitiated, ruthlessly cast overboard. The permanent heritage of liberalism has been bartered for the essentially ignoble notion of national security, in itself a gross illusion. These liberals are loath to conceive of the present war as one waged by barbarism against civilization. Though many of them were moved by the plight of the Spanish Republicans, they have managed to insulate themselves from any human feeling over the fate of the humiliated and bullied Czechs, the tortured Jews, the murdered Poles, the basely threatened Finns—or the French and English who may next face extermination—just as many of them have managed to keep supremely cool about the horrors that have befallen the Chinese. They have eyes and they see not; they have ears and they hear not; and in their deliberate withholding of themselves from the plight of humanity they have even betrayed their own narrow values, for they are witnessing the dissolution of those worldwide co-operations upon which the growth of science, technics, and industrial wealth depends. This corruption has bitten deep into pragmatic liberalism. The isolationism of a Charles Beard or a Stuart Chase or a Quincy Howe * is indeed almost as much a sign of barbarism as the doctrines of a Rosenberg or a Gottfried Feder. No doubt the American liberals mean well; their good intentions are traditional. But they cling to the monstrous illusion that they can save themselves and their country by cutting themselves off—to use Hawthorne's words in Ethan Brand—

* Mr. Howe repented; Dr. Beard wrote his Basic History of the United States.

from the magnetic chain of humanity. Their success would spell the end of every human hope they still share.

In a disintegrating world, pragmatic liberalism has lost its integrity but retained its limitations. The moral ardor of the eighteenth-century liberals, who faced difficult odds, strove mightily, risked much, has gone. The isolationism that is preached by these liberals today means fascism tomorrow. Their passivism today means militarism tomorrow. Their emphasis upon mere security today—and this applies especially to the current American Youth movement—means the acceptance of despotism tomorrow. While their complacency, their emotional tepidity, their virtuous circumspectness, *their unwillingness to defend civilization with all its faults—and with all its capacity for rectifying those faults*—means barbarism tomorrow. Meanwhile, the ideal values of liberalism lack support and the human horizon contracts before our eyes. While the barbarians brazenly attack our civilization, those who should now be exerting every fiber to defend it are covertly attacking it, too. On the latter falls, perhaps, the heavier guilt.

What are the prospects, then, for the Western world's surviving the present crisis, with even a handful of the scientific discoveries, the inventions, the literary and esthetic and scholarly achievements, the humanizing patterns of life, that the last three centuries so magnificently created or expanded? On any candid view, the prospects are poor. Barbarism has seized the initiative and is on the march. But as the crisis sharpens, as the evils that threaten us become more formidable, one possibility remains, born of the crisis itself: the psychological possibility of a large-scale conversion. Are the pragmatic liberals shattered enough yet to be ready for a reintegration? Are they capable of rededicating themselves to the tasks of ideal Liberalism? If so, there is at least a ray of hope: the optimism of pathology, a commonplace of both religion and psychoanalysis.

To achieve a new basis for personal development and communal action, the liberal need not abandon his earlier concern for science, mechanism, the rational organization of society. But he can no longer regard the world that is embraced by these things as complete or all-sufficient. The sphere of political action must transcend that of the Economic Man: it must be as large as the fully developed human personality itself. No mere revision of Marxism, no mere ingenious political program with a few socialistic planks added or taken away, no attempt to make five disparate economic systems produce profit in a community where new social motives must take the place of dwindling or absent profits—none of these shallow dodges will suffice. What is demanded is a recrystallization of the positive values of life, and an understanding of the basic issues of good and evil, of power and form, of force and grace, in the actual world. In short: the crisis presses toward a social conversion, deep-seated, organic, religious in its essence, so that no part of personal or political existence will be untouched by it: a conversion that will transcend the desiccated pragmatism that has served as a substitute religion. For only the living—those for whom the world has meaning—can continue to live, and willingly make the fierce sacrifices and heroic efforts the present moment demands.

To the disoriented liberals of today one must repeat the advice that Krishna offered Arjuna on the eve of battle, as reported in the Bhagavad-Gita. Like the liberals, Arjuna hesitated, debated, had specious moral scruples, remembered his relatives and friends on the other side, clung to the hope of safety in a situation that did not permit him to enjoy it. Victory, Krishna pointed out, is never guaranteed beforehand;

and what is more, it is irrelevant to the issue one must face. What is important is that one should attend to the overwhelming duty of the moment, in a spirit of clear-sighted understanding. "Counting gain or loss as one, prepare for battle!" In that spirit—*only* in that spirit—can civilization still be saved.

# THE REASONS FOR FIGHTING

[The following is the text of a radio address, No. 20 in the Let's Face the Facts Series, delivered over the network of the Canadian Broadcasting Corporation on 1 December 1940. I would underline the date on which it was given; and the only further comment I would make is that there is not a word in it that I should care to change today.]

## 1. THE DEMAND FOR ACTION

Were it not for the fact that our countries are already joined in acts of civil and military co-operation for our common defense, I should be loath to speak to you about the ultimate issues of the present war, even in response to your cordial invitation. As an American I have not yet earned the right to talk to you about the future. That future involves decisive action, great political responsibilities, whole-hearted personal sacrifices; and my countrymen have yet to assume those responsibilities and make sacrifices in anything like the fullness that the hour demands.

At present, we Americans hover at the water's edge, like someone who watches a brave swimmer battling with a school of man-eating sharks. A great many of us have enough intelligence and enough sense of moral obligation to know what the human demands of this moment are: we know that we shall have to plunge in and help kill the vicious creatures. To leave you threshing around in the water, no matter how cool you may be, will not permanently get rid of the sharks

unless we lend our fresh strength to your efforts: unless we
arm ourselves not just for defense but for attack, and swim
boldly into the danger zone.

Not everyone in the United States, it goes without saying,
has either the clearness of vision or the moral resolution to
understand this. There are still some who prefer to turn their
eyes away from the scene because it is so painful to the spectator. There are others who hope that some turn of the tide
will cause the sharks eventually to swim away or that some
miraculous fatality will cause the most dangerous of the
sharks to sink to the bottom through self-inflicted wounds.
Still others say that after all our chief business in life is not
to kill sharks but to enjoy the water as swimmers. They even
talk about allotting special feeding grounds to the sharks, or
they say we shall have to get used to swimming in shark-
infested waters, even if we lose a limb or two: after all, sharks
must live too, and one must keep on the right side of them.

If you have followed the trend of public opinion in the
United States as recorded by various objective polls and sur-
veys, you will note that the number of people who believe that
the United States must be prepared to step into the war and
to fight the Axis powers has been slowly and surely growing.
But what I should like your permission to do is to assume
for the moment that we Americans, before it is too late, will
take this decisive step against the spread of Fascism: that we
will throw all our moral weight and physical power openly
on the side of the other English-speaking peoples.* Just as
overnight last June we abandoned the theory and practice of
isolation, so perhaps overnight we will abandon our self-

* This was more than six months before Hitler took the initiative in
bringing Russia into the war: an act that decisively brought on Germany's defeat, but muddied the issues, because of Russia's own absolutism.

defeating policy of aloof self-defense and benevolent neutrality.

At some point during the next month, the next winter, or the next year, my countrymen will, I believe, have the courage and the intelligence to take the initiative out of the hands of Hitler and his accomplices. At that moment the American people will scorn to hold our political representatives to their foolish pledge that they will under no circumstances permit our country to be drawn into the war. We will demand rather for our honor and our safety and our common love of humanity that our government shall use the might of our navy and our air forces to subdue the totalitarian powers and to redeem Europe and China from the heavy yoke of their aggression.

This is not a promise, of course, for I have no authority to make promises. It is an assumption that I make on the basis of past history and experience; above all on the basis of my general knowledge of my countrymen and of the profound spiritual change that has taken place in them during the last six months. We Americans now see very clearly that we cannot permit this war to end in the defeat of democracy, for that would be a crushing blow to our way of life, as it would commit us to the need for military organization and regimentation on a scale that would far outpass the craziest dreams and enterprises of Hitler. Neither can we stand by impassively and permit the war to come to a premature end through the compromise and appeasement of exhaustion. That course would leave the sharks still alive and still preparing new raids on their victims.

Nor yet can we permit the present war to drag on interminably until all the precious memorials of Europe are bombed into powder, until millions of innocent victims in Great Britain and on the continent are annihilated or turned into physi-

cal wrecks by the inhuman punishment of lawless attack from
the air which they must endure.

I assume that the American people will rise up with all
their manhood and their moral convictions and declare their
unmitigated enmity against the Axis powers, against the
ferocity, the brutality, the lying, the treachery, and the systematic barbarism for which totalitarianism stands. In short,
we will fight, and we will not content ourselves with a policy
of hemisphere isolation and passive defense. We are beginning to understand that an ounce of attack is worth a pound
of defense, and that, as the editor of the Louisville Courier-
Journal pointed out a few weeks ago, as few as twenty thousand American aviators and mechanics brought into action at
the right moment may turn the scales in the present war.

So, though I am anticipating the future in assuming that
the United States must and will enter the war before it is too
late, I am nevertheless not letting my imagination or my
hopes run away with me. We *may* hold back, we may falter,
we may allow optimism or unenlightened self-interest to keep
us in check until it is too late. But I think not. For I have a
higher opinion of the essential decency and humanity of the
average American than either the Fascists or the isolationists
have. I am convinced that we will be fighting at your side
presently without waiting for further assaults or aggressions
by the Axis powers, and we will do this for a simple reason:
because there is no other course open now to free men and
women who value their democracy, who believe in justice and
freedom and truth, and who realize that outright death is preferable either to slavery or to constant terrorism.

## 2. THE ISSUE IS PLAIN

The men with mechanical hearts may argue otherwise; the Stalinists and their fellow-travelers may argue otherwise; fascist agents in our midst, whether paid or unpaid, whether native or foreign-born, may seek to confuse the issue, but the issue itself has long been plain, and every day is getting plainer. Democracy cannot hope to survive in a totalitarian world. We *could* not survive in that world if we *would*, and when we behold its corruption and debasement, its deliberate cruelties, its boasted hardness of heart, its sinister befoulment of the human personality, we know that if survival meant acquiescence in that regime, we *would* not survive in that world even if we *could*.*

War has become the price of peace; fighting has become the price of security; and the victory of the English-speaking democracies over the stale tyrannies and the moldy despotisms that threaten them is the minimum requirement for a decent life in a world fit for human beings to live in.

Having made this large assumption, I have thereby given myself provisional license to deal with the main subject of this discussion: what ends should we be fighting for, and what sort of world can we reasonably hope to create at the end of the present conflict? Note: I do not ask what we can get, I ask rather what we should demand. There is a school of political thought that prides itself on its realism and that never dares to put a political question in ideal terms because it is afraid of being considered impractical and idealistic. The leaders of

* Though the American press and radio did their part in concealing or playing down fascism's calculated atrocities, no informed observer could, without self-imposed blindness, have been ignorant of them. Their belated exposure by our GI's in 1945 only multiplied the evidence and made it forever irrefutable. The surprise was that anyone was surprised.

this school always abandon their ideals before they have had the courage or the opportunity to test them out. They do their compromising and cutting and trimming in advance, and as a result when they encounter a practical problem they have already given in so completely to their opponent or to existing circumstances that they then do not even achieve the little they modestly demand.

I belong to the opposite school of political thought, the one which assumes that without rational ideals one can no more get what one wants than one can cross the ocean without charts and compasses. For I remember to this day the valuable advice that was once given me by an older colleague whom I was consulting about my course in life. I had laid before him various practical openings and opportunities that had presented themselves to me; but he shook his head. "The first thing to do," he said, "is to know clearly what you really want and to go directly for that. You will be surprised how much easier all these practical decisions become."

That holds as true in political affairs as I have found from experience it does in the life of the individual. Indeed, whatever successes the totalitarian states can flatter themselves on achieving have been plainly due to the fact that their leaders knew clearly and unmistakably what they wanted, whereas those who opposed them had no clearcut notion as to where democracy was going or what it was trying to do. Lacking convictions these so-called leaders of democracy lacked direction; lacking convictions and direction they lacked courage. They tried to oppose violent ideals with comfortable habits.

## 3. DEMOCRACIES MUST PLAN

Now, we who belong to the free democracies must have a program of action and a plan of reconstruction for our own countries and for the world—a plan and a program just as daring, just as comprehensive, just as world-shaking, if need be, as anything that the totalitarian leaders can conceive. I do not mean that we must console ourselves for our present ineffectiveness and our past errors by treating ourselves to political fantasies and figments. We can leave that sort of thing to Hitler, who now promises millions of non-existent houses to his followers to atone for their non-existent conquest of England.

Still less do I mean that we should repeat the mistake people made at the end of the last war when they assumed that peace, order, prosperity, and good living could be willed into existence overnight. If we win this war we will momentarily prevent slavery and totalitarian darkness from covering the whole planet; and *that will be a great victory indeed, worth the mountains of effort that will be needed to achieve it.*

But nothing that we can do now will make the world safe and easy for our children to live in. Nothing that we can do now will lessen the need for further effort. If we wish to live easily the cheapest course of all is to accept totalitarian slavery; that involves no further sacrifice than the loss of our manhood and freedom. Once the initial act of spiritual castration is over, we can live in peace and harmony, the harmony of the chain gang and the peace of death.

But the life of freedom and democracy makes strenuous demands upon us, demands for self-discipline and self-sacrifice. And because people at the end of the first World War did not understand this, they fell back into a state of hopeless disappointment, bitterness, and cynicism. They became the parents of the young men and young women who say now, "What's the use of fighting to save democracy again? We didn't succeed twenty years ago and we probably won't succeed now. What's the use?" * The answer to that question is that the expectation of a permanent and final victory over the forces of evil has no meaning in the actual world. Democracy, like every other human institution, is subject to change—to corruption no less than to improvement. Nothing on earth is wholly perfect or can for long remain perfect. And there is no success so complete, as Walt Whitman reminds us, that it does not demand further effort.

You cannot save democracy once and for all, no matter how drastic your sacrifices, if immediately after this effort you turn over and go to sleep. It is not enough, either, to be prepared to save civilization every twenty years. You must be ready to save civilization every twenty minutes if need be. In short, without continued care, steady readjustment, active choices and decisions, creative plans, and the courage and social vision to carry them out, we cannot survive and our civilization cannot survive, even if we should achieve a military victory.

I believe accordingly that we must be much more positive and much more drastic in our demands for a new world order than were the people who emerged victorious from the last war. But at the same time we must be more patient. † If our demands are intelligent ones they will involve radical and decisive changes in every part of our civilization; they will include the economic order no less than the political order; for political democracy and political freedom, without eco-

* Once our men were in combat, most of them promptly discovered what they were fighting for, though, as General Stilwell racily suggested, they might be reluctant to put their faith in words.

† The atomic bomb over-rules this otherwise judicious counsel. Nevertheless, the incredible mental and moral inertia of our present political leaders in the United States must not tempt us into premature discouragement. Only a dogged unwillingness to admit the possibility of failure will see us through the dark hours ahead.

nomic democracy and social justice, would be just a shadow of the full-bodied reorganization of our society that alone will provide an enduring order.

Just because our program must be such a fundamental one, however, it cannot be realized at once. No group of diplomats, scientists, and technical experts will be able to prepare those plans and organize this world-wide change. With the best will and the most concentrated devotion in the world, the needed transformation cannot take place in half a dozen years.

The better we plan for the future, the more that we demand, the farther off will be the full-scale realization of our plans. So there will be a great temptation, even on the part of those who do not belong in the camp of the appeasers, to accept half-measures so that they may quickly say that the war is done and over and a new order has begun. But economic and political half-measures will not provide the basis for a new order. They will only provide the basis for the same kind of disappointment, bitterness, cynicism, and spiritual defeat that followed the last war.

## 4. WHAT ARE THE GOALS?

What, then, are the minimum goals that we must set ourselves? Let me begin with the negative conditions. First: We cannot live in a world that is part totalitarian and part free. There is no possibility of security in such a world. There is no possibility of co-operation in such a world. Two systems of ideas are now at war; they are fighting for the right to organize the world, as the armies of the Christians and the Saracens when they met on the battlefield of Tours were struggling for the narrower right to organize Europe.

This is a knock-down fight between these two ideas. If the totalitarian states win, the nations of the world will, one by one, be enslaved and looted for the benefit of their barbarian conquerors, as Czechoslovakia, Poland, Denmark, and every other conquered territory in Europe has already been enslaved and looted. If the English-speaking democracies win, our task will be, not the restoration of the world that existed before 1930, nor even the restoration of the world that existed before 1914. It will be nothing less than the establishment of a democratic world society in which each nation and region will play a co-operative part.

Nothing short of a world union will justify the losses and the sacrifices of the present war, and no effective world union can be envisaged except one between peoples who speak the same political language and practice the same kind of loyalty to moral right and to objective truth.* This means that if the English-speaking democracies emerge triumphant from the ordeal of battle, they will have to assume the imperative task of organizing life on a democratic and co-operative basis throughout the planet. No other peoples will have the necessary combination of moral authority and physical power. We cannot continue to view with tolerance or indifference the continuation of obsolete systems of government, the prevalence of barbaric ideas of public order and right; and we cannot admit the possibility of active collaboration with governments that do not rest on the free consent of the governed. And this means that the governed, in turn, shall be equipped by adequate education and by the institutions of free speech and free assemblage and free criticism, to accept the full measure of their responsibility. Effective world organization, in other words, demands a community of equals.

Second: We cannot live in a world that permits nations to be suppressed or mutilated or wiped out of existence, or treated as hewers of wood and carriers of water for the bene-

* See note at end of this chapter.

fit of some master nation. *But neither can we live under an order in which nations proclaim for themselves the right of absolute independence of action and absolute freedom from the moral authority and political power of the rest of mankind.* The notions of national sovereignty and national isolation go together. They are both insolent fictions that contradict the real condition under which human beings and communities actually live. No human being can live to himself. To attempt this, as Aristotle once said, man must be either a brute or a god.

And similarly, no nation, no empire, no continent can live to itself; or refuse to take on the duties and responsibilities of international intercourse and international collaboration. Nations, like individuals under St. Paul's injunction, must be members one of another. Continental isolation is as unreal as empire isolation or national isolation. Nothing less than the earth itself is now a big enough place for any community to live in; nothing less than the lands and the waters of the earth —all its continents, all its resources, all its peoples, all their treasures of culture and history—are sufficient for the education of man.

In this war, no single nation can survive by itself. That is plain enough from the desperate efforts that the Germans are making to bring into their company every country within reach of their bribes or their bombardments. And in the world that will exist after the war, no nation or continent can live to itself or survive by itself. The continuance of our civilization depends upon our ability to conceive, work out, and to operate a world-wide union of peoples. Today mankind is one —one in misery or barbarism, or one in co-operation and human development.

The closed world of the totalitarian states is the symbol of darkness and regression, closed to trade, closed to ideas, closed to foreign radio communication, closed to foreign newspapers, closed to foreign travel; even in peacetime that is a world only one step away from the insane asylum. Or rather it is a world whose hallucinations and suspicions and corrupt fantasies are the veritable marks of the denizens of an insane asylum.

We must expand our parochial horizons, even we in the United States and Canada who think so easily in continental terms, but still shrink from world-wide responsibilities. Solon, the great Greek law-giver, was once asked for the mark of a well-governed city, and he replied that it was one in which a citizen felt as much resentment against a wrong or an injury done to another as he would feel if the crime had been committed against himself. That is likewise a definition for a well-governed world.

It follows from all this that something more than a *European* settlement will have to come out of this war: something more than that Federation of Europe of which people still too timidly dream. Europe is important, North and South America are important, but the security and well-being of the peoples of China and India and the rest of Asia, Malaya, and Polynesia, to say nothing of the peoples of Africa, are equally important. Nothing less than a Federal Union of the free and democratic peoples who are bent on establishing a world order will be sufficiently strong and decisive to serve as a starting point for the long process of reconstruction that lies ahead.

That reconstruction will be a many-sided one. It will involve the equalization of advantages between continent and continent, between region and region, by a planetary rationing of resources. It will involve the equalization of advantages between economic classes within the community now spread far too widely apart in their incomes and their social opportunities. It calls for the transformation of a system of production based chiefly on the pursuit of profit to one based on the pursuit of human well-being; in other words, to a system capable of working effectively even when profits have shrunk or have altogether disappeared.

## 5. RESPONSIBILITY OF VICTORY

The present war brings to a head—and let us hope to an end—four hundred years of unscrupulous power politics and reckless physical conquest. The so-called youth of fascism, which proposes to renew the grandiose dreams of power conquest and booty that inflamed men's minds in the sixteenth century, is in reality not youth at all, but the second childhood of the Power Man, with his dreams of predatory achievement and despotic rule. We are approaching the Era of Resettlement, the era of balance, cultivation, and co-operation; an era that will be marked less by its mechanical inventions than by its social and political experiments.

We will need strength and hardihood to build this new order on a world-wide scale, no less strength, no less hardihood, than our ancestors showed when they spread over the planet as missionaries, as explorers, as immigrants and pioneers. But we now have a different ideal before us, not the exploitation of man and the conquest of nature, but an organic partnership based on men's permanent needs for security, freedom, justice, and truth. Victory over the Nazi-Fascist barbarians will not mean that we have a smooth and easy journey ahead of us on the road to world order. Victory will merely mean that we have earned the power to make decisions and to go ahead.

As an American, I want my country to contribute to that victory. I want to have the privilege of sharing the sacrifices that the peoples of the British Commonwealth of Nations are making. I want us to earn the right to work on the plans for the future and to take part in the difficult work of reconstruction that lies ahead. Nothing that is worth doing today will come easy. Nothing that needs to be done can be done without running terrible risks and enduring painful sacrifices. But that is the way of birth, that is the way of life and creation. Only those who have taken part in this travail have earned the right to carry on—humbly, patiently, wholeheartedly— the work that those who are now heroically fighting and dying to preserve civilization must leave behind them.

NOTE

*Soviet Russia's mighty contribution to the victory of the United Nations, for which all the democratic nations must be grateful, for which generations to come will still be grateful, makes one reluctant to press this point; namely, that a World Organization must be based on a common morality and a common conception of law, which transcends all national and class stratifications. This is the essence of democracy. Russia's lack of internal political liberty and democratic responsibility makes co-operation, for the present, embarrassingly tentative and guarded. Democracy has nothing to fear from Russia's communism: it has everything to fear from Russia's absolutism, not less in the form of a single-party government than in the historic form of Czarism itself. While Soviet Russia remains totalitarian and isolationist, the efforts toward responsible World Government will be handicapped.*

*Our chief problem is to keep the present situation from intensifying into active fear and animosity. Therefore one of the most urgent tasks of American statesmanship is to dis-*

arm Soviet Russia's justifiable suspicions and to remove every conceivable occasion for distrustful belligerence. This does not call for appeasement: it does call for a candid confession of our own sins and a rectification of our own errors, in order to clear the path to a common understanding and to make it easier for Russia to forego some of its own no less devious practices.

First: We should admit the error of our hitherto muddled official attitude toward fascism, from our shameful collaboration with Darlan, a political disaster out of all proportion to its military success, to our unprincipled support of the fascist Argentine dictatorship's plea for admission into the United Nations Organization—a betrayal of democracy which brought to a climax our policy of conniving with fascism in Brazil, Bolivia, China, and elsewhere.

Second: We should withdraw any claim to unilateral control over bases in the Pacific or the Atlantic that Soviet Russia might reasonably interpret as directed against its own security. If our plea of "defense" were tenable, a Russian claim to Hawaii and the Aleutians would be equally valid for the same grotesque reason. (Today any form of unilateral defense rests on a balloon-bubble conception of security: there is no effective military defense without world co-operation, acting through a common police force. The admirals and generals who have not learned this lesson should be promptly retired.)

Third: We should signify our readiness to surrender all thought of independent proprietorship of the atomic bomb, for military or industrial purposes, on condition that Soviet Russia join with us in renouncing our one-sided domination of international affairs and in creating a common world authority, capable of maintaining law and order throughout the planet, with every issue between governments subject to arbi-

*tration and final decision before an impartial authority. Despite the ABC atomic bomb declaration, our present official attitude (Autumn, 1945) on all these matters is an invitation to war, catastrophe, and, incidentally, to national suicide, for we are still trusting the obsolete structure of the pre-atomic United Nations Organization to do work for which its framers did not fit it.*

# THE AFTERMATH OF UTOPIANISM

[This essay, written at the request of Dr. Reinhold Niebuhr, was published in Christianity and Crisis, on 24
March 1941. Such insight as it may show was due to
the severe examination I had made of my own past as the
world crisis rose to its climax; for the levity, the political indifference, the deep-seated isolationism of my own
generation had, when our individual sins were multiplied
by the tens of millions, plainly helped to bring on catastrophe. Few of us, no matter how alert we were after
1933, could escape self-castigation for our beliefs and
behavior during the previous fifteen years. I trust the
reader will find this essay as useful as I myself found
it during the past year, in forfending premature discouragement over the weaknesses and errors of our present
leaders.]

## 1. THE RETREAT FROM RESPONSIBILITY

One of the difficulties about the present war is this: people
have never faced with candor the issues and results of the
great World War. Our contemporaries read Under Fire, All
Quiet on the Western Front, The Road to War; they brooded
over the horrors and tortures of fighting; they became acutely
conscious of the ineptitudes and blunders committed by the
victorious powers, and in particular, they recognized the im-
placable selfishness of the ruling classes. But they lost sight
of what the war itself was about; what it actually *did* achieve,
and what it eventually *could* achieve.

Even those who had entered eagerly into the World War

did not as a rule survive the shock of the post-war deflation. They had hoped for a new heaven and earth to descend from the skies; and when they found that they had only cleared the ground for the City of Man, they were unprepared to survey the site or to set the cornerstone. The two decades that followed the first World War will be known to posterity as a period of ebbing energies and dwindling hopes. Its efforts for peace and co-operation were half-hearted: there was a general retreat from responsibility, symbolized at its worst by the passive non-committal observers the United States sent to the League of Nations.

The agreement to treat the World War as an altogether disastrous and meaningless episode in the life of mankind was a bad preparation both for facing the duties that rose out of the war, and for avoiding the present repetition—this time with the odds heavily weighted against freedom and democracy, by reason of the very cynicism which was encouraged by that agreement. But why did this mistaken judgment become popular? Why was this retreat from responsibility all but universal? Why did the war leave only an image of vindictive imbecility on the minds of most people; so that those who were on the victorious side were ashamed of their cause and looked back sheepishly to their participation, as to a dementia that had unaccountably seized them?

These questions are worth asking; for they cast a light on our present weaknesses. The answers will, I think, bring out a fatal naïveté in the social and ethical philosophies that still govern the behavior of most democratic peoples; and in particular, the more enlightened, the more humane, the more liberal groups.

For a dozen years after the war I shared many of the typical attitudes of my generation; our beliefs were symbolized by the polemics and the predictions of Randolph Bourne. So

I am entitled to speak with candor about the sins of the post-war generation: in part they were my own. Bourne had prophesied a permanent disaster from America's participation in the war; he thought, in contrast to Thorstein Veblen and John Dewey, that it would bring an end to all social progress here. His view proved false. Many evils indeed accompanied the war and persisted long after it had ended. But the worst disaster of all was not the direct result of fighting: it was the consequence of our withdrawal from social and political responsibility. America's participation in the military struggle had given us the right and the duty to take part in the establishment of a more just and stable world order. But we refused. Perhaps the greatest catastrophe of the war was that those who emerged from it accepted, consciously or unconsciously, the romantic defeatism that Bourne had preached in 1917.*

My generation, old and young, smug and cynical, was wrong; it expected too high a reward for its virtue and sacrifice; and it was prepared to give too little. Above all, it failed to understand the task that history had given it; and it thus did not rise to the demands of peace as those who had been maimed or killed had risen to the demands of war. In an orgy of debunking, my generation defamed the acts and nullified the intentions of better people than themselves. If only to prevent a similar miscarriage of effort from happening today, it is important that we should understand the reasons for that earlier failure.

* In its worst form, this showed itself in the actions of Mr. William Bullitt, who betrayed Woodrow Wilson to Senator Lodge at the Senate hearings on the League in 1919.

## 2. GREAT EXPECTATIONS

Those who attempt to account for the disillusion and cynicism that followed the World War usually think they have accounted for everything if they refer it to the Treaty of Versailles. They contrast the high hopes and the ideal expectations that had been enunciated by Woodrow Wilson with the terms of the treaty. And they find in that contrast an excuse for the bitterness, the apathy, the resentment, the indignant sense of betrayal that followed.

But this explanation is more in need of an explanation than the fact it supposedly explains. Did people reject the war itself because the Treaty of Versailles was not a perfect treaty? Or because they discovered, by May, 1919, that the politicians who pieced the treaty together were not saints and philosophers? Or again, was it because they suddenly discovered that the moral and humanitarian claims of the Allies were disfigured by the rankest sort of national egoism, and by undisguised lust for economic and financial power?

When one examines the attitude that grew up among the democracies as to their own share in war and peace, one discovers that a great part of the disappointment arose out of the illusions they had nourished about human nature and society. The mistakes that were committed in the peace treaties were due to conflicting economic interests, to political ignorance, and to sheer stupidity and chicane. But the people who were appalled by these things did, apparently, hope for a peace treaty that would, after six months' conference, be perfect: they did indeed believe that capitalism, enormously over-stimulated by war production, would affably bow itself into oblivion and permit the Bolshevik revolution to spread; they did indeed hope that national egoisms, swollen to the bursting point by the very act of fighting, would suddenly dissolve, and permit a quick, world-wide co-operation.

These were singular hopes and expectations. They suggest that the liberal and progressive groups in the democratic countries had told themselves a fairy story. They indicate that people expected more to be achieved through the peace treaty with regard to international affairs, than had been heretofore achieved through peaceful education and co-operation within any one country. Unfortunately, in 1919, the world was full of pert young men who believed that in less than six months, immediately on top of a war of unparalleled brutality, rancor, and violence, a perfectly just and generous treaty could be composed. These indignant people did quite as much to sabotage the post-war political tasks as the most vindictive isolationists, like Senator Lodge. They formed an unholy alliance with the forces of reaction, comparable to that formed in our own day between the groups of the extreme Right and those of the extreme Left.

In short, the war-weary countries were full of yearning utopians who looked upon Woodrow Wilson as a savior, capable of transforming the souls of his contemporaries. But Wilson's fellow-statesmen were limited men, who saw in the great leader only what he actually was—another limited man. The war generation was bitterly disappointed because their Moses did not lead them into the Promised Land; but that disappointment was highly premature. Moses's followers were forced to endure forty years of wandering in the wilderness: the utopians were not prepared to endure forty months.


## 3. THE DOGMA OF HUMAN PERFECTION

What was the source of this wishful utopianism? What brought on this long period of morbid disillusion? The an-

swer lies a long way behind the first World War: it lies in
the social and religious philosophy that became popular in
democratic countries from the eighteenth century on. Though
the war itself, with its ugliness and its heroism, temporarily
displaced this utopianism, the latter attitude finally had its
revenge.

For the last two centuries the liberal and humanitarian
groups in the Western World have been governed by two lead-
ing ideas. One of them was the belief in mechanical progress,
more or less openly accompanied by the conviction that there
was a positive relation between material improvements and
moral perfection. The other was the belief that, through the
free use of the human reason, the world was ripe for a sudden
transformation that would establish peace and justice forever.

The first of these ideas buoyed up the capitalist classes and
gave a sort of missionary fervor to their most routine activities. The second set of beliefs accompanied all the reformist
and revolutionary movements of the nineteenth century; its
promise of social salvation had a millennial undertone even
in the prophecies of Marx, for whom the classless state was
a final resting place which suspended all the dialectical movements and oppositions that preceded it. The first doctrine was
gradualist; the second was apocalyptic. Both rested implicitly
on a third doctrine, the dogma of the natural goodness of
man. Theologically speaking, the last belief is, of course, the
Pelagian heresy.

According to this belief in natural human goodness, the
purpose of social reform is to shake off evil institutions and
restore man to the primeval paradise in which he could once
more "be himself." The self, as such, was above suspicion.
Rational men, once they are in possession of the facts, will act
in accordance with reason on behalf of the common good:
given enough rational men, one might enact the millennium;

or, if one needed force to effect the change, the need for it would disappear as soon as the last king was strangled by the entrails of the last priest.

This optimistic belief in the automatic reign of reason found steady reassurance, from the 1850's on, in the succession of improvements that took place in mechanical industry; the perfection of machines and the ennoblement of man seemed parts of a single process. Did not Mark Twain, a naive mouthpiece of the age, couple the birth of the "steam press, the steam ship, the steel ship, the railroad" with the emergence of "man at almost his full stature at last"? Though rational invention was not nearly as automatically beneficent in its general social applications as the utilitarian philosophers proclaimed it to be, the sense of power that was derived from conquering space and time and commanding great energies spread into every department of life. If machines could be improved so easily, why not men? In Bellamy's Looking Backward, that typical mixture of humanitarianism and mechanism, utopia is voted in at a Presidential election.

None of these hopes was altogether absurd if one accepted the basic premises. Before 1914, people watched the spread of socialism from country to country, without the faintest tremor of suspicion that socialist ends might become the excuse for the most savage despotism, as in Soviet Russia, or that socialist means might become the agents of barbarous and archaic ends, as in Nazi Germany: in both cases, a hideous travesty of rational hopes. Only reactionary writers like Dostoyevsky were acute enough to predict that a humanitarian materialism might result in Shigalovism (The Possessed). That human nature might go wrong, that people might consciously cultivate barbarism and restore torture, was before 1914 unthinkable; indeed, so unthinkable that those who still cling to this older ideology in its original purity will not let themselves admit the existence of barbarism and torture today.

On the same humanitarian premises, again, it was equally difficult to accept the war itself. Into this world of mechanical progress and human amelioration, the World War came like a baleful meteor from outer space: a meteor that landed, not in a Siberian desert, but in the midst of a populous city. What was shocking about the war was not merely that it cut across the path of social improvement. What was even more dreadful, from the standpoint of a utopian rationalism, was that it brought into action emotional drives, animal loyalties, irrational surges, outrageous capacities for bloody exploit that had long been hidden from popular view: acts that were supposed to belong to the unenlightened past. Man's complete nature, not his rational side alone, now became visible. Plainly he was a creature with greater capacities for good and evil than the utopian had pictured. In war, he reached sublime heights of heroism and self-effacement; he also sank to depths of brutal egotism and animality that only the dregs and outcasts of society had explored.

The discovery of man's seamier nature was to many people a deep humiliation; what is more, it contradicted many of their most sacred beliefs and hopes. But instead of understanding themselves better, they made the war bear the burden of their frustrated idealism. If this barbarous ordeal was to justify itself to reason, it must become the repository of all men's idealisms. If the war were not to mock them forever, it must produce the rainbow; and the rainbow must also point to an authentic pot of gold. Unless all this was assured in millennial terms, the whole business was just a futile horror.

## 4. THE FALLACY OF ABSOLUTISM

In short, a good part of our contemporaries accepted the World War on condition that they should be given, for fighting through it, a free pass on an express train to the Promised Land. Their desires for the future were in proportion to their shock and outrage over the brutal present. For them, only an absolute good could justify such an absolute evil.

Need I point out the twofold misconception? First: the war itself was not in its outcome an absolute evil. Those who opposed Germany's tribal plans for conquest, though not guiltless themselves of exploiting economically a domestic no less than a colonial proletariat, nevertheless stood on their records as the exponents of far more humane and co-operative and democratic methods of government than Germany exemplified. Germany had not undergone the liberating processes of the English, the American, and the French revolutions: hence the German government, backed by a long line of German thinkers from Luther to Fichte and from Treitschke to Houston Chamberlain, stood for conquest as a mode of life, and the beast of prey as the pattern for a conquering ruling class.*

Compared with Germany, the Allies stood for universal principles of justice: principles that would eventually liberate India, Africa, China, no less than the internal proletariat of their own countries. The immediate result of the

* The epithet Hun, generally applied to the Germans during the first World War, was not the invention of an Allied propagandist. It was first used in an intentionally "eulogistic" sense, by Kaiser Wilhelm II, in bidding the German soldiers who sacked Pekin to terrorize the Chinese in such a fashion that their name would never be forgotten. Facts of this nature are usually conveniently overlooked by those who steadfastly believe that these ugly traits were never shown by the Germans until after 1933.

Allies' victory was the restoration of dismembered Poland, the redemption of submerged Czechoslovakia, the liberation of the Baltic states from Germany's recent conquest, the lifting of the yoke of slavery from Belgium, and finally—not least—opportunity to throw off the incubus of Junker military rule from the new republic of Germany itself. All these were beneficent results; they prepared the way for a more co-operative international society.

The second misconception was the belief that the peace treaty, to justify the high aims that Wilson had uttered, must be absolutely good; that only a perfectly just peace, without stain, without blemish, without human error, could justify the four long years of slaughter. This belief in an absolute good is the fabrication of people who have no understanding of the human personality, of the processes of human society, of the inevitably relative and mutable quality of all human effort. For the kingdom of absolutes is not of this world; human life knows only partial or momentary fulfillments. The post-war settlement was full of specific evils and specific goods. On the whole, the goods greatly overbalanced the evils, because a method of co-operation and the beginnings of a system of effective public law between nations had been laid down. If the mechanism of the League of Nations was feeble and imperfect, it was no worse than the Articles of Confederation which came out of our own Revolutionary War.

The notion that the World War had been fought to no purpose by the Allies and in particular by the Americans—who might have stayed out of it—is false both in theory and fact. Life presents one with innumerable situations in which one's most strenuous acts and duties produce nothing good: at most by taking up one's burdens, one keeps something worse from happening. A surgical amputation is not in itself good; it is a frightful evil; but it is usually preferable to the complete loss of life. A flood is an evil that might often be prevented by human foresight; but once the flood breaks, salvage and rescue become one's duty; and one does not help matters by crying out loudly against the Legislature's failure to provide reservoirs and reforestation belts in time.

So with the World War. Its long list of negative results is no proof whatever of its unreason or its purposelessness. This was an irrational solution of unbearable military and political tensions that had been forming for fifty years. Had Germany accepted repeated British offers of co-operation, the war might have been averted: that choice lay in human hands. But once the war itself had broken out, the duty of decent, intelligent men was to keep this irrational event from being pushed by a German victory to an irrational conclusion: a conclusion in which power alone would triumph over reason and justice. The Treaty of Versailles did not fully succeed in this aim; but one has only to compare it to the German-dictated treaty of Brest-Litovsk to realize that both wisdom and justice were preponderantly on the Allied side.

To perform the duty of resisting collective aggression, it is not necessary to hold that the morally worse cause is altogether evil, or that the better cause is wholly pure. When one helps one's neighbor to resist the assault of the gangster, the assault itself is open evidence of the relative merits of the two parties; even when one is ignorant of the gangster's history: but one need not deceive oneself as to the moral beauty of one's neighbor's character. The fact that he needs succor does not prove he is a saint; and the fact that he is not a saint does not establish one's right to withhold succor. In helping one's neighbor one vindicates the dignity of the human soul, in its refusal to submit to unreason and injustice. No reward has been promised for such an action; no reward can be demanded. But a penalty is attached to non-action in such a situation; for a human society in which men will not help their neighbors to resist evil and struggle for justice, will presently cease to exist as a society, since it will lack even the animal loyalties that are necessary for survival.

The second point against the argument that no good came out of the World War is that two tremendous results, both potentially beneficent, did indeed come out of it. One of them was the world-wide disgust and hatred for war, as an instrument of asserting and enforcing the will of nations. The hatred became so deep in the common people of the world that it has already had a fatal result: it has caused them to treat peace as an absolute good and to surrender to evil, rather than to resist it at the price of war. Thus this salutary reaction against war has lent itself to perverse manipulation by the totalitarian tyrants: Hitler has boldly exploited its capacity for demoralization.

The other great positive result of the war, achieved in the very act of fighting, was the world-wide co-operation against the Central Powers. This was a unique event in mankind's history. It made possible the League of Nations, and had the United States accepted its share of responsibility as a world power—even to the extent that it is now belatedly doing—it might have made possible a far more effective union of mankind than the League of Nations. This was no small triumph. It was the first recognition of the fact that mankind had, for practical no less than for religious purposes, become a working unity. Hence aggression and injustice in any part of the planet must eventually be a threat to law and order and peace in every other part of the planet. Through this world-wide co-operation, the Central Powers were defeated by a moral as well as a military coalition.

Here was an occasion for profound rejoicing. Its moral

meaning and its further political uses should never have been
lost sight of in the years that followed.

Apart from all the particular goods that did in fact come
out of the war, these two larger results would, if carried
through, have justified the tragic sacrifices that men had
made. But because our more idealistic contemporaries hoped
for an immediate, wholesale regeneration of mankind, they
shirked the further duties and further renunciations that the
situation demanded. What is worse, in order to justify to
themselves their own irresolution and irresponsibility, they
cast the blame wholly on the diplomats, the capitalists, the
munitions manufacturers—as if the natural and inevitable
conduct of these people did not precisely constitute the great
challenge of the post-war situation. So the outraged utopians
held that since perfection was not achieved, nothing whatever
was achieved; and that since low aims as well as high ones
had characterized the victorious powers, the high aims were
non-existent, and the low ones alone had reality.

## 5. MORAL FOR THE PRESENT

The natural letdown that followed the World War was
debilitating enough in itself. But such a letdown is almost
the inevitable physiological result of the hypertension and
superhuman effort such a great crisis demands. What made
the letdown worse was the fact that the results of the war
were measured, not against human probabilities, not against
the dire results that would have followed a German victory,
but against "ideal" results, born out of exorbitant hopes and
expectations, founded on a juvenile conception of human nature. A good part of the liberal gullibility about the achievements of the Russian revolution, in the face of its patent tyranny and totalitarianism, was due to the fact that, having

been cheated of an absolute at home, the utopians needed a surrogate heaven which they could worship at a safe distance.

Unfortunately, the spirit of utopianism has not yet been exorcized. It still continues to infect much of the thinking that has been done about the present war. And it is therefore necessary both to see its mischievous effects in the past and to anticipate them once more in the future. Unless we head off these false hopes, lazy wishful attitudes, and perfectionist illusions, we will continue to defeat all our legitimate expectations and deplete the moral energies we will badly need to achieve the relative goods that will be open to us.

We must remember, to begin with, that the immediate aftertaste of the present war will, without doubt, be repulsively bitter, even if the Axis powers should be decisively beaten, beyond any possibility of their plotting a second comeback. Consider the peoples of Europe; peoples who have been bullied and blackmailed, robbed and raped, bombed and tortured and enslaved, who have been flung here and there like so much rubbish, peoples who have been betrayed by their Quislings and Lavals, and who have been ruled by the cold sadists that Himmler has created for his universal inquisition. The sense of intolerable wrong and outrage felt by the people who come under the totalitarian rule will not at once disappear. If their hearts are to be softened, the Germans must show a capacity for repentance commensurate with the wrongs they have inflicted: an attitude of humble contrition that they gave no sign of, as Friedrich Foerster reminds us, after the last war. Humility, contrition, repentance will probably not come quickly in a land where the human soul has been barbarized and defaced to the extent that has by now happened in Germany.

In the meanwhile, the democracies, if victorious, will be condemned to take over the ignominious duty of policeman and jailer, exercising a strict vigilance, not only over millions of Nazi gangsters, well-hardened in crime, but over large tracts of the earth that have become barbarized and demoralized by the actions of these people. We must not expect the victims of Nazi rule to shake hands with those who have terrorized them: on the contrary, we must make allowances for the resentments the totalitarian governments have awakened, and we must not be unduly impatient when hot hatred or uncharitable impulses of revenge stand in the way of rational plans and reorganizations. We cannot expect more of the peoples of Europe than actually came from our brothers in the South after their country had been overrun by Grant and Sherman. And if it took fifteen years to get rid of the poisons generated politically in the first World War, it will probably take twice that time to recover from the present conflict. Only charlatans will promise a quicker recovery; only inveterate sentimentalists will let themselves even privately hope for it.

With similar realism we must face the demand for immediate world peace and world disarmament. I mention this matter here because the failure to fulfill the original promise of disarmament is often taken as one of the most outrageous breaches of international promise that followed the Versailles Treaty, and as one of the great failures of the League of Nations. Even so astute a statesman as President Roosevelt has repeatedly publicized the view that world disarmament must take place after the present war. If "after" means during the next twenty years, the demand is based on a serious misconception. The fact is that security, under law, is bound up with the existence of force; as law becomes more universally observed, more habitual, the need for force is diminished, though never entirely removed. Disarmament is not a cause of security; quite the contrary, security is the condition of disarmament. Not merely must one disarm the gangsters and bandits before one can establish the reign of international law; one must be careful *not* to disarm those who will be responsible for keeping the gangsters from building up another racket.

Before universal disarmament can take place, the states of the world will have to submit to the reign of law.* They must embody their desire for law and justice in an ordered international government, with an executive, a legislative, and a judicial authority; and this government must be capable of superseding the wills of individual groups and states. Disarmament cannot precede the establishment of a world authority; and since the working out of a planetary organization is an extremely complicated and difficult task, the maintenance of armaments by the democratic states who will serve as a nucleus for world order is vital to the success of a peaceful constitutional regime. Disarmament can proceed as fast as the non-democratic states transform themselves into constituent republics, obedient to international law: no faster. On any other terms, disarmament is an invitation to banditry and a pledge of insecurity.

The moral of this should be plain. The end of the present war must not repeat the pattern of the first World War; and to avoid that tragic error, we must banish the spirit of immature utopianism that proved so self-defeating when the first great catastrophe was ended. If the ideal goals we must work toward are to be achieved, we must be prepared for a century

* This is precisely what the United States, Russia, and Great Britain refused to do in the Dumbarton Oaks proposals. That refusal is embodied in the present charter with its domination by the Security Council whose members not merely effectively stand above the law, but are prevented by the single veto clause from disciplining or restraining one of themselves without resorting to war—the very measure that must be avoided. Unless these unwise provisions are rectified immediately insecurity will remain chronic and war itself be all but inevitable.

of resolute struggle. There will be delays, mistakes, misman-
agements, weaknesses. Unless we take these things in our
stride—along with the human partialities and prides that
threaten all good efforts—we will be disheartened once more
with the nature of the materials with which we have to deal
and we will once more shrink from the burden of responsibility.

When the war is over we will not enter utopia; we will pass
into the next phase of life. Such goods as we achieve will not
be ultimate and absolute: they will always be relative; and
we shall be in danger of losing them at the very moment they
seem most secure. There are no final solutions to human problems: what seems a final solution is only the courage to take
the next step.

# PROGRAM FOR SURVIVAL

[This essay is, in effect, a continuation of the final chapter in The Condition of Man. The opening section of that chapter might be profitably read in connection with the present argument, since it shows that it did not need the actual invention of the atomic bomb to convince intelligent observers like Burckhardt and Henry Adams that the elements that might lead to a complete disintegration of modern civilization were already at hand.]

## 1. THE CRISIS OF THE CRISIS

*At the present rate of progression since 1600, it will not need another century or half century to tip thought upside down. Law, in that case, would disappear as theory or a priori principle and give place to force. Morality would become police. Explosives would reach cosmic violence. Disintegration would overcome integration.*

Those words were written by Henry Adams in a letter to Henry Osborn Taylor in 1905; and he elaborated them in his essay on the Phase Rule in History. However outwardly arbitrary the formula upon which this prediction was based, Adams's forecast was the product of the keenest historic insight that has been recorded in modern times; for not merely did Adams date the turn in the transformation of the physical sciences and technics almost to a year, but he understood the nature of the political and moral changes that would accompany that event.* With the invention of the atomic bomb every

* Adams predicted a change of phase in 1917; actually, Rutherford's critical discovery of the possibility of smashing the atom by striking the nucleus took place in 1918.

item in the prediction was fulfilled except one: the disappearance of law and morality. That took place when the bomb was actually used.

Every human being must now consider the implications of this cosmic event; for we have now to devise, under pressure of the greatest crisis mankind has yet faced, the political and moral protective devices that will keep our knowledge, not merely from ruining civilization, but from causing life, in all its organized forms, to disappear from the planet. No previous crisis in mankind's history can compare with this: even the Ice Ages, because of their slow coming, were less of a menace to the biosphere. The question is no longer whether this or that nation, this or that civilization, can survive. The question is whether mankind has enough imagination to mobilize, on behalf of peace and co-operation, forces men have hitherto conscripted only for war and destruction. Unless the crisis produces such a dynamic will, man himself is lost.

There is one element in this problem that makes the outcome especially hazardous: the element of time. Since Henry Adams's formula has already proved to be accurate, we must have sufficient respect for his historic judgment to note that in the series of epochs into which he divided the modern age, the length of each period became progressively shorter. The age of atomic energy opened with A. H. Becquerel's discovery of radioactivity in 1896. With the invention of the first machine for releasing atomic energy on a large scale (the atomic bomb itself) that age has possibly already almost reached its end. If we fail to establish the necessary political controls and to impose the necessary moral disciplines, our world will come to a close in a quick orgy of annihilation, brought on by unsupportable anxiety and fear.

But if we learn the art of control soon enough to prevent the suicidal misuse of scientific knowledge, we will, by that very fact, have outlived the Atomic Age itself, the age of unqualified, indiscriminate power. The unification of knowledge and life will put an end to the current pursuit of power divorced from the ends of life. In the very act of saving the race, man will be compelled to master the perverse impulses that caused him to regiment and repress life itself; and that conquest will make the Atomic Age, in which the machine dominated and threatened the existence of man, obsolete.

Grave as the situation is in itself, the time element infinitely increases its gravity. Mankind, already weakened and debauched by war, cannot give itself time to idle on the oars, while deliberating at length over the changes that must be made in our educational and political institutions, if we are to control the terrible genius that has risen out of the cyclotron and the atomic bomb, as the jinn rose out of Aladdin's lamp. We must think swiftly, plan swiftly, act swiftly. And our thinking must be as unsparing of our foibles and habits as the atomic bomb itself is unsparing of all the structures and organisms within its range of disintegration. *This means that there is no part of our modern world that we must not be ready to scrap, if the need to scrap it is the price of mankind's safety and continued development.*

Nothing is sacred but human life. If the dismantling of every factory, if the extirpation of every item of scientific knowledge that has been accumulated since 1600, were the price of mankind's continuance, we must be ready to pay that terrible price. It would be foolish, indeed, to urge such a voluntary withdrawal now. But it should not be unthinkable: for only the readiness to think unconditionally about our dearest institutions and to take whatever actions the situation demands will enable us to grapple with the forces that threaten us.

The age of atomic disintegration cannot tolerate absolutism in any form: even in the form that regards scientific knowledge as an absolute. If science itself were the main obstacle to mankind's continued existence, reasonable men, fully awakened to the danger, would demolish science as readily as they would demolish a Congo fetich. They would know that if intellectual progress had caused mankind to reach the edge of the abyss, it is better to recoil than to take the last step that will send us hurtling downward. If that were the price of survival, we would have to pay it, as cheerfully as the Erewhonians did when they made the invention of machines a criminal offense.

In the first moment of appraising our situation it would be premature, to say the least, to advance the abandonment of modern science and technics as the only way out: that is far from my purpose. But our only hope of ensuring mankind's safety at a smaller price lies in our willingness to think in terms that would be as drastic and unconditional. If we cannot control ourselves sufficiently to create a harmonious world order, then we shall have to destroy our machines, as the only other means of guaranteeing our survival. But note: the most complete transformation of the self must take place among those who have been least concerned with the psychological and moral nature of man. If our leaders remain fossilized and fixed, if they remain unimaginative, limited, brutish, if they continue automatically along the path on which they have been going, they will bring on catastrophe.

This is not an idle threat, nor is it the panicky reaction of mere laymen: it has come first from those whose theoretic and practical knowledge of atomic energy gives them the fullest authority to predict the consequences of its misuse. In the course of an atomic war, as one of the distinguished Nobel prize winners, Dr. Irving Langmuir, has pointed out, the planet itself may be made permanently uninhabitable—the countryside no less than the cities. As a result, not only man's civilization but the human race, not merely human life but all forms of life, may be exterminated forever. That doom would be a heavy price to pay for the promotion of untrammeled curiosity and unbridled power.*

Never has mankind faced such a total danger before. In the race between education and catastrophe, which Mr. H. G. Wells pointed out long ago, we can already see the finish line. And at the moment, catastrophe is in the lead.

## 2. *IS* HUMAN LIFE SACRED?

Nothing is sacred but human life. I have affirmed this dogma as if it were indisputable; but in doing so I do not deny or forget that Dr. Sigmund Freud has found a death wish in the heart of our civilization; so there is a possibility, if not a probability, that part of mankind itself is now in a psychotic state and is possessed of a strong impulse to work destruction upon the world and death upon itself. To measure the destructive potentialities of the atomic bomb it is not enough to estimate the amount of energy a single machine may release: we must also make some appraisal of the forces of love and hate, creation and destruction, that are at work in the user, in modern man himself. To what extent does modern man act on the premise that life is sacred?

Two sets of forces have worked side by side in modern civilization; and they have likewise operated side by side

* See Dr. Langmuir's address at the American Philosophical Society, Philadelphia, 16 November 1945.

within science and technics themselves: one negates life, the other affirms it. The physical sciences, as first formulated by Galileo and Descartes, displaced the whole man from the investigation of the physical world. By eliminating the human equation, as far as possible, by repressing not merely emotions and desires but even the secondary qualities of matter which touched these emotions and desires, they achieved an astounding measure of skill in observing, measuring, and controlling the processes of nature. In developing along these lines they followed the classic path of capitalism.

The results had great human significance and produced measurable human benefits: an increase in power, goods, vitality. But the results were the by-product of a method that was not, as such, concerned with human benefits beyond those that accrued directly to the scientist in his search for verifiable truth.

The very success of the physical sciences in their applications to technics has given support to their metaphysical assumptions and their daily regimen. Projecting this mechanical world out of one side of his personality, man has in turn been influenced by it: in the act of contriving automatons he himself has become one: he has conceived a personality whose main characteristic is the displacement of the human by the mechanical.

Under the influence of a more humanitarian Christian insight, Leonardo suppressed the invention of the submarine, because, as he wrote in his Notebooks, man was too devilish to be entrusted with such an invention. This kind of inhibition has become almost inconceivable to the orthodox scientist or engineer. In the pursuit of truth or in the pursuit of practical success, there is no road that they will not follow to its end, even should that end prove inimical to man. Professing to eliminate questions of value and purpose from scientific thinking, this kind of man attributes value and purpose chiefly to one kind of human activity: that which he himself practices. It needed nothing less than the atomic bomb itself to shatter the shell of this orthodoxy.

Under the guise of rejecting absolutes, the technician has made science an absolute. One might smile on this charitably as a natural human foible but for this fact: Western man has accepted the scientist at his own value. The piety and superstition that led men once to worship the Golden Calf now leads them to worship the machine. For most Americans, certainly, almost any religious heresy might be uttered without awakening a word of protest, except the heresy that I am now actually uttering—the assertion that the machine is a fetich: an object of irrational devotion. Yet it is in this very irrationality of our reaction to the machine that one of the main problems of controlling it lies. If the machine is indeed our true God, what worshiper would dare to control it? The very suggestion savors of blasphemy.

From the standpoint of the physical scientist, as scientist, the notion that life is sacred is meaningless. The highest exponents of physical science, from Kepler and Newton to Clerk-Maxwell and Einstein, have never accepted the mechanistic dogma that robbed man himself of primacy and bestowed value only on his creations. But for all that, it is the guiding principle of modern research. In the physicist's world, life is non-existent, and the values of life are, if anything, merely accessory to the triumphs of physical science. This, at least, is the traditional view. Significantly, a succession of physical scientists in our own time have challenged the dubious assumptions upon which this dehumanized worldview was built up; and one may regard this reaction, which I shall refer to later, as a protective development within sci-

ence itself, against the forces of disintegration it had un-
leashed.

But there is another side to science and its applications,
fortunately for the world. This side of science has its origins
in medicine, whose first object is the maintenance of health
and the healing of disease; and here a radically different conception has flourished. Biology has established, not only the
interdependence of the entire world of life, but the fitness of
the planet itself for the nurture of life. One of the most tough-
minded of biochemists, the late Lawrence J. Henderson, demonstrated the fact that the very distribution of the chemical
elements on this planet was as if directed toward life, as if
life were the object of blind natural processes. From this
standpoint, the potentiality of entering into those unstable
combinations which constitute life is an essential aspect of
matter; and the once rigid dividing line between matter and
life has disappeared.

With these biological interpretations have grown up an increased respect for all living organisms and an increased tenderness for human creatures in particular. A desire to alleviate the sufferings of men, to wipe out disease, to eliminate
unnecessary death, to sustain health and prolong life, has
been the guiding motive of a vast amount of biotechnic research: anesthetics, aseptic surgery, dietetics have all regis-
tered enormous gains during the past century. In the application of medical insight to mental illness, Freud and his suc-
cessors have gone even further: they have demonstrated that
love is the very principle of all integration, biological, psychological, social. Without erotic love, without parental love,
without brotherly love, the destructive impulses that have
been engendered by man's struggle to survive might gain the
upper hand. Originally, the care of the sick and the outcast was one of the chief functions of the Christian Church,

with its doctrine of universal love: today the doctrine of love has become one of the most practical concerns of those devoted to the care of the ill and the mentally disrupted.

In biology, medicine, and psychology, the maintenance and amelioration of man's life is one of the main purposes of scientific activity.

Even in the biological sciences, the knowledge that is available for the development of human life may be misapplied and corrupted: that almost goes without saying. A prejudice against natural processes, abetted by scientific pride, may cause physicians to dissuade mothers from nursing their young, or the technique of contraception may lead to the wholesale practice of sterility. But on the whole, the advance of knowledge in these fields has been accompanied by increasing tenderness, increasing sensitivity, increasing practical regard for maintaining the balances of nature that help sustain, not only human life itself, but all man's millions of co-partners and helpers in the animal and vegetable world. All creatures live by complicated partnerships; but in man, the dominant creature in the hierarchy of living organisms, the circle of his responsible control and conscious co-operation has widened, and without the counter-balancing development of love and understanding his powers of annihilation would now be boundless.

Part of our technics (not the least part), part of our science (also not the least part), are deliberately on the side of life. When we give ourselves to the control of the destructive processes that the age of atomic disintegration has released, we must summon up the aid of this powerful ally. Biotechnics alone will not be enough to offset destruction. But if we are to find a substitute gratification for our present infantile worship of the machine, we shall perhaps find it in the further application of the biological sciences to the arts of life. Without that counterweight, our political and moral devices might prove too feeble to move the world.

## 3. BACKGROUND OF MORAL DISINTEGRATION

Had the atomic bomb been conceived in the year 1300, the scientist who released this thought would have been imprisoned and the opportunities for working would have been denied him. This is not a wishful judgment; it is on record that Roger Bacon, who merely dreamed of automobiles and flying machines, was treated in precisely this fashion. Without exception modern thinkers have sided with Bacon against his ecclesiastical superiors; but in its distrust for the kind of thinking the experimental Bacon introduced, it is possible that the conservatism of the Christian Church was more realistic than the sublime faith of the believers in progress, from Glanvill to H. G. Wells, that the untrammeled applications of science would automatically bring about a heaven upon earth. We can now see that the end of this automatic development may not be heaven but hell. Christianity, which had witnessed the disintegration of one civilization, knew something about the pride and destructiveness of man which modern man, precisely because of his pride and destructiveness, has resented being told. This knowledge we must now be humble enough to face.

If, from the standpoint of human safety, the thirteenth century might have been the best time for inventing the atomic bomb, the eighteenth century was perhaps the last moment in modern history when there still existed sufficient restraint, sufficient self-discipline, to ensure temporary safety. Even then, human insolence would have made the secret of atomic disintegration an incalculably dangerous toy to place in man's apelike hands. But certainly the invention of the bomb at the very climax of the second World War raised its potential of destructiveness: for atomic disintegration has been preceded by a fateful moral disintegration.

We Americans, thinking of our momentary safety, may congratulate ourselves on the foresight, the intelligence, the scientific penetration, and the international co-operation that put this illimitable power in our own hands, rather than in those of our enemies. But we must sober ourselves by recalling one fact: in the act of fighting the war we have already succumbed to our enemies' principles. We have used our invention with criminal levity, with childish impatience. Let us review the events that made this frightening transformation possible.

In the eighteenth century, as A. J. Toynbee has demonstrated, wars were fought with limited means for equally limited objectives. War brought suffering and death; but both the means and the ends of fighting were under human control. This was the result of a long effort to reduce the area of violence, broken by such mass horrors as the Albigensian Crusades and the Thirty Years' War. As a result, even such uneven contests as those between Louis XIV and the Netherlands, did not result in the swift, overwhelming defeat of the Dutch, still less did it result in the elimination of the Dutch as a nation. Military power, though used for irrational political purposes, was still subject to moral control. Nobody held the fallacious notion that war itself was so bad it could excuse any degree of violence or butchery. Law had not yet, in Henry Adams's words, disappeared as theory or a priori principle.

These hard won conventions remained in operation until the Civil War. That was an early contest between democracy and a proto-fascism which rested on slavery, racism, and belief in the finality of military power. Sherman's march through Georgia was an attack, not only upon armies, but upon the enemy's ability to make war: it was the first large-scale application of totalitarian warfare in recent times. As with our use of the atomic bomb, this evil was perpetrated by the side that justifiably boasted the preponderance of moral good in its purposes. Though the Civil War was fought for a good end, part of the process by which victory was achieved was a bad process. The total demoralization of life in the South visited penalties upon the whole country from which we have not yet recovered. Not the least penalty was the insolence and self-righteousness exhibited by the victor: the little men who took over after Lincoln's death lacked both his imagination and his magnanimity. There are obvious parallels to this situation today.

Despite this grim episode, the attempts to restrict the savage possibilities of warfare, which mechanical invention had brought with it, continued right up to the first World War. Before that war broke out, men's consciences had become extremely sensitive to violence in any form, despite its sporadic outbreaks in pogroms, lockouts, and strikes. Accordingly, when a German military officer knocked into the gutter a lame cobbler who did not make way for him, in the little town of Zabern, the incident was reported throughout the world; and the public's reaction to this exhibition of military ruthlessness was overwhelming: so overwhelming that the German Reichstag itself dared to censure the German army for this conduct of one of its members. Which, indeed, is more incredible to our case-hardened consciences today—this universal reaction to a *single* act of violence that did not involve either torture or death, or the fact that even an autocratic government was still sufficiently under the sway of public opinion to give heed to the protest?

One must ponder well this Zabern incident to realize the gap which separates the moral sensitiveness of even 1915

from that of 1945. For what was the chief reason for the
United States' entrance into the first World War? It was
essentially the practice of unrestricted submarine warfare,
which the Germans opened by the sinking of the *Lusitania* in
1915. The world gasped with horror at this savage lack of restraint. It gasped, not alone at the loss of life, but at the
abandonment of rules and limitations. The transformation of
warfare, from acts of violence between opposing armies to
unlimited terrorism and total destruction of the enemy nation, was now in full swing. The open enslavement of Belgian
workers, the Zeppelin raids on England, were of the same
order: likewise the attempt on the part of the English to bring
the German armies to terms by cutting off the food supply of
the entire homeland.

What has happened during the last thirty years? Nothing
less than the dropping of the very principle of restriction. We
have dehumanized ourselves and no longer accept any limitations, inner or outer, upon our will-to-annihilation. Within
fifteen brief years every restriction has been removed: first in
theory by our fascist enemies, then in practice by the same
enemies: but finally *by ourselves* on an even more destructive
scale. The fascist theory of total warfare was first put forth
by the Italian General Drouhet—volubly parroted by Major
Seversky and others in the United States. The believers in
this theory held that wars could be won by unlimited aerial
attack upon the civilian population. The demolition of War-
saw and the center of Rotterdam brought this theory into
action. Instead of recoiling against it and concentrating our
whole might on the fighting area, we imitated our enemies.
By the practice of obliteration bombing (alias strategic bombing) we lost any edge of moral superiority we originally held
over the enemy with regard to our *methods* of fighting. (Our
*ends* were still measurably more human.) This general moral

disintegration paved the way for the use of the atomic bomb.

Nihilism had set up a chain-reaction in the human mind: by a succession of bombardments our last inhibitions were removed.

This change did not come about overnight, nor without considerable reluctance, even on the part of military commanders. The question as to whether it was morally defensible to achieve victory over Japan by wholesale destruction from the air was still debated in Washington as late as the spring of 1942: it was not yet a closed question. When the American Air Force first operated in Europe, it boasted of the accuracy of its so-called pinpoint bombing. It did not take long for the observer to realize that this was an empty boast. The excellence of the Norden bombsight was considerably abated by poor visibility, by flak, by inability to find the target, and by false identification of the target: the number of neutral or friendly civilians killed by our bombers—to say nothing of our own combat troops—runs into thousands, on the basis of scattered newspaper reports alone.*

Long before the war came to an end in Europe the Army had abandoned all pretense of bombing military targets alone: we resorted to devastation and terror on the largest

* The report of the United States Civilian Survey Board, released 31 October 1945, on the effects of strategic bombing in Europe establishes the following facts: 1. Only twenty per cent of our missiles fell on their targets. (So much for the air arm as a weapon of precision.) 2. We did not severely damage Germany's industrial production until her air forces had been completely reduced. (Indeed, according to German figures, German production rose higher in 1944 than at any other time.) 3. The most decisive blow struck against Germany by air was the attrition of its fighter planes by our own planes at the rate of over 1000 a month at the beginning of 1944. The last item undermines the whole theory that our success in reducing Germany was due to strategic bombing: for *even in the air* it was due, rather, to the deployment of our forces, in an orthodox military manner, against the enemy's forces, not against cities, industries, and civilians.

scale possible. All our carefully built up inhibitions against unrestricted warfare had broken down. We concealed our abdication by smugly clinging to the letter of the Hague conventions with regard to the feeding of enemy prisoners of war—even though at the moment our Allies were actually starving at the very gates of the camps where such prisoners were fulsomely fed. Despite our army's readiness to kill civilians by the tens of thousands in air attacks, we refused to reduce the, diets of prisoners of war by even a few hundred calories in order to alleviate general starvation. With utmost punctilio we remained faithful to a minor convention of recent date, whilst we ruthlessly abandoned a far older and far more sacred convention. People who think in this fashion simply cannot be trusted. But it is precisely people who do think in this fashion who have the political and military disposition of the atomic bomb.

A.E.'s dictum, that man becomes the image of the thing he hates, has been fully borne out in the present war. While the pre-war fears that resistance to fascism would turn Britain or the United States into fascist countries have been proved an empty bugaboo with respect to their internal affairs, those fears have proved correct with regard to the practice of war itself. Now our methods of fighting have become totalitarian: that is, we have placed no limits upon our capacity to exterminate or destroy. Morality has become police: a mere tool of the state. In the act of grappling with fascism, the enemy has forced into our hands his most dangerous weapon, his moral nihilism. *That nihilism is the social counterpart of the atomic bomb.*

Though the transformations I have described have been swift, they have been accomplished, apparently, without any great moral shock: it needed the dramatic destructiveness of the atomic bomb itself to bring home the extent of our danger

and our demoralization. Many "good" people, many "innocent" people, accept as commonplace acts which even thirty
years ago would have been regarded as examples of unbelievable barbarism: they accept these acts as if no alternative
were conceivable. We swallow as daily food, we good people,
practices that would, a generation ago, have nauseated us
almost beyond recovery if done only once in a lifetime.

We have, indeed, reason to be proud of the scientific genius
that penetrated the secrets of matter's constitution and devised the means of disintegrating the atom. On this plane,
modern man has achieved the ultimate miracle in physics:
far beyond the wildest dreams of the medieval alchemist.
During the century that opened with Faraday's researches in
electricity, we have endowed mankind with godlike powers;
but unfortunately we have not at the same time become godlike men. The ultimate physical means of disintegration have
been discovered at a moment when our moral nihilism has
brought us down to the level of Genghis Khan, or, if that is
possible, somewhat lower. Even before the atomic bomb had
been used, we had accepted, as a normal instrument of warfare, the practice of exterminating civilians. As with the
Nazis, our lack of a sense of guilt was almost as great a sin
as the sin itself.

Because the lives of their sons and husbands were at stake,
many Americans, perhaps a majority, quickly found a way
to justify the use of the atomic bomb; that first impulse was
a natural one. But Mr. Truman and Mr. Churchill, who had
taken upon themselves the decision to exploit this new invention without specific warning, sought also to pacify their
fellow citizens' consciences. The very glibness of their words
proved their unfitness to make such a grave decision. Our
leaders pointed out that the use of the bomb reduced our possible military losses, perhaps to the extent of a million and

a half lives. For a while, the alleged humanity of atomic bombing was stressed by official publicists. As to the first point, we have now learned that the enemy was actively suing for peace before the bomb was employed. We used the bomb when we were neither in military extremity nor even in a stalemate. As for the instantaneous death of the civilians bombed, which put the method almost in the realm of mercy killing, our comfort is a little abated by the reports of the shocked, the maimed, the burned, who were not quite exterminated. But when once success becomes the sole justification of the means, there are no conceivable limits to human deviltry. The history of the Catholic Inquisition proves that fact.

Do not blame the institution of war for this ultimate mischief. It is not the rising tide of physical destructiveness that has caused war to overflow our moral levees: rather, it is our complete unreadiness to build higher and stronger levees that has kept us from containing these forces. We ourselves have breached the dykes that held back barbarism. There is no moral code in existence that could excuse the indiscriminate and wholesale slaughter of men, women, and children, no matter how instantaneous or painless that butchery might be.

The wantonness of our apologetics has not been diminished by the fact that Japan's surrender took place nine days after the first bomb was used. While one may doubt that the use of the atomic bomb alone shortened the war, other forms of obliteration bombing, equally great in scale, surely hastened the day. But the very success of the methods only increases their menace. In any short term view, wholesale extermination pays higher dividends to the successful user of the method than any other form of warfare. That in itself is a powerful, almost irresistible temptation to its further use.

On a long term view, the results of our success are less

entrancing: we have widened the province of fear, and instead of a local anxiety we have produced a universal one. The unrestrained use of terrorism and extermination reacts upon the user as well as the victim: if it does not cause revulsion, it must deepen his debasement. Our victory will be a deceptive one, if the present absence of inhibitions shortens the life-span of the human race. For mark this: the ultimate weapon of annihilation has been put in the hands of practicing nihilists, ourselves. Once we become theoretical nihilists, too, as we must when we attempt to justify our methods, then both the degradation and the danger will be multiplied. At that moment the last step in the process described by Henry Adams will take place: disintegration will overcome integration.

## 4. NIHILISM IN PRACTICE

There was once a piece of parlor casuistry which went this way: If you could acquire a million dollars by pressing a button that would kill, without pain, a man on the other side of the world, would you press it? We have found such a button and to win, not a million dollars, but a war, we have used it. In two raids, one with incendiary bombs on Tokyo, and one with an atomic bomb on Hiroshima, we killed on a modest estimate more human beings than were killed in England by Germany's continued bombing over a period of six years.

This quantitative change has proved to be a qualitative one. By increasing our own capacity for annihilation we have, paradoxically, lessened our sense of horror. Here we are faced with one further result of modern technics: even our own forces no longer make visible contact with the enemy. This process began with the invention of long-range weapons long ago; but it has now reached its limit with stratosphere flying, the rocket bomb, and the atomic bomb. The ideological insulation of the technician from normal human considerations perhaps reaches its height in the training and practice of military aviators.

The consequences of this insulation are extremely treacherous. Attack from the air upon cities is usually made from such a height that only the threat of flak reminds the airman of the presence of human beings below. When he sees flame or watches explosions he beholds them—as Mussolini's son did in the war on Abyssinia—as esthetic spectacles, not as scenes of infernal torture and pain. Unlike the infantryman, who eventually confronts his victims, the aviator is deliberately cushioned from this human shock, in the interests of preserving his mental balance. Suppose our flyers had been compelled to check in each Japanese they killed at the door of an extermination chamber. Could they have killed as many as fifty visible civilians without suffering a mental breakdown? *

In this merciless form of warfare we have justified our acts, as President Truman justified the use of the atomic bomb, on the ground that the Japanese themselves have been a cruel foe. No doubt they have been so; their acts are on record: not merely our own, but countless thousands of Chinese dead testify to this. But if evil is to be retaliated by equal evil, what should prevent us from imitating the practices of

* The rocket-bomb and the automatic, remote-controlled plane will complete this development. The airman, to his honor, risks his own life: if we permit war to exist, as a result of our selfishness and feeble-mindedness in not creating an effective world organization, the principal operatives in our next war will be screened from all contact with the enemy: safe until they are annihilated by the same means of long-distance attack. Such a war might well begin—and end—without the victims' being able to identify the enemy, or even to identify the direction from which the bombardment came.

the German extermination camps? For every rule of war the Japanese broke against us on the scale of hundreds, we have broken an equally valid rule on the scale of thousands.

To understand what we have done, let us ask what we ourselves would now feel had we been subject to the same treatment that we meted out to the Japanese. Would we not have reached new heights of moral indignation over our enemy's barbarism? Then let us ask ourselves one further question: What kind of people were we ourselves in process of becoming as the war mounted to its climax? Were we actually as innocent as we felt we were? Or had we merely hardened our hearts to the point at which we were capable of committing the Unpardonable Sin?

These are harsh words to address to a people who hated the idea of war and entered this one only at the extreme provocation of their enemies. They are even harsher words to address to a people who, in the moment of victory, naturally feel a grateful release: people who have keyed themselves to high-speed production and battle strain, and who have a natural desire to relax. Finally, these are terrible questions to ask men in combat whose lives have been spared by the method of wholesale annihilation we have practiced on the Japanese. In victory itself most of us are likely to find sufficient justification for our manner of winning it. Is this, then, the moment for drastic self-examination and self-criticism?

Yes; this is the moment for self-criticism. For it is precisely at the hour of our greatest success that we must beware the terrible sin of *hybris*, or untrammeled pride, which the wise Greeks knew, even before the Christian theologians, was the chief source of man's moral undoing. We are men and we have erred. In the very act of fighting the enemy we have let his evil become our good: a sinister transvaluation of values. Let us be strong enough to acknowledge our sins; let us be prompt to repent of them before they become habits. All the errors men made before the war, from Munich to Pearl Harbor, continue to fester because those who committed them have lacked the grace to say openly: "I was wrong." And so with this almost universal relapse into barbarism. Unless we can arouse our imaginations sufficiently to picture the consequences of our acts and to appraise rigorously their actual character, there is no further enormity that we might not, as a people, be ready to commit.

For mark this: if we can use one atomic bomb, we can use two and have done so. If two, then twenty: if twenty, then enough to wreck the world. Once we have lost the principle of control, once we have deadened our moral responses and released our inhibitions, we have lost everything. This is one of the facts that makes the present situation so serious. Modern technics, so far from helping to create a race of enlightened supermen, as Mr. H. G. Wells sentimentally dreamed, has produced a race of moral robots: their archetype is the Man with the Mechanical Heart. It is not an accident that this man was an ardent supporter of the Nazis, their willing messenger boy, and a believer in the Nazi Wave of the Future. As that wave is now receding from our shores, we must take care that we are not dragged down in the undertow.

All of Henry Adams's predictions have come true. Explosives have now reached cosmic violence and, within the international sphere, law, as *a priori* principle, has disappeared. Unless our moral recoil becomes equally violent, there is nothing to prevent disintegration from overcoming integration. This may well take place at the very moment when we are most sure of our own good purposes, our moral sobriety, and our ultimate beneficence.

## 5. THE NEED FOR CHECKS AND BALANCES

The moral recoil against the atomic bomb has already begun to take place. Horror and fear may restore us to moral sanity. Even those who apologize for its use realize that it is a double-edged weapon. If the recoil goes far enough, it may set in action the human forces and impulses that will save us. But if we cushion the recoil with specious excuses and self-justifications, if we are reluctant to respond to the challenge of our own actions with sufficient promptness and sufficient zeal, mankind may be lost. Since we have the honor of possessing, for a brief time, the technological secrets of smashing the atom on a sufficiently large scale, the duty of taking the necessary political initiatives remains ours.

Perhaps the hardest thing for us Americans to realize is that we are no longer confronted by external enemies: the most dangerous enemy we face lies within us. The high religions have always acknowledged this enemy, in the human heart itself, and modern psychology has unearthed the same foe. In the depth of man's unconscious life lie the forces of destruction he projects outside himself and externalizes. As an infant he cherishes illusions of omnipotence, and the actual achievement of physical omnipotence may cause him to relapse into infantile modes of behavior. The history of every great concentration of imperial power, from Nebuchadnezzar to Alexander, from Ivan the Terrible to Hitler, bears witness to this threat of regression. "Absolute power corrupts absolutely."

To grapple with the enemy within, we must rapidly reconnoiter and reorganize our personal conduct: that is the first step toward adequate measures in the political and economic fields. Unfortunately, we find ourselves as unprepared for this effort as we Americans were unprepared for war in 1940, when our army was drilling with wooden rifles and wagons labeled as guns. But it may help us to accomplish the profound and rapid transformation that lies ahead, if we recall the way in which a peace-loving, somewhat self-indulgent people, used to their securities and comforts, actually met the situation. What accomplished the change? Two things: self-imposed coercion and external danger. The danger justified the coercion and the coercion made it possible to face the danger. In actual battle, danger produced the effect of a wholesale conversion.

Even in the factory, still more on the battlefield, men learned to displace their individual feelings and their individual purposes, to meet the common need. Easygoing men learned to give orders; irresponsible men learned to accept weighty responsibilities; soft men learned to harden themselves to carry burdens and to perform acts that nothing in their civilian experience had fitted them for. In 1940 our country was full of cagey defeatists who would have been as easy a pushover for the fascists as the French were. By 1943 we had produced millions of highly disciplined, excellently trained men and women who were equal to the most exacting ordeals of war. The outward pressure and discipline produced an inner change.

The process that began in the training camp was completed in the field, in the air, on the sea. In the presence of danger, men learned that *the price of survival was unconditional cooperation.* "We lived only by helping one another." "You stood by the other guy and some day he might be there to help you." Those are the commonest thoughts our fighting men have brought back: it was the secret of both survival and victory. Danger made the common soldier and sailor live from day to day as only saints had lived under less terrible conditions. No one used the word love; but the fighting men kept going under fire only because they loved one another: because they loved one another more than they loved life itself. There were exceptions; there were breakdowns; but the rule survives them.

The incalculable powers of the atomic bomb have put the whole world in a situation more desperate and dangerous than that on any battlefield. The consciousness of this fact has fortunately been widespread; it tempered our exultation, even in America, over our provisional conquest of atomic energy. In warfare, we have now carried the will-to-annihilation to its logical limits. Now mankind must rapidly learn, after the pattern of the camp and the battlefield, how to unite effectively to master this danger. No nation, no group of nations, is powerful enough to stand alone: none is sufficiently disciplined and moralized to be trusted. *Today unconditional co-operation is the price of mankind's survival. If we are sluggish in our response to this situation we may forfeit the immense human blessing that the very danger, a danger on a cosmic scale, carries with it.*

## 6. THE NEED FOR LIMITATIONS

The solemn feeling that war has become more bestial by nature than cannibalism is, perhaps, the first step toward our remoralization. The kind of war every decent person hates is not alone that which the Axis powers have waged: it is that which *we* have waged. The enemy no longer lies in Berchtesgaden: he has captured the very citadel of our hearts.*

* The most disconcerting proof of this fact was brought to light in a Fortune Magazine poll, whose findings were published by Mr. Elmo Roper in the New York Herald Tribune, 8 November 1945. According to Mr. Roper over fifty-three per cent of the civilian population "believe

But it is not the menace of war alone that imposes the need for limitations, inhibitions, rigorous controls in the use of atomic energy: those conditions are imposed by the nature of the force itself. Many commentators have concealed the potential dangers of the process by picturing the unimaginable prosperity and well-being that might ensue from harnessing such vast quantities of energy to peaceful uses. But the fact is that even in the pursuit of this peaceful goal, we may encourage our scientists and technicians to embark hastily on experiments from which there may be no withdrawal: experiments that might possibly produce a chain of physical disintegrations which, so far from lending themselves to man's welfare, would rub out our centers of civilization, perhaps make life impossible on the planet itself. Too late we would learn from those experiments that knowledge, like patriotism, is not enough. Man's nature is threatened by the diabolical powers he now possesses: the history of the present war demonstrates this fact. But even were man wholly an angel, he would still need to control the smashing of the atom.

Now, the history of Western man's technical improvements during the last thousand years has been the story of his accelerated expansion of physical energy. Unfortunately, at no point in this process have we developed the political controls and the social goals that would diffuse this gain and make everyone the beneficiary. If any people should know this fact it is we Americans; the very vastness of our material resources tempted us to perversions and wastes on a comparable scale. Our one-sided belief in mechanization, as a good in itself, even concealed from us the need for controlling devel-

that we should have used this secret weapon in exactly the way we did," while "a majority of all sexes, all age groups, and people in every part of the country subscribed to this feeling of satisfaction over our use of the atomic bomb."

opment of the machine in relation to our capacities for assimilating it. The prospects of profit closed our eyes to this need. Did we not introduce the radio, the long range bomber, and the atomic bomb in a decade still governed mainly by isolationist minds? Have we not produced the technical means of world-wide communication without devising a world language?

The great problem of all mechanical improvement is the problem of tempo. Our mechanical inventions have multiplied at geometric ratio, so to say, while our social skills and moral controls have increased at an arithmetic ratio, when they have not, in fact, gone backward. If this disparity had not existed, job insurance would have been invented the same time as the factory system, and an active Union of Nations would have been produced, in lieu of the half-hearted and abortive Hague Conferences, during the decade when the Wright Brothers perfected the airplane.

The disproportionate development of the physical sciences, right down to our own day, has increased the threat of the atomic bomb, and greatly lessened the likelihood that good would immediately come of its industrial applications. The two billion dollars that was ungrudgingly voted by Congress for the perfection of the atomic bomb should have been accompanied by an equally large sum for the promotion of such knowledge and understanding and skill as would control such a weapon. The first measure spoke for itself and needed little extraneous support beyond General Marshall's say-so. The second measure was so far from our habitual evaluations that it would have seemed bizarre had anyone even proposed it. While we spare ourselves no effort on the physical perfection of our weapons and machines, we are still content to blunder and tinker with their human applications.

Now, the miraculous knowledge which has made it possible to use atomic energy has been in existence less than fifty years: indeed, the critical experiment which put this power in man's hands is hardly more than half a dozen years old. In view of the present rate of acceleration, the first act of prudence, the minimum precaution against a world catastrophe, would be the deliberate curbing of further activity until adequate positive controls can be worked out. Even to preserve the scientific knowledge that has unlocked this new source of energy, we must first take care to preserve the civilization that encouraged it. Far-sighted engineers, like Sir Alfred Ewing, saw the need for such a moratorium on invention half a generation ago.

What are the obstacles to declaring such a temporary respite? Mainly these: disbelief in danger and disbelief in the principle of control, or even in its possibility. I have already pointed out the consequences of an unqualified worship of the machine; but perhaps nothing so well indicates the danger that threatens our civilization today as the absence of response to danger signals. That was true of the original fascist attack on civilization: apparently intelligent people refused to believe the plain evidence of their senses, and dismissed as hysterical war-mongers those who pointed out that the Nazis were planning a wholesale attack. Though in many quarters the response to the threat of the atomic bomb has been far more adequate, there is no guarantee that it will remain at its original pitch, or that, once the first breath-taking realization is over, complacency and inertia may not once more prevail.

The first step toward control of atomic energy must be an international one. No one country, with the best will in the world, can establish adequate controls. I shall go into the details of that reorganization presently. Here I would emphasize that there is nothing new or untried in the proposal to put restraints upon invention: *such measures are daily commonplaces in the business world.* Our great industrial monopolies do not hesitate to suppress an invention which may result in diminution of current profits, no matter how advantageous the invention might be to society at large. The automatic telephone-exchange, for example, was suppressed for a whole generation because of this fact.

If inventions are curbed by private corporations for their own benefit, at the expense of the consumer, by what foggy canon of conduct are we bidden not to suppress temporarily the invention of the atom-smasher, when that invention may result, not in a loss of profit, but in the wholesale extermination of the human race? In this matter, who are the chirping idealists and who are the hard-headed practical men—those who would go ahead blindly with these forces of destruction or those who would freeze our present knowledge until education and law and personal discipline had become adequate to control them and direct them toward valuable human ends? Only life is sacred. Knowledge and inventions are mere by-products of life.

Probably, now that the secret of the constitution of matter has been plumbed, the co-operative intelligence that achieved this first result will also find methods to release intra-atomic energy by more economic methods: possibly in smaller installations than the present ones. No one man, no one group, no one nation, is wise enough to carry this responsibility; while if the knowledge becomes further diffused before we have devised adequate controls, we have but widened the grounds for fear, and planted potential booby traps behind every closed door.

Even if the military threat of the atomic bomb were overcome by an adequate world organization, its peacetime uses must still be under surveillance. Curiosity once killed a cat.

It is conceivable, with the means now at the scientist's disposal, that untrammeled curiosity might kill the human race. The probability of this happening may be low; but it cannot altogether be neglected. Let no one cheerfully recall the ominous predictions once made about the disastrous effect of rapid transit on human health: there is no parallel between any older type of machine and the powers now at our disposal. Minute radioactive particles of low intensity, introduced into the worker's system while painting luminous dials on watches, resulted in the destruction of tissue and the death of many such workers. Our safety so far has lain only in the infinitely small quantities of such energy that were available. In dealing with forces of cosmic violence our previous calculations are as inapplicable as using ten fingers would be in reckoning astronomical distances.

Freedom of research, in other words, should not apply to this field; nor may the control of research be left even to the most responsible group of scientific workers. Who will control the controller? There might come a time when one psychotic worker in the realm of atomic disintegration would possess the power to blow up a city—and might use it. Such power has never before been in human hands: it is the equivalent of the imaginary lever which Archimedes described as capable of lifting the world.

In the face of such power, we must perfect an equally superhuman discipline to govern its use; and we must not attempt to exploit the power prematurely, before we have developed such a discipline. What is more: the extent and rigidity of our political and moral controls must be directly proportional to the power and speed of the process of atomic disintegration. This is an elementary theorem, and it should be self-explanatory. What are not self-explanatory are the means that will promise, if not guarantee, success in this effort. We have still to take the first step.

## 7. THE ATOMIC BOMB AND WORLD ORDER

If the development of atomic energy requires the strictest kind of control, even in the peaceful arts, the demands it imposes in the realm of war are even more drastic. The continued acceleration of destruction in modern warfare has now reached a point where, through the use of the atomic bomb even in its present limited form, every major center of civilization might be wiped out, and all that we recognize as civilization might disappear in that process. Mr. H. G. Wells pictured these dire events in The Shape of Things to Come with consummate accuracy: his imagination failed him only when he sought to rescue the world from disorder and abject barbarism by giving authority to the same kind of personality that had made this disintegration possible.

Fortunately, even in the United States, a timely sense of foreboding has restrained our elation over our prior invention of the atomic bomb. Even the ignorant know that it is only a matter of time, probably a very short time, before the same skill and the same capacity for terrorism will be in the hands of peoples who, if the world remains unregenerate, will be potential enemies. Within ten years a combined perfection of the atomic bomb and the rocket bomb might make destruction absolute: no spot on the planet would be out of range, and this fact would destroy every conceivable immunity of defense. This is no empty threat, no terrified fantasy: once more the wishful dreamers are the "practical" men who continue to labor under the hallucination that nothing essentially has changed. In the present state of mankind, chaos is already breathing down our neck.

The best authorities on this question are the physicists and chemists, particularly those who have developed the atomic bomb. On the absoluteness of our present danger, and on the radical need for organizing an effective world authority, their considered opinions are practically unanimous. Indeed, the superb response of the physical scientists to the human threat of their most significant single advance in science and technics is one of the few encouraging signs in the present situation. Their bold and prompt reaction offers a stark contrast to the pitiful inertia, the limited perspectives, and the bumptious isolationism of the so-called practical men in politics.

Those who know most about the results of releasing atomic energy also know how close we already are to final catastrophe. They have likewise shown an exemplary capacity for personal reintegration, upsetting their well-formed habits and sacred conventions in order to deal unreservedly with this emergency. Overnight, as it were, the recluses of the laboratory have become citizens: world citizens, morally awake and active, serving their country best by thinking first for humanity. Their demand for a World Organization as the first step toward responsible control is all the more effective because it has been preceded by this profound personal break with their own hitherto inviolable routines: what they ask of the National State they have done in themselves.

Dr. Reinhold Niebuhr has appraised the response of the physical scientists with great acumen: "The humility and moral sensitiveness of the scientists who developed the bomb, proves that the atomic bomb heralds the end of one age and the beginning of another in more than one sense. For this humility proves that the era in which science assumed that all of its discoveries were automatically beneficent to mankind, is past. The scientists are beginning to understand how all the achievements of a technical age contain potentialities of evil as well as of good; and that sometimes the evil is more obvious and immediate than the good." *

The knowledge that has made the atomic bomb possible cannot, under present conditions, be concealed or hidden: it was the product of an international scientific co-operation, and the threat of its widespread use can be averted only by international control. The moral disintegration which has made it possible for "civilized" men to practice obliteration bombing has likewise become universal: the hideous practices of fascism have attacked, like cancer cells, the sound tissues of democracy. Men are now psychologically prepared to attack human life in the same spirit that they use DDT to attack insects: the planet itself is now, potentially, an extermination camp. Those two facts form the baseline for every rational plan to safeguard the future.

Let us examine, first, the immediate problem of control: the effective outlawry of war itself. The English-speaking nations are the present custodians of the atomic bomb. We who belong to those nations must be devoutly grateful for this one-sided blessing; at least the secret is not in the hands of our enemies: indeed, we can even thank our enemy's irrational racial prejudices for delivering into our hands some of our essential scientific collaborators.

But how secure, how grateful, can the rest of the world feel? Other nations do not regard our intentions as so immaculate as we regard them; neither do they regard our virtue as so sustained, our motives as so incorruptible as we do. When our country was led by a Wilson or a Roosevelt it was generous, magnanimous, co-operative. But what if the United

* The Atomic Issue. In Christianity and Crisis. 15 October 1945. For a brief, effective statement by representative scientists see: The Atomic Scientists Speak Up, by Dr. D. H. Hill, Dr. E. Rabinowitch and Dr. J. A. Simpson, Jr., in Life. 29 October 1945.

States were led by a Huey Long, a Robert Reynolds, a Charles Lindbergh? A country that can produce such people might, by some freak of human perversity, put one of them into the presidency. At that moment the other nations might well shudder at their prospects—and redouble their feverish research on bigger and cheaper atomic bombs.

What organization is capable of controlling the use of atomic power and securing its potential benefits for humanity? The present organization of the United Nations? Obviously no: that institution was already twenty years out of date when it was formed: the very terms of the Dumbarton Oaks proposals show how little the politicians and the diplomats and the so-called experts had been awakened by the events that had taken place before their eyes. The invention of the atomic bomb has merely made the weaknesses of the San Francisco Charter flagrant; one might as well attach an old-fashioned wagon brake to a 100 h.p. motor car, as apply its provisions for control and co-operation to the regulation of atomic energy.

There is nothing in the constitution of the United Nations that would enable the rest of civilized mankind to bring the principal user of atomic energy under control. Quite the contrary, the charter specifically provides that the United States, as a member of the Security Council, may veto any effort to establish such a control. The three big powers have, in actuality, placed themselves above the law, and above the necessity for showing a decent respect for the opinions of mankind. But the very invention of the atomic bomb has made it imperative, for the good of the whole world, to put these powers—ourselves above all—strictly under the judgment and the surveillance of the rest of the human race. Humanity's future, not ours alone, is at stake.

In other words, we ourselves have put the world in peril;

and as an indication of our own sense of responsibility, we should take the initiative in inviting the world to reconstruct the charter of the United Nations, so that no one big power shall sit in judgment on its own righteousness, or escape responsibility for offenses that this power itself may commit. Such an initiative would be a little like the sane impulse of a person threatened with a manic attack, to commit himself, during his lucid periods, to the hands of a physician, lest he might lose control of himself at some unexpected moment and become a danger to society.

For us to take the initiative in making the United Nations charter an instrument of universal law, rather than the instrument of a temporary concentration of power in the hands of the Big Three, is nothing less than an act of self-preservative prudence. For unless present national sovereignties are liquidated, the world organization we have created will lack the authority necessary to give even ourselves security. The United States is no less vulnerable than the tiny state of Luxembourg to the weapon we have created. So long as the preparation of atomic bombs may go on in secret, we have no guarantee that our own cities might not, in five years or ten years, be wiped out without warning by an enemy that had caught up with us in technical research.

Certainly people who were demoralized enough to use such a weapon would not hesitate to attack without warning in a time of professed peace: even the routine flights of commercial planes might be used to effect a simultaneous attack without warning on a score of different cities. That would realize Mr. Stuart Chase's Two Hour War fantasy with a vengeance: the inevitable reprisals would not undo this damage but would widen it. Once explosives have reached cosmic violence, there is no middle point between world order and annihilation.

The only guarantee of our own safety as a people, then, is a world governed by law, in which protection against violence is enforced by police, acting as the obedient agents of a common judicial and moral authority. Such a world must be, by definition, an open world: that is to say, no nation can hold itself immune to the processes of world government. The authority of the United Nations must be unqualified and universal: every last laboratory and factory must be open to investigation by authorized international agents, responsible to the central world authority. The power to spread, limit, or even outlaw scientific investigation must reside in such a body no less than the power to outlaw completely all national armies. Privacy, secrecy, sovereignty must be unconditionally surrendered to a common body whose prescribed powers must override all local administrative organs at every point that is necessary to ensure freedom from fear and freedom from unlawful aggression. *This is the minimum price of security. No state can be permitted to stay out of this organization; no state, no group of states, can be permitted to dominate it.**

But now we must face the major problem that the Dumbarton Oaks proposals studiously avoided: the problem of assessing political power, which is the first step toward its responsible distribution and its effective expression. In practice, the San Francisco Charter concentrates power in the hands of the three nations that momentarily possessed the maximum amount of military effectiveness. If this was done at the insistence of Soviet Russia, the joke is now sadly on that country; for if military power is to be the sole weight, the English-speaking nations now effectively dwarf Russia and

* See Dr. Niels Bohr in Science. 12 October 1945. In his analyses of the danger of the atomic bomb and in his suggestions for positive international control Dr. Harold Urey has shown a statesmanlike grasp of the situation so far apparently denied to most professional statesmen.

without forbearance could make Russia's formal veto as meaningless as Salvador's. But in a few short years our own preponderance of power might become equally absurd: by some unexpected scientific discovery, Switzerland might possess the power to manufacture five times the number of atomic bombs we can make.

The alternative to giving a preponderance of power to the Big Three is not to give equal power to each of the so-called sovereign nations: that is a manifest absurdity at the other end of the scale. One cannot equate the power of an elephant and a mouse. One nation one vote is a formula for inequality and injustice. In order to give effective representation to the principle of equality and to the fact of power, power itself must be weighted. The temptation to give voting power to nations in accordance with their populations has the precedent of the national ballot box; but it is not capable of representing the real forces that are at work in great collective groups. Though there remains an element of arbitrariness in every assessment of power, a point score can and must be worked out. Such a score would give weight to each of the following factors: population, literacy, industrial capacity, resources, responsible participation by the governed. Thus on the score of population the United States would be inferior in voting power to China or India; but that would be equalized, as of the present moment, by greater literacy, greater industrial capacity, and a greater measure of organized political responsibility. Russia would stand high on the first two counts; but under her present system of government would stand low on the fourth item.

Without any other form of coercion, this voting principle, once instituted, would contribute in every country to those reforms in education, government, and industrial life which would further international co-operation. The assessment of power is the first step toward the international control of power. Once a just and equitable system of voting is worked out, which takes account of political realities, mankind will be able to bring legal authority, moral wisdom, and police force toward the solution of problems that have hitherto been left to inertia and arbitrary coercion, to accidental changes and to one-sided interference with such accidental changes.

The absolute destructiveness of our new weapons has destroyed forever the notion of absolute national sovereignty. All the struggles and oppositions that will take place between nations and groups, must take place, as civil quarrels now do among individuals, within the frame of a common law and a commonly accepted procedure for peaceful settlement, in which the strongest must bow before the weakest, when the latter has justice—and the rest of mankind—on his side. Such an organization must be ready, in Augustine's words, to "spare the lowly and strike down the proud."

Nothing could be plainer than the fact that cagey non-co-operative political thinking has brought on the catastrophes of the last thirty years. But if that was true even in 1919, it has become infinitely more true now. Has the atomic bomb awakened our leaders to the need for another approach to the problem of world organization than that which was actually taken? Will atomic energy serve as the catalytic agent that will make possible a profound transformation of human society? . . . If an atomic bomb had fallen in every country, one could perhaps hope that the shock would be universal and effective; failing that, failing action in the near future while the shock is still operative in our thinking, we may too easily sink back once more into a false sense of security, based on a willingness to accept only conditional and limited surrenders of national sovereignty.

Accordingly, something more than shock will be necessary

before mankind learns the art of co-operation. As in times of plague, people often make virtuous resolutions under the threat of immediate death, which they not merely forget, but actually flout, once the danger has lifted. Moral shock therapy may, as it were, make us ready for a fresh integration; but it will not by itself provide us with the resources that will ensure mankind's survival. That goal requires total mobilization.

## 8. MOBILIZATION FOR SURVIVAL

Admittedly, the political measures I have just sketched are not easy to work out in detail. So crude is the world's social organization still that the very census data essential to a just apportionment of votes is lacking for large areas. But if this initial difficulty is great, the obstacles to carrying through a scheme of world-wide government, within the time span that the atomic age itself presents, are even more serious; for we must conquer our aggressiveness, our pride, our insularity, as well as our inertia, not merely to institute a new charter of government but to ensure its continued operation.

Whereas, with marvelous scientific resourcefulness, man has unlocked the secrets of outer nature and so achieved control of nature's arcane forces, he has not yet fully unlocked the secrets of his own constitution. The sciences and arts of conscious human development are still in their infancy, though they are both probably older than the use of fire or the systematic observation of the stars. Samuel Butler's jibe at Christianity, that as an implement of morality it is but a flint instrument, holds not merely for orthodox religion but for all the disciplines that operate on man.

On the human side, there are two places that call for self-preservative effort. Negatively, we must impose restraints and restore inhibitions. Positively, we must overcome our frustration, our hatred, our aggressiveness by removing both the inner and the outer blockages to sympathetic understanding and loving co-operation. The inner blockages are the result of man's willful egoism; many probably spring from failures to grow out of infantile illusions, to live down early injuries, or to assimilate life's later humiliations and disappointments. The outer blockages are chiefly the projections of these weaknesses in institutions, institutions that often continue in operation, as war itself has continued, even when the impulse they originally represented is no longer present.

What resources are in humanity's immediate possession toward the achievement of these ends? In answering this question, I would stress the word immediate, for such knowledge as man might possess a hundred years from now, or even a generation from now, if the psychological and social sciences were widely pursued, would be too tardy to guarantee survival. Furthermore, in looking for helpful agents we must not commit the characteristic mistake of looking for knowledge alone; for it may be that it is only at the instinctual or pre-rational level that we shall get an adequate response on a scale sufficient to combat the disorders that threaten society. The reaction of the intellectual classes to the present war shows how little their special discipline is to be trusted in the appraisal of realities. In the spring of 1940 a big group of distinguished scientists begged the American government to keep out of the war on the ground that our participation would hamper scientific research! Their naïveté was as incredible as their logic.

We already have enough knowledge of the human organism to understand that further knowledge may not be the answer we most need. Yet so engrained is our reliance upon science itself that a multiple approach, though grounded in a deeper knowledge of human nature, runs the danger of being automatically dismissed.

Any forthright analysis of this problem finally must come to the conclusion that we are concerned with the radical making over of the personality of modern man. If love is to replace aggression, if the Virgin is to supplant the Dynamo, if integration is to overcome disintegration, every institution and organization through which human beings operate must address itself to the task in hand. The re-education of man is the key to his immediate safety and his ultimate salvation. Our fatal error would be if we thought that world organization alone could see this job through. Quite the contrary. There is no single device for making love work or for controlling the flood-waters of hate and aggression. As with destructive rains that man must harness, part of these energies must be absorbed by the soil, part must be conducted into natural reservoirs, part must be held back by dams, part must be made to work turbines, and part must be used for irrigation. All these operations have institutional counterparts in human society; but the place where the controlling transformation must take place is in the individual personality. When society is in danger, it is the individual who first must be saved.

This last statement may seem either an outmoded commonplace or a vapid paradox. Actually, it rests on a mass of demonstrable historic evidence, much of which has been gathered together in A. J. Toynbee's classic A Study of History. Yet so remote is this point of view from the intellectual folkways of our time that few educated people can even understand the theorem as a simple proposition, and fewer are ready to accept it for themselves, even if they finally realize that it does not mean just the opposite of what it professes to say. Because of their faith in automatic and depersonalized processes, because the scale of our institutions makes men feel dwarfed and irresponsible, people look for changes to take place, if at all, in the form of organized mass movements. Above all, they look for change to take place outside the human ego. "Science" will find the answer: "organization" will find the answer: we are reluctant to believe that, first of all, "you" and "I" must find the answer. We are perhaps ready to change the whole world, but only on one condition: that we do not have to touch or transform our selves.

But the fact is that wholesale changes can take place only on a piecemeal basis. There is no solution of Carlyle's tantalizing problem: given a world of thieves, to produce an honesty out of their united action. Given a world of infantile and aggressive personalities, one cannot hope to produce political union and brotherly love out of their collective operation. Change, therefore, must be multifold; it must take place on every level that will further the renewal of the human personality. Political change is no more vital than religious change; economic change no more essential than educational change; for all these changes are, first of all, processes in an integrating personality. Changes that mankind will require perhaps a thousand years to translate adequately into working institutions, must first manifest themselves within the human heart. Only there can the initial transformation operate with sufficient swiftness; by contrast, every institution is by definition a society for the *prevention* of change.

In short, man must achieve wisdom before he can use his knowledge: he must be transformed at the core before he will be able to control the periphery. On this matter, I can think of no better counsel than the reflections of a young Frenchman (killed by the Germans in 1942) when he faced the debacle of Munich. "It is indeed," wrote Jacques Decour, "the moment for us to remember love. Have we loved enough? Have we spent enough hours each day in marveling at other men, at being happy together, at feeling the value of contact, the importance and the worth of hands, of eyes, of the body? Do we still know how to dedicate ourselves to tenderness? It is time, before vanishing without hope in the earthquake, to be entirely and definitely for love, tenderness, friendship, because there is no other thing." * This is but a modern variation of the essential insight of Jesus of Nazareth: a prelude to effective action on the scale of our present needs.

What is the upshot of this analysis? One must impose the duty of saving mankind from its own potential self-destructiveness, not upon a single savior, not upon a group of statesmen or experts, still less upon some new institution: this analysis throws the burden, first of all, on each individual. Only if the challenge is widely accepted, will the human reaction be equal to the present situation. Without this personal change all the necessary institutional changes will be crippled at the start.

For mankind at large, there is no time to discover new knowledge before we control the forces that now threaten us: we must work with the existing means, and transform those who operate these means—ourselves. Eventually we may hope to create a world religion, but immediately we must rely upon the Hindu becoming a better Hindu, the Mohammedan a better Mohammedan, the Christian a better Christian, the Communist a better Communist. Eventually we must create a world society; but first we must rely upon the leaders of our national states giving to man's welfare the zeal they have hitherto given to party or country. We may hope for a unified science, too; but first we must demand greater self-discipline, greater social responsibility, greater capacity for mutual aid, on the part of the individual scientist. To each and all of our

* Unedited Memorandum. In Twice a Year. New York: 1945.

fellow-men, first of all to ourselves, we must now repeat Father Zossima's words in The Brothers Karamazov: "Every day and every hour, every minute, walk around yourself and watch yourself, and see that your image is a seemly one."

## 9. DEDICATION TO LIFE

Even under the limitations of his present development, modern man possesses enough life-furthering impulses and life-directed goals to save himself. But only on one condition: that a change in attitude overcomes his inertia and makes these impulses and goals operative. Man cannot save himself without first healing his split personality, without giving up his current habit of pursuing at the same time two different and incompatible goals. Power must become the willing servant of love.

No new principles of morality, no new devices of politics, need be invoked in order to achieve this psychological change, much though we might welcome them were they already at hand. What we need rather is the dynamic capacity to apply old principles and old devices to the situation we now face: to apply them and keep them vigorously in operation, even when the first threat of danger has seemed to subside. To effect this change on the world-wide scale our very technology demands, each individual must dedicate himself to his own self-improvement. It is the continued rule of the complacent and the unawakened ones—most of our present leaders in politics, business, and education—that we must fear, rather than the immediate outbreak of the more disintegrated and destructive types our civilization also produces. As in the 1930's the blindness of the first paves the way for the sadistic exploits of the second.

Since our first problem is the problem of control, let us

begin with those elements of control which are still operative within the dominant pattern of our civilization; and first of all, let us consider the sciences themselves, which have developed, within their own fields, an adequate technique of control. The basis for this is the co-operative sharing of knowledge and the institution of the experimental method, whereby the findings of any particular man or group can be subjected to independent verification. This technique itself is a moralizing practice. Within the field of nature it has caused men to replace their random guesses or their untutored prejudices with instruments of measure and order from whose finding there is no appeal, except by a resort to similar methods. The humility of the scientist in the face of observed fact is the equivalent of "Thy will be done." The method of science, in other words, neutralizes man's local biases and partialities; it normalizes his rationality.

The world-wide diffusion of the scientific technique has fostered co-operation and mutual confidence among those capable of employing it. As far as they go, these controls are useful; but it would be presumptuous to think that the scientific method replaces other means of control: as presumptuous and unwise as the statement of a distinguished historian, as late as 1930, that science had forever removed the possibility of a recurrence of barbarism. The techniques of science only apply to the method, not to the end; they control the process of research, not the direction of research; and they discipline a fragment of the human personality, not the whole personality, many parts of which are untouched by this method and immune to its processes.

Indeed, the very over-emphasis of a method that displaces human wishes and desires in the pursuit of truth may create a compensatory willfulness in other aspects of the personality. In the evolution of science and technics to the dangerous state they have now reached, the scientist himself has often shown an incapacity for both self-criticism and self-control. Holding himself strictly responsible for processes, he has been incurious about the ultimate results of his work. Outside his own narrow realm, he may be a barbarian, and to the extent that he is concerned only with that narrow realm he is in fact a barbarian. Even in the social sciences, where the very subject matter should erect a safeguard against dehumanized thinking, the adoption of a more exact methodology has often been accompanied by a loss of direction and purpose, on the false assumption that true science has no human concerns.

Now, the emergency that confronts mankind demands that there should be a change in the direction of research itself. Until man's personal disciplines and social controls are capable of mastering the immense forces he now commands and putting them to wise use, he must desist from aggravating the danger by fostering further effort along the lines that have brought on the present crisis. Here our institutions of learning, our engines of research, must govern their apportionment of budgets and their selection of staff on a principle not hitherto generally respected except perhaps in Soviet Russia: the principle of social need. Such an effort would multiply the number of anthropologists, sociologists, and psychologists, while it would diminish their opposite numbers in the physical sciences: it would endow Schools of the Humanities and curtail Schools of Technology.*

There is, of course, no magic in such a change unless it be accompanied by a new sense of urgency and responsibility, and a fresh capacity for distinguishing between the trivial

* See The Making of Men in Part Two. I do not suggest that any of our existing Schools of Humanities, despite many superficial changes now taking place, will meet our need.

and the essential. But this effort would be at least a deliberate attempt to rectify our one-sided preoccupation with mechanical invention and purely material improvements. In the end, a balance would be established; and the physical sciences themselves would probably benefit by this curb on their random productivity and by the opportunity for assimilating their own headlong advances.

Men act long before institutions move. The change I am advocating here has already taken place, in token form, through the redirection of effort by individual mathematicians and physicists. The humanistic studies of the mathematician, A. N. Whitehead, with his criticism of the mechanical world picture itself, were typical acts of reorientation. As if in a self-preservative effort to guard against the life-threatening knowledge that physics possessed, even before the atomic bomb was devised, men as eminent in physics as Erwin Schroedinger, as able as L. L. Whyte, have sought, as physicists, to ally their own findings to biology. All over the world such men are attempting to create a body of unified science, which would not alone adequately describe physical nature, but give their due primacy to life and mind and spirit. The quiet researches in optics of Professor Adelbert Ames at Dartmouth College have re-instated value and purpose at the most primitive level of physiological activity—that of supposedly pure sensation. Such work in many different fields lays the groundwork for a new age, not a new Age of Technics, but a new Age of Man, fortified by a technics that is under the control of man and is directed to man's survival and development. This age is still waiting for its new Bacon, who will re-write the Advancement of Learning with the human elements, which Bacon did not in fact exclude, in a dominant rather than a subordinate position.

But the reorientation of the sciences touches only one

aspect of the human personality. The change that will make world organization effective must operate on many different levels of the personality; and to put all our trust in science would be to show that we have not learned as much about the human personality as the psychologist and the sociologist have already demonstrated. Perhaps the most we can ask of the scientist today is that he transfer his capacity for self-abnegation, his well-trained inhibitions, his rigorous respect for controls, to wider areas of knowing and doing. His knowledge must be oriented toward life; for only life is sacred. Here his insight and his example will have a powerful effect upon his contemporaries; for the mass of mankind today his authority is as absolute and as awful as that of a primitive medicine man.

Not the least important force we must mobilize, in the interests of survival, is an ancient one: that of religion. Both Benjamin Kidd a generation ago, and Henri Bergson in our own time, interpreted religion as a self-preservative effort, on the part of life, to guard man against the discouraging effects of his own achievements in knowledge. There is a profound truth in these interpretations. Though most of the classic religions have dwelled on the familiar facts of man's limitations and frustrations, centered in the ultimate mystery of death, they have all guarded life itself, as zealously as the vestals guarded fire. Hinduism, Confucianism, Buddhism, Judaism, Christianity, even Mohammedanism, have sought to curb man's impulses to destruction and disintegration: each of them interdicts random killing, each of them encourages procreation, each of them has sought to foster love.

In this moment of common peril, we should do well to overlook the hypocrisies and failures of the orthodox: their very superstitions have nevertheless kept the ignorant, the willful, and the destructive under some limited sense of order and some minimum system of control. If the symbols of religion do not always stand up under rational examination, if their myths are more mysterious than the mysteries they would explain, that is not necessarily a proof of their inability to penetrate and control the irrational elements in man. Religion's function, in fact, is to redress man's pride in his intellect, to reduce his conceit and his complacence, so that he will be better fortified to face the ordeal of reality. Mankind is a-float on a frail life-raft. Religion understands the monsters of the deep and the storms that come up in the night.

Religion reminds man of his creatureliness and his creativeness, his impotence and his power, his cosmic littleness and his cosmic preciousness—for the tiny spark of consciousness man carries in his soul may be, up to now, the final event toward which the so-called physical universe has moved. Religion's cosmic time sense, achieved long before astronomy sustained the intuition with exact calculations, is a brake against the possibility that man might sacrifice his own long future to some temporary gratification or some temporary triumph. Here is a latent power for man's self-preservation: on the whole, theologians have made a more prompt response to the atomic bomb than any other group except the atomic physicists themselves, though they have still to show the capacity for unified effort that will make a wider renewal possible.

Morality is Sancho Panza to religion's Don Quixote; for morality develops out of the customs of the tribe and those customs, too, are usually life-preservative ones, though they may clash with those of other tribes. Modern man, proud of his fearless investigation of every part of the universe, conscious of his increasing powers to control his circumstances, has shown something less than forbearance to those primitive cultures whose daily acts are limited by taboos. But in throwing off the irrational object of most taboos, modern man has also forfeited the very habit of inhibition that the taboo imposed. He has thus forgotten one of the most essential secrets of man's advance: the practice of restraint. Whereas the older midbrain is the seat of man's instinctual energies and his explosive emotions, the newer forebrain, which takes care of his higher behavior, is also the seat of his inhibitions. Without the development of these inhibitions man's untempered curiosity might, long before this, have proved suicidal.

In little matters, modern man acknowledges taboos: he does not spit in a subway car, blow his nose in public without using a handkerchief, or enter a house with a quarantine notice posted on its door. But in general, his plan of life has resulted, not in exchanging taboos for rational restraints, but in exchanging taboos for equally irrational habits of relaxation. For the last two hundred years a long succession of thinkers, from Diderot and Rousseau onward, have urged man to throw off his ancient taboos: to act on his impulses, yield to his desires, abandon measure in his gratifications. If man were wholly rational and wholly good, these counsels would perhaps have been profitable: but Dostoyevsky, who understood the demonic in man, pointed out long ago the dangers of this moral nihilism; and in our day those dangers have assumed cosmic dimensions.

Morality, in the elementary form of accepted inhibitions, is the first step toward the conscious control of the powers man now commands: without this lowest form of morality, engrained in habit, no higher form can be practiced. What Irving Babbitt called the inner check—the vital restraint—is essential to our survival. Promptly we must reverse Blake's dictum—we must bless braces and damn relaxes.

This moral tightening of the bit comes very hard to modern man; for it is no exaggeration to say that he has attempted in

the past generation to live by the pleasure principle: he has
tried to establish a regime of limitless gratifications without
accepting deprivations or penalties. The very quantification
of life through machine production has lifted many natural
limits that once prevailed. So self-indulgent have we become
that even a temporary shortage of cigarettes in America
evoked a response far more irrational in character than any
religious taboo on smoking would be: in the midst of a biting
blizzard, crowds waited in line for a whole hour in order to
purchase their quota of cigarettes. The indecent haste with
which the American Government threw off the rationing of
foods after the Japanese surrender, at a time when the rest
of the war-battered world was close to starvation, is an indication of a popular unwillingness to exercise self-control: an
unwillingness most prevalent in the very circles that exercise
most political influence.

Morally, such people are as unfit for the control of atomic
power as a chronic alcoholic would be for the inheritance of a
vast stock of whiskey. Those who have lost respect for taboos
of any kind are most in need of their self-preservative principle.

Now, experience demands that we should recognize the
place of negative stimuli in human development. Pains, ab-
stentions, renunciations, inhibitions, are perhaps as essential
for human development as more positive nurture. During the
war, fighting men learned this lesson; it gave them power to
confront danger and surmount it; and where civilians were
placed under the same stresses, as in cities that endured aerial
bombardment, they learned the same hard lessons. The imaginative widening of this experience among people who are
still unchastened is an essential measure. To recover the very
habit of restraint, to subject every act to measure, to place
limits even on goods that may be offered in limitless quanti-

ties—this is the communal response we must make to the challenge of both physical and moral disintegration. The very processes of democracy, which it is so essential to extend to world organization, demand a high degree of conscious moderation. That is possibly why the most restrained of peoples, the English, are also the best exemplars of democratic processes. Every civilian must master, as the price of society's survival, the lesson that military organization teaches the soldier: group survival requires the acceptance of sacrifice.

In thirty years of public writing, I have perhaps never put forth proposals more shocking and more inacceptable than the present ones: I can remember how I myself was shocked by them, more than twenty years ago, when I first encountered similar ideas in Irving Babbitt's Democracy and Leadership. Our mechanistic folkways are at war with these assumptions and conclusions. In every Western nation, the devices of publicity are constantly used to break down our inhibitions in order to make us more susceptible to the allurements of the advertiser: narcotics, stimulants, aphrodisiacs in large quantities, both in the form of symbols and the form of material goods, all conspire to this end. The goal of the advertiser is to make the consumer say Yes to his every suggestion. Under the pressure of a totalitarian ideology, the breakdown of inhibitions became absolute in fascist countries: there was no conceivable fiendishness which the Nazis did not practice in their extermination camps. Along that road, we ourselves have gone no short distance; and if we are nearer Hell than we had dreamed, it is partly because we thought that by abandoning inhibitions we were approaching Adam's ancient paradise.

The restoration of rational inhibitions and purposeful sacrifices is now one of the conditions for human survival. Men must institute these practices in their daily routines before nations will collectively follow their example. Our capacity for restraint must be proportional to the power we now command. On no other terms will we be able to control the malign forces that exist, not so much in the atomic bomb itself, but in the human soul: forces whose eruption out of the unconscious has already brought this otherwise highly disciplined and highly co-operative civilization to an advanced stage of visible disintegration—visible in terms of the hundreds of cities ruined, the countrysides that have been devastated, the millions of souls that have been starved and tortured, maimed and killed. If our morality is not adequate, if our daily habits are not informed by rational purposes, if our inhibitions are not, when necessary, inviolable, the means that will validate our political controls will be lacking. Every institutional change will be insufficient unless we bring to it a fully awakened and constantly renewed personality. Love must transform aggression into sacrifice; and sacrifice must put aggression at the service of love.

Each of us must remember his humanness: it takes precedence over our race, our economic class, our politics, our religion, or our nationality. Only to the extent that the nations cultivate this humanness, becoming members one of another, can our civilization achieve peace and security, to say nothing of the well-being and creativeness that will eventually issue forth from them. If we do not put humanity, in every sense of this word, before all petty and limited ends, nothing can be saved.

If man is to survive on a high level, not like the diminished primitive hordes Mr. H. G. Wells pictured, our reaction to this challenge must be unqualified and universal. Every day, and every hour, every minute—I quote once again—we must walk around ourselves and watch ourselves and see that our images are seemly ones. No habits must be uncriticized; no values must remain unexamined; no institutional procedures must be regarded as sacred; no life-denying goals must remain unchallenged. It is not this or that group, elected or self-elected, that must carry the burden of mankind's salvation. Every individual person must first mobilize himself to meet the danger, with a more unconditional acceptance of responsibilities and sacrifices than even the British did when they stood alone, facing imminent destruction, in the summer of 1940. Our best will hardly be enough to guarantee survival. Less than our best will be treason to humanity.

BOOK TWO:

# ADDRESSES ON EDUCATION

You do not educate a man by
telling him what he knew not,
but by making him what he was not.

JOHN RUSKIN: MUNERA PULVERIS

# THE SOCIAL RESPONSIBILITIES
# OF TEACHERS

[This address was read before the Bennington Planning
Conference held by the Commission on Teacher Education of the American Council on Education, in August,
1939. Here the concept of a world-wide change from an
era of expansion to an era of stabilization, already outlined in Technics and Civilization and in The Culture of
Cities, was applied to educational institutions.]

## 1. THE NEED FOR SOCIAL UNDERSTANDING

During the past generation, many of us have worked in the
light of a new notion of education. Instead of being content
to hand on the stereotypes and fixed patterns of past stages
in our culture, we have held that a valid education must enable the student to face a changing world. And we have also
thought of social change and movement as being directed,
more or less, by some immanent process, that left it outside
human choice, human desire, human will; so that a certain
conformity to external change was expected from intelligent
people. Ogburn's widely adopted doctrine of the cultural lag
crystallized this belief.

This notion of the role of education, new though it is, already is due for a revision. Our earlier conception of trans-
mitting the social heritage provided the student with a rigid
outline of formal studies that had become progressively irrelevant to the world in which people actually lived: so much

is true. But the latter-day conception of education as a means of meeting an indefinite series of changes—mainly mechanical and external changes—is hardly less irrelevant today than the system it replaced. It was, in fact, a belated recognition of the volcanic social displacements and mechanical improvements that had characterized the last century. But meanwhile that original situation has profoundly altered. Mechanical invention, industrial improvement, the spread of colonial enterprise and capitalist methods of exploitation, in short, the whole movement that was characterized indiscriminately as progress before 1914 is now coming, rapidly and definitely, to an end.

Today our civilization faces conditions for which neither the rigid patterns of the earlier past, nor the hopeful fluidity and optimistic expectancy of the recent past, provide a sufficient educational orientation. Instead of indefinite possibilities of change, we face a strictly limited number of alternatives. Instead of looking upon change as being due to purely external pressures, mechanical and institutional, we face the need for building up personalities who are capable of dynamically reacting upon their institutions and their physical environment. For our society is going through a crisis: that has been plain for the last two decades. Our very chances of survival rest upon a surer insight into the nature of society itself, and the demands it makes for co-operative understanding and co-operative action.

By now the very realm of significant invention has altered. Man has conquered the physical world, to a degree that surpasses the wildest hopes he held in the seventeenth century, when most of our modern activities were first systematically projected as fantasies and dreams. In achieving that conquest, he has overweighted the role of mechanical invention; he has overemphasized the part played by purely physical alterations in the environment; he has made physical power itself an absolute; and as a result, while industry itself has become more refined, more scientific, more delicately co-ordinated, man himself has become barbarized. Rationalization in industry: irrationalism in politics—that is the order of the day.

Plainly the cultural lag has worked both ways. People are still trying to make mechanical inventions that will do away with the need for social purposes, for religious and psychological and ethical controls. This faith in purely mechanical progress itself represents a cultural time lag. In the crisis that we now face, it is critically important that each one of us should understand the nature of modern society and be capable of taking an active share in directing it; for collective decisions, as John Dewey has pointed out, are the cumulative result of thousands of minor choices, made day by day. Before I can discuss the social responsibilities of the teacher, therefore, I purpose to describe briefly the type of society Western European man has been building during the last three centuries. We must realize why this social order has now failed us, and what is required of the new order we are already, blindly, fitfully, timorously—but so far ineffectively —attempting to build up.

## 2. THE CAPITALIZATION OF EXPANSION

The prime characteristics of the passing social order were derived from the growth of capitalism. I speak of capitalism not merely as a system of economic enterprise, but as a tissue of values and purposes, which largely displaced the immaterial goals of a transcendental religion. Now capitalism means many things in many contexts. But it is primarily an accountancy of numbers. It springs into existence in an economic situation where it is possible—and even necessary—

to translate real goods into an abstract unit of measure called money. This abstraction, because it can be transported, transferred, and conveniently stored becomes (as capital) the foundation for further economic enterprise.

Merchants and money lenders have, of course, existed as a caste or a functional group from almost the very beginning of civilization. Under capitalism, however, the interests, the preoccupations, and the habits of the merchant become universal ones. Every other social group is affected by the accountancy of numbers: timing, measuring, counting, labeling, ticketing; translating human gestures into mechanical movements and human desires into the calculus of price, the capitalist quantification of life creeps into every department. Education records this change no less than science: marks, examinations, annual inventories are its contributions to the new bureaucracy.

Though the goal of capitalist production is private profit, please mark that this profit motive has never been a universal one. Only in the exceptional instance is the profit motive invoked to stimulate the work of the farmer, the mechanic, and the clerk, to say nothing of the soldier, the physician, the scholar, or the priest. Even under capitalism, the humbler members of society work for a living, work to escape starvation and a penurious age, not for profit. But the accountancy of numbers and the absence of any positive social goal except the aggrandizement of the individual enterpriser did indeed signalize the advent of capitalism. If social gains were achieved—and undoubtedly they were—they came as a by-product of actions which the theologians of medieval Europe, imbued with a higher sense of human values, had branded as the sins of greed, avarice, luxury, and pride.

As the mode of a whole society, capitalism is definitely dated. Its main span lies between the sixteenth century, with the invention of the Bourse and the spread of double-entry bookkeeping, and the twentieth century, with the world-wide disruption of trade, finance, and production. For the material triumphs of capitalism were everywhere associated, we can now see, with social impoverishment. Society under capitalism was like a plant that is overfed with nitrates and deprived of potash and phosphates: its spindly stem growth was gigantic, but it lacked the elements necessary for a healthy leafing and efflorescence.

Capitalism belonged to an era of expansion; it helped that expansion and in turn profited by it. In the desire of our political and financial conquistadors for abstract riches and power, the resources of the planet were quickly pillaged. Mine and forest and farm land were stripped of their contents, without thought of replacement or of continuous human culture. So, too, in the same ruthless fashion, whole peoples were condemned to slavery or to a routine of life, marked by dull mechanical toil, mean living quarters, anxious desolate periods of unemployment—periods that even lacked the security of slavery, without lifting much of its compulsion.

That whole movement is now at an end. That is to say, it can no longer continue as an instrument of civilization; expansion in the world today is possible only by restoring and countenancing barbarism. We have reached a period in which the original social premises of capitalism no longer apply.

Why has capitalism, as a complex of values, methods, purposes, and means, become the anachronism that it now is? The essential reason is that during the last generation the era of expansion has come to an end. First of all: territorial expansion has reached its natural terminus with the exploration and world-wide recolonization of the planet itself. Nothing remains for the explorer except barren mountain tops or polar wastes. What new areas remain for settlement are negligible: regions of difficulty like Manchuria, Siberia, Alaska, are the last important frontiers.

Even more significant than this, population expansion is rapidly coming to an end. In the United States, between 1945 and 1965, if present tendencies continue, the population will reach stability. Except for a few countries, notably Soviet Russia, which is still in a pioneering phase, this holds true for every industrialized country. That great tide of births which thundered in during the nineteenth century, overflowing national barriers, uprooting millions of human beings, making Europe rival Asia in sheer fecundity—is now again ebbing toward slack water. The greatest modern achievement in mass production—the mass production of human beings—is coming to an end.

And finally, partly as a result of territorial restriction and birth control, partly by natural self-limitation, industrial enterprise has reached its own broad limits of expansion. The profitable manufacture of plant, equipment, machines, utilities, which made such vast demands upon our resources during the nineteenth century has now come to an inevitable terminus. The greater part of our mechanical plant is now on a replacement basis: we have willfully to cause obsolescence by introducing shoddy materials or vapid changes in style in order to ensure even a minimal continuous demand. In terms of production for profit, of goods produced for the individual random consumer, we are overexpanded and overbuilt. Today, expansion can take place only by raising the standard of living. That is mainly a collective, not an individual matter, and if it is to be handled successfully, private profit can hardly even be a secondary consideration. The three chief places where this standard must be raised are in the consumption of food and the building of family dwelling houses and the provision of well-equipped communities whose social and educational resources will further every citizen's development.

Expansion, then, is no longer, as it was for three centuries, a social goal so obvious that it needed no further justification. Territorial expansion, population expansion, industrial expansion—above all, the expansion of pecuniary values and private power—that was the dream and accomplishment of an age that is almost past. We are now probably in the midst of its last great crisis. For we are now entering a period in which, *if civilization is not to perish*, the habits of expansion must give way to a belief, equally bold and persevering, in the need for balance, intensive cultivation, stability.

Socially speaking, if we are not to accept barbarism as a permanent way of life, production must go on and achieve higher levels of both material and cultural well-being for the mass of mankind. But we must not deceive ourselves about the terms for such advancement. With expansion no longer possible, with disparities between region and region, between class and class, growing smaller, profits must inevitably fall toward zero. Continued production is possible, in other words, only by minimizing profit and by conjuring up alternative social motives and individual rewards. This change is indeed already in process. During the last generation there has been a steady shift from individual demands, satisfied mainly by the conventional machine industries, to collective demands, expressed in goods and services that are supplied by the community to all its citizens. Private industry itself depends for steady employment upon the continued shift of larger quantities of otherwise unemployable savings into civic enterprises of a nonprofit-making nature: housing, city building, park construction, regional cultivation, into schools, museums, theaters, into all manner of public services and public works.

Now these new demands and opportunities cannot be attached to a capitalist ideology: on the contrary, they challenge it, and they are bound to displace it. But the ability to integrate all these new social and economic demands into a self-renewing system taxes our ingenuity today. And one of the reasons why the problems of this transition have so far been spottily handled is the fact that we are all still working within an obsolete frame of reference. Above all, we have not yet introduced into our schools the knowledge, the working methods, or the personal discipline that will insure success in formulating and fulfilling our new social objectives. In an age that demands social balance, stability, equilibrium, realization, we have continued to use the shibboleths of the nineteenth century, and against the irrational attacks of the barbarians we have pitted a thin and timid and overhopeful rationalism. This is perhaps one of the reasons why the barbarians have the upper hand; and by attacks from within and without threaten even our own democratic foundations.

## 3. SOCIAL BALANCE—BY DICTATION OR EDUCATION?

The acknowledgment of this situation is looked upon, by many who cling to the older order, as a sort of defeatism, almost an act of treason. Boyishly, these people look backward to the days of aimless expansion as ideal ones; the manipulation of machines still recalls to them the wild exhilaration of playing with buckets and shovels by the seashore. They wish to make perpetual a state that was, at its best, limited, temporary, and extremely unstable. All the obsolete, self-defeating preoccupations of the businessman are indeed deeply embedded in our waking consciousness.

But the real defeatism is to abandon hope because our

familiar institutions have ceased to be relevant and to fail to see that our new needs create new opportunities.

The watchword for the new age is not conquest but cultivation: not more power but more life, and only so much power as directly serves life. We must turn from the wisdom of the machines, contrived for specialized tasks, to the wisdom of the body, to use a phrase that Professor Cannon has popularized: the wisdom of the living organism, prepared to establish its own inner equilibrium in an environment that itself must be kept in balance if every creature in the partnership is to achieve its optimum share of life. The age of expansion was the age of unbalance: unbalanced environments, unbalanced activities, unbalanced men. In facing the new demands for stability and dynamic equilibrium, we must prepare to modify profoundly our conceptions of both the personality and the community. And this means, in turn, that we must make fundamental changes in our entire educational program.

Most of us flinch from appraising this situation in all its bearings. Those who are aware of the economic needs fail to see the applications to education; those who would admit the validity of a more balanced program of education do not see its close connection with economic circumstances and with the need for progressive modification of our economic regime. But the great problem for all of us today is not whether we shall resign ourselves to the end of the era of expansion. The real problem—perhaps the only problem, now that it has been raised in an acute form by the fascists—is whether balance is to be achieved by regression or whether it is to be achieved by integration at a higher level. To put it boldly, the choice is whether the new order will be conceived by the *dictator* or by the *educator*.

So far most of our attempts to achieve balance in political

society have been crudely empirical ones. Indeed, in industry, the efforts to achieve balance have been attempts to secure profit at the expense of social welfare by violating even the old canons of capitalist enterprise. The growth of economic monopolies, the attempts to achieve national self-sufficiency by the use of governmental loans, subsidies, tariffs, have been of this nature. All these efforts have been quasi-fascist in their economic allegiance, though they have often been carried out by people who, in their conscious philosophy, are opposed to the very hint of state interference or despotism.

In fascist countries, however, stabilization by regression has been carried on much more desperately and systematically. For the fascists have deliberately lowered the popular standard of living, in order to maintain profits, and they have widened the area of military conquest in order, paradoxically, to erect a self-contained economy. Under fascism, stability is achieved partly by sheer repression and partly by giving a new lease on life to the forces, like population expansion and territorial expansion, that favored a power economy in the past.

Even if stability, rather than complete chaos, were to result from fascism, the cultural and human loss would be too heavy to tolerate. Half the humane potentialities for living would disappear, as they did in Sparta, as they always do under violent regimentation. Yet fascism, on its positive side, is a reaction against the moral weaknesses of capitalism: particularly its indifference to the social results of its impersonal mechanisms and instrumentalities, and above all the blind operation of the free market. To this extent, fascism, for all its degrading characteristics, shows a more complete sense of the social order than capitalism did.

A little while ago the Regents of the State of New York— for some mysterious reason I have not yet divined—circulated a letter of Lord Macaulay's, stating the classic doctrines of capitalism in all their bald ruthlessness. Macaulay upheld the old thesis that property is more important than human life, and he said in so many words that in order to insure the automatic rectification of the capitalist system, by the blind working of supply and demand, the ruling classes must be prepared during an economic crisis to let thousands starve and to shoot down ruthlessly all who rebelled, or attempted by political pressure to alter the balance of wealth.

Now the interesting fact is that hardly anybody would *publicly* support this theory today. Even in fascist countries, where the state is prepared to ruin millions of lives on behalf of its sacred egoism, the most cynical of fascist dictators does not openly dare avow such a doctrine. When the dictator introduces starvation measures, he makes a show of inflicting a *common* sacrifice; and though he abolishes the right to strike, to protest, even to hold private opinions, he nevertheless also takes cognizance of the human need for security, for decent family life, for recreation and for what passes, under the fascist order, for cultural opportunity.

We cannot hope to achieve social balance unless we acknowledge the economic implications of this new nonprofit order. During the age of expansion, capitalism gave cream to the few, whole milk to the middle classes, and a blue watery residue to the majority of farmers and industrial workers, agricultural laborers and slaves. The highest hope of capitalism, its most sacred incentive, was the hope that a fractional few of the skimmed-milk drinkers might, by elbowing and pushing, claim a place for themselves among the cream drinkers.

In an age of economic balance, on the other hand, we must look forward to a widespread distribution of whole milk for everybody. This means a restoration of economic parity between country and city; and it means a steady increase in economic parity between classes, groups, individuals; so that, no matter what their economic contributions or responsibilities, a decent minimum level will be the birthright of every member of that society. These premises are not new ones. Theoretically, at least, they have long been accepted in education, although already, not merely in fascist countries, but in democratic America, there have been outright assaults upon these principles. But the assumptions themselves derive from the very nature of modern society; for today the most valuable forms of property are communal ones, and the system as a whole, with its great surplusage of power and goods, is unworkable unless every member of the community can participate in its benefits. The richest man in the world could not hope to acquire a library for his private use that would equal the resources of the New York Public Library; and even all the millionaires on Long Island could hardly have afforded to build for their private and exclusive use one of Mr. Moses' new parkways. If we reject regressive stabilization through fascism, with its order that enlarges disorder, we must work toward an integration that will be based far less even than fascism upon the characteristic purposes of capitalism.

## 4. THE ACTIVE ROLE OF EDUCATION

I have attempted to paint a very broad historic picture of the change that now confronts us for a very simple reason: it is impossible to see the interrelation of details within a narrower frame or against a shallower background. The essential work for the statesman and the educator today, if this diagnosis is correct, is to achieve a dynamic, self-renewing social order that shall remain, through all its changes and adjustments, in a state of balance: an order in which harmony shall be achieved by the expression, rather than the repressive regimentation, of social diversity, and in which co-operation will take the place of one-sided dominance by despotic individuals, classes, or nations.

Education cannot attempt to remain aloof and impassive during the present transition. For only by intelligent preparation and participation can the problems that confront us be solved in rational rather than irrational terms. That preparation is pre-eminently the task of the school. Precisely because old objectives still have a delusive hold on our minds, it becomes the duty of education to recast its program, not merely in order to preserve valued elements from the past, not merely in response to dynamic pressures in the present: but also to work out a program in terms of emergent social possibilities, realizable step by step in the future.

We cannot hope to get practical co-operation from those who are used to having their own way at any terms, like a spoiled child; we cannot get intellectual co-ordination, which is equally needed in any fundamental social program, if we must rely upon the skill of those who are mentally confined to some small compartment. To reduce our problem to the briefest compass: we cannot have social synergy without emotional synaesthesis and intellectual synthesis. This bald formula is, of course, merely a mnemonic one. I shall use the rest of this paper in tracing out its implications for teacher education.

Perhaps the active role here assigned to education in the present social crisis would be accepted a little more eagerly if people realized how great a part education played in the general series of social transformations we have learned to call the Industrial Revolution. For it was not an accident that the nation which put into the hands of every child the fable of Robinson Crusoe became the chief exponent of his utilitarian virtues; nor was it an accident that the countrymen of Locke and Hume, who had made a blank sheet of the human mind, were so quick to depart from traditional ways and to invent purely mechanical equivalents for the organs of sense, intelligence, and muscular effort.

Even in university circles the superstition still lingers that the social changes begun in the middle of the eighteenth century were essentially the outcome of mechanical inventions like the spinning jenny and the steam engine. This interpretation puts the whole initiative in the hands of the industrialist and the engineer and the inventor; but actually it does not belong there. Watt's steam engine would have been as innocent of social results as was that of Hero's of Alexandria, if it had not been accompanied by ideological and institutional changes. One of these was the development of the modern army; another was the development of the modern commercial and political bureaucracy; and still another was the quantification and isolation of experience that came in originally with capitalist accountancy. These changes gave mechanical invention a social vehicle and a social goal. Our need today is for equally radical innovations that will give social inventions and cultural contrivances an integral place in the new social fabric.

Obviously, I cannot attempt to cover all the requirements for synthesis and social discipline in the course of this short outline. So I will be forced to concentrate on two or three parts of the field, in the hope that yourselves will follow out and contribute to its ramifications. And first let me deal with the profound and all pervading change that must take place in our world-picture.

A prominent university president is responsible for reviving the notion that a metaphysical orientation is an important basis for a higher education. I agree with him in this general belief; but I would not leave the conception of metaphysics so vague that it might mean anything one chose to pick from the ragbag of past cultures, including glosses on Aristotle and St. Thomas Aquinas. When I say that our metaphysical basis, our fundamental categories, our abstract world picture are important, I mean something quite definite: namely that the first important change in education today, if it is to meet the challenge of our time, is a change from the metaphysics of the machine, derived from the needs and interests of capitalism, to the metaphysics of the organism, directed to the needs and interests of the co-operative social order that is now emerging.

This reorientation is a fundamental one. It means a shift from the belief in a science of dead things, analyzed, isolated, dissected, reduced to a tissue of simple abstractions, to a belief in a science of living things. In this new science, a qualitative understanding of pattern, form, configuration, history, is as important as statistical analysis; and in terms of the method that accordingly develops, no situation is fully resolved and no problem is fully explored until it is seized in all its ultimate social relationship to human values and human purposes.

Let me clarify this description with an elementary illustration. Take a doctor who examines a young man with a functional disturbance of the heart. From the standpoint of oldfashioned medical science, the main facts to be determined were: the rapidity of the heart beat, its strength or weakness, regularity or uncertainty, and the pressure of the blood. All three points could be investigated by means of accurate mechanical instruments: a watch, a stethoscope, and a pressure gauge. The problem for the physician, on the basis of this exact knowledge, was to choose a particular chemical compound that would by purely physical means clear up the disturbance.

Mind you: I do not say that any good doctor ever made such a simple diagnosis or utilized such a limited means of correction. Indeed medicine, precisely because it unavoidably deals with living creatures, has always tended, even in the days when the standards of physics and chemistry were supreme, to deny the universal use of their oversimplified abstractions. Nevertheless, these one-sided scientific attitudes left their mark even upon medicine: almost a century ago it was already possible for Oliver Wendell Holmes to make the joke about the specialist who dealt in diseases of the right leg and not in diseases of the left leg.

Now a true physician, guided by the philosophy of the organism, has a much more subtle approach to the ailing heart. He thinks, not of the abstract anatomical heart that is more or less like a thousand others he has cardiographed: he thinks rather of this particular heart, in relation to the boy's history, which is a biological and social fact, in relation to habits of nutrition, which is a physiological and social fact, in relation to his occupation, which is an economic fact, in relation to home environment, which is a geographic and personal fact, in relation to psychological problems which may include anything from an infantile trauma down to the fact that he has just been rejected by a girl he loves. In short, this philosophy restores the heart to its integral position in the organism, and it restores the organism to the total environment in which and through which it functions. Permanently to effect any change in the heart itself, the physician may have to suggest different habits of recreation or a psychoanalytic consultation.

If our social goal is a dynamic equilibrium, achieved within a co-operative social order, the first place to make an approach to it is in the organization of thought itself. And the main responsibility for all of us—above all for the teacher—is to learn what Patrick Geddes used to call the art of simultaneous thinking: the habit of thinking in the many-sided and interrelated way in which a good physician approaches the life of his patient.

But mark the difficulty that we all face. This type of organically related thought, the kind that deals with whole situations rather than isolates alone, the kind that deals with concretions as well as abstractions, is obviously less expeditious than mechanical thinking. Fragmentary, unrelated thought gives a quick response to a pressing situation. There are times when this may indeed be the only response possible. If someone must be rescued from a burning house, only an idiot would think of asking first how he got there or how lately the fire underwriters had passed on the wiring.

The point I would make, however, is that we need no longer act, in general, as if the world were a house afire: the occasion for haste has gone, along with the original pressure toward capitalistic expansion, which so largely occasioned it. Some of our haste was due to our overvaluation of mechanical contraptions and mechanical performances, so that we disparaged areas of experience that lay outside this scheme; and some of it was due to the mere shortness of the individual's life.

All these conditions have radically changed, and they are bound to change more in the immediate future. For one thing, the average man has twenty years more of life than he had to look forward to at birth a hundred years ago: the need has diminished to specialize at an early age, achieve quick eminence in a narrow field, and sheer away from esthetic and domestic and political concerns in order, by this resolute contraction of interest, to enlarge the individual's income and his sense of power over his rivals. Though the individual life-span has not increased, the number of people who, barring military extermination, will enjoy a full life-span has multi-plied. This enlargement of the mature group provides new challenges and opportunities.

As educators, we must understand that the capitalist who knows only his markets, the engineer who knows only his machines, the teacher who knows only his books, are all intel-lectually crippled people. The fatal weakness of their edu-cation and training is that it makes them incapable of dealing with the real world: they are helpless except in dealing with the series of abstractions in which they have achieved a minor competence. This weakness was no weakness under capital-ism. On the contrary, it was rather a condition of success: a lopsided personality was at home in a lopsided environment because it made no inconvenient demands for opportunities that the environment could not supply. Today, the need for orderly and interrelated advance in both thought and social action, which would have curbed profits under capitalism, is the very condition of success in a more humanized society.

## 5. REGIONAL SURVEY AS SYNTHESIS

During the last generation a movement toward synthesis, both in philosophy and science, has been gradually taking shape. The very fact that it exists is itself a subtle indication of the fact that the underlying social and economic pattern of society is already in process of further alteration. The specific science in which this social point of view was first achieved was in plant ecology, but the recognition of related and inte-grated wholes has made its way into thought at many points. In geography it is the concept of the region; in sociology the concept of the community; in psychology it is the concept of

the person, now emerging from the atomistic study of dis-
sociated modes of behavior.

In the field of education itself, one of the most promising
contributions toward synthesis, it seems to me, has come from
the development of the regional survey. This was first devised
by Patrick Geddes, at Edinburgh, as far back as the 1890's.
During the last twenty years it has been tried out, at the primary level by Caroline Pratt and Lucy Sprague Mitchell, and
at a more advanced level by John Gaus, in the experimental
college at Wisconsin. The utilization of regional material has
now been made the subject of an excellent monograph, many-
sided and exhaustive, by a group at Stanford headed by Professors Hanna and Hand.

About the regional survey two main facts should be noted:
facts that distinguish it from purely verbal or schematic attempts at synthesis. The first fact is that the introduction to
orderly knowledge comes directly from the student's observation of, and participation in, the activities of man and nature.
Some writers, like H. G. Wells, have expressed the hope of
achieving a common background and a coherent point of view
through some vast encyclopedic massing of specialists' contributions. This impulse has doubtless been responsible for various collaborative textbooks and for the general orientation
courses that are now appearing in our schools and colleges.
But although much good comes from these efforts, the method
has a serious defect: that is, it proceeds from results already
given, results wholly external to the student's experience,
whereas what is needed is a unified *approach*, in terms of the
*process* of study, rather than a unified *result* through the mere
systematic massing of already formulated knowledge.

Do not misunderstand me: regional survey is not something to be added to an already crowded curriculum. It is
rather (potentially) the backbone of a drastically revised

method of study, in which every aspect of the sciences and the arts is ecologically related from the bottom up, in which they connect directly and constantly in the student's experience of his region and his community. Regional survey must begin with the infant's first exploration of his dooryard and his neighborhood; it must continue to expand and deepen, at every successive stage of growth, until the student is capable of seeing and experiencing, above all, of relating and integrating and directing the separate parts of his environment, hitherto unnoticed or dispersed. Social action, in a balanced society, rests upon this sort of balanced understanding.

There is another important attribute of the regional survey that distinguishes it from more specialized kinds of field study. Each part of the environment, when studied momentarily by itself for the sake of clarity and orderly definition, is correlated with every other part of the environment not merely in space but in time: not merely by association but by filiation. Thus historical survey complements regional survey. This is a necessary corrective to what one may call, in diplomatic parlance, unilateral and unitemporal thinking. Thanks to the methods originally developed in seventeenth century science, we now have ample intellectual means for dealing with single areas of experience, with isolated sets of facts; and such thinking has immeasurably increased our power over the forces of nature. But we are incapable of dealing effectively by this method with interrelated and implicated objects; and this means that we are incapable of dealing with the real world and achieving rational power over the forces of society. For in communities, associations, regions, groups, personalities, the facts of interrelation are as primordial as the parts that are related; and the specific pattern that emerges has a reality no less significant than the fiber and color of the individual threads.

Finally, let me call attention to one further fact about the regional survey that distinguishes it from specialized investigation in narrower fields: it includes the facts of man's life and activities as the culminating point in the study of nature itself. The structure of society and the dynamic processes of human history, the world of culture as conditioned by nature and the world of nature as modified by human culture, enter into this final picture. The knowledge of where people live, what they do, how they feel and express themselves, what types of association they form, in what realm their fantasies play, is an integral part of the regional survey: like self-knowledge, like the appraisal and direction of the personality—which is in effect the subjective, individual aspect of the regional survey—*such knowledge must begin at home.* One cannot start too young on such a survey; one cannot push it too far or carry it on too long. Comte's great formula is implicit in the method of the regional survey: See to foresee: foresee to provide.

Regional survey itself is a program of acting and doing, as well as knowing: it utilizes the student's personal interests and places them in a common frame, which puts them in a more significant relation to neighboring interests. Regional survey carries with it, as part of its method, the habit of thinking interrelatedly and acting co-operatively: it makes the fact of society real in practice as well as constant in thought. And this in turn breaks down the disabling breach between facts and values, between past conditions and future possibilities. Rational co-ordination and purposive planning, with widespread participation at every stage of the process, constitute the only alternative to arbitrary compulsion; for a society in which social needs are uppermost cannot be run by random private efforts. Because regional survey is a study of social processes and activities, it leads inevitably to critical revaluations, and finally to the formation of policies, plans, and projects that will alter the existing situation. A generation that had really grasped its region and its community would know what to do about them. It is ignorance— ignorance of goals and purposes as well as ignorance of conditions—that handicaps desire.

Note here that the need for social balance inevitably reverses the place of the physical and the social sciences, even as it changes the focus of leadership from the province of the private businessman, seeking profits, to the sphere of the public servant, seeking the common good. Instead of continuing to accord primacy to the physical sciences, with their almost infinite capacity for suggesting fresh mechanical inventions and their complete innocence of social motive—instead of this we must give primacy to the biological and social sciences. An active knowledge of the social environment and of the behavior of men in social partnership, their needs, their drives, their impulses, their dreams, is just as indispensable for working our new social order as reading, writing, and arithmetic was for those trained to capitalism. And so equally the arts of society—the art of politics, the arts of purposive behavior and significant communication, must become the main field for new inventions. What we need today is not so much a moratorium on mechanical inventions as a large-scale transfer of interest and of personal talent to the fields of community and personality. This positive measure would serve as one of the surest brakes on the irrational expansion of the machine.

## 6. MANUAL EXPERIENCE AND ESTHETIC EXPRESSION

So far I have been discussing the need to devise conceptual and scientific instruments appropriate for dealing with the

complicated social conditions that confront us: I have gone
into these matters further in two of my books, on Technics
and on Cities; and I have discussed the educational reference
of the regional survey in a paper published in a Bulletin of
the University of the State of New York (No. 1143).

But even if I must trespass for a moment on Dr. Prescott's
particular field, I must point out that the social discipline we
seek must be worked out, at the same time, in the education
of the personality. Here I come to the very core of the
teacher's social responsibility. It is important that he should
understand his civilization and his community in all their
concrete diversities and unities. It is important that the concept of society and organism should be fundamental to his
systematic thought. But it is also important, in this new
regime, *that the teacher, as the public servant par excellence,
should exemplify the social man.* It is the teacher who must
first of all be educated into the opposite of the barbarized
*Teilmensch,* or subdivided man, who as soldier, industrialist,
financier, or scholastic specialist, has reigned over capitalist
society.

The fragmentary man, concentrating upon some narrow
proficiency, eager for power in the form of riches or direct
command over other men, was a product of capitalist and
militarist ideals. He was conjured into existence at a definite
period in European history: he was trained to command, not
to co-operate; to obey, not to participate. Full men would not
work well as cogs in the factory, the bureaucracy, or the
army; their very potentialities stood in the way of their
success.

Now it seems to me that there were three places in particular where the ideal of the whole man was lost in our program of education. The first loss occurred as early as the
Renaissance: it was the displacement of manual skill and the

daily discipline of manual effort in the training of the so-called educated man. The inability to work with one's hands became a point of pride among the educated classes. In the meanwhile, a sort of surrogate labor in the form of sport came to take the place of manual activity; but by that very fact labor was made trivial and play itself lost its special quality of being irresponsibly aimless.

The restoration of manual labor as a daily discipline should, I believe, stand high in any attempt at social integration. Already, psychiatrists have come to realize the uses of carpentry, weaving, painting, modeling, and gardening in the cure of nervous disorders; and it is time to realize that, as great teachers from St. Benedict onward have recognized, it is perhaps equally important in the prevention of disorder. In active manual labor the body becomes well exercised, the hand and eye co-ordinated, the spirit accepts the discipline of routine, whilst in the concrete activity itself—a bed of flowers, a path hewn through the woods, a rug or a cabinet—the worker achieves a result far more rewarding than the abstract numerical score that is the sole outcome of success in sport. Above all, in co-operative tasks, the worker achieves comradeship.

In Europe, some of these ends were achieved through compulsory military service in the army. And there were pioneer educators, like Dr. Rosenstock-Huessy, who, perceiving the educational value of work discipline and work comradeship, founded the labor camp movement in Germany to give these modes of behavior a higher social content. At the secondary level, work camps like those of the Society of Friends and of the Ethical Culture Society in New York, are beginning to make a similar contribution.

This kind of labor must not be confused either with the older academic schemes of manual training or with the sort of shop experience sometimes provided in engineering schools. Our primary concern with manual discipline is a humanistic and cultural one. One of its most useful by-products, however, would be its giving the teacher greater insight into the economic activities and the social usages of farm and factory and household, whereas—unless poverty has driven him to other spheres of work—the teacher's life-experiences unfortunately tend to make him at home only in classroom and office—a clerk among other clerks.

The next place where we have lost balance is in the relation of inwardly conditioned to outwardly conditioned activities. Our whole civilization has become patently extroverted: we ascribe to our thoughts and feelings a lower order of reality than we do physical objects and external organizations. Our capitalistic culture, indeed, was the work of men who had given up the hope of achieving holiness, beatitude, or beauty, in order to conquer the forces of nature and master the external world. The mechanical arts flourished in this transformation. But the work of the humane arts was progressively emptied of meaning and social dignity. All that was intimate, personal, non-utilitarian, all that concerned the poet and the painter, the musician and the gardener, the friend and the lover, all that arose out of an inner life of fantasy and dream, was regarded both by the businessman and the natural scientist as essentially discreditable.

In the light of our extrovert philosophy, the subjective was the equivalent of the unreal, or even worse, of a neurotic failure to face reality.

In restoring the balanced personality, capable of giving heed to all the dimensions of experience, it is important, it seems to me, to restore the balance between the outer world and the inner world. Instead of taking the capitalist disparagement of subjective modes for granted—as if capitalism itself were not riddled with dubious subjectivity—we must be careful to place no higher value upon fact-finding, acquisition, external activity than we do upon the inner responses of contemplation, fantasy-building, evaluation, and expression. The great task of the expressive arts is to socialize this otherwise private inner world: to bring it out into the open and to project it in forms that have quick meaning for other men.

During the last century we have done much to build up the orderly, rational, fact-finding, emotionally equable personality. We have rigorously trained people to displace their emotional reactions, to overcome their ingrained prejudices, sacrifice their pet wishes, conceal their desires: we have created on an unbelievable scale people who accept with becoming modesty the objective conditions laid down by nature and society. But there is a sense in which this emotionless moral neutrality is a sterilizing device: a device opposed to creative expression and confident constructive activity.

Those who are most adept in displacing themselves lack precisely the emotional impetus that gives rise to new goals and to new fulfillments not provided in the immediate situation. Such people regard the will-to-create as essentially immodest. Aware of all the tangled intellectual complexities that fact-finding itself reveals, desiring to *know* rather than to *do*, these passive individuals distrust the quick syntheses and brilliant shortcuts that the artist always makes in proceeding from reflection to action. For these people, there is an element of impudence, even of charlatanry, in the characteristic habits of the painter, the architect, or the statesman, for the latter, if they are good at all, always have the faculty of building better than they know. In the political field, some of the strength of fascism undoubtedly derives from its legitimate criticism of the feeble desires, the deep-seated self-distrust, that this neutral type of personality—the very paragon of the academic virtues—exhibits when he is faced with the responsibility for any kind of action.

And here is why the expressive arts have a particular message for our generation. For a great part of the work that needs to be done, whether in building cities or in recasting social institutions, is of a formative nature. Mere knowledge, mere fact-finding, mere technical skill will not lead to these new forms: they will lead only to some minor modification of past forms. If our social order is to achieve balance, if rational men are to create an alternative to the barbarous fantasies and irrational goals of the fascists, it will necessarily be the work of people who have a robust inner life: confidence in the validity of their dreams and projects. It will be the creative expression of people who are capable of giving form to their social needs as completely as the artist creates, out of the chaos of experience, a painting, a poem, or a symphony. Social invention is by its very nature closer to these esthetic activities than it is to mechanical invention; and if society itself is to become, as it were, a work of art, that is a product of deliberate human effort and creative contrivance, we must not be content to leave the field of expression to the nursery school, and then to see it dwindle progressively as the student matures.

## 7. POLITICAL ROLE OF THE TEACHER

I come now to one final place that has been seriously neglected, the culture of the social man: a key position. Here we must correct a weakness that has long been visible in education, and above all in the education of the teacher. Though we have made many diverse (but on the whole feeble) attempts to train for citizenship, we have rested too easily content with the addition of new courses, or with a damnably iterative emphasis on the bare concept of democracy. But we have so far failed to break down the fundamental contradiction that threatens our potential democracy, and that is, the present partition between private and public life. We have failed to correct even symbolically the state of unbalance that exists between these two phases of the human personality.

Now belief in the sacredness of private property and the private personality appeared at the same time. It was part of that general gift of privacy that came in with the seventeenth century and resulted in the private house, the private bedchamber, and private activities generally: part of that politically irresponsible life which was left to the subject of the absolute despot, once his privileges as a citizen and a member of a guild had been reduced or taken away altogether.

Even when the republican movement of the eighteenth century recaptured political responsibilities, the habits of privacy persisted. So it has come about that the major portion of each citizen's day is still devoted to private activities: his individual work, his individual family. Effective participation in the guidance of the community is reserved for election day, while social service and education of any sort is at best a sporadic matter—a call to jury duty or a demand to serve on a local committee for raising charitable funds.

Now the first thing for us to realize is that the type of social economy we are creating will demand far more constant political activity on the part of the individual citizen. The sole alternative to repressive regimentation, whether by a personal despot or by an impersonal but equally tyrannical and irresponsible "system," is steady, unrelaxing participation. In any organic community, public life will necessarily embrace at least a third of a citizen's wakeful existence; it cannot be otherwise.

Unless public activity embraces this large area, we shall all be subjected to a servile absolutism, which will place all effective direction in the hands of a distant administrative bureaucracy; and through sheer burden of detail this bureaucracy will not be able to perform even its useful functions of co-ordination and standardization. But the great meaning of modern machine production, as a means of release, here appears with all its profound promise. Its meaning does not come mainly from its capacity to supply more goods than ever before: if that were all, mankind might exceed its optimum demand and die of overeating, luxury, and boredom. No: the great meaning of mechanization is the fulfillment of our most pressing political want: the need for leisure. Only an economically secure leisured class can serve as enlightened and incorruptible public servants; and only through the disciplined political use of leisure can a democracy that includes millions function as such, except in name. Our very success in socially utilizing the immense power of the machine rests on this political transfer of power. Without it, even communist regimes must be despotic, and the class struggle will continue, with office-holders and bureaucrats and soldiers serving instead of capitalists and financiers.

Plainly, it may be necessary to keep politics out of the schools, in order to prevent their being used as a football for partisan interests. But it is simply impossible, if we are to build up a social order advantageous to life, to keep the schools out of politics. For the school, first and last, is the modern institutional organization for interpreting social change and for converting brute compulsion and arbitrary routine into rational, enlightened, and purposive participation and control.

From ancient Greece one gets perhaps the clearest image of the alternative political roles of the teacher: the regressive or the progressive role. One picture is that of the servile Greek pedagogue, a house-slave, one degree perhaps above the cook in social reputability: the pedagogue handing down by rote the prescribed forms of the past. The other is that of Socrates, challenging the old gods, examining the institutional basis of Athenian life, and seeking to guide the changes taking place: passing on, first to Plato, then through him to Aristotle and a whole school of minor men, the conceptions of man's responsibility for self-knowledge and for communal guidance: conceptions that have renewed validity, in other terms, today.

As the servile pedagogue, the American teacher need merely keep close to his classroom, fill out his reports punctually, follow the prescribed syllabus of studies, and in general not go out of his way to court trouble. The more readily he can by his habits of thought, language, and actions resemble the petty businessmen of his community the more secure will be his position.

The role of Socrates, on the other hand, calls for courage and audacious initiative. For it means that the teacher must, up to the limit of his capacities and opportunities, have a fresh vision of the world of landscapes and cities and social institutions. This is the world that, ultimately, must inform every aspect of his teaching: and this is the world that his teaching will help to form anew, to re-form, to transform. On one hand he must be capable of responding to the social environment as a whole, understanding and feeling all man's social dilemmas and social purposes; on the other hand he must help to create balanced personalities, capable of handling life more or less deftly at any point, capable of giving an integrated—and therefore fully energized—response to the challenge of any particular situation.

As a representative of the social and spiritual forces in his community, the teacher in our age has now the role that the clergy alone once fulfilled in the congregations that founded New England. Potentially, the teacher's part can be even more decisive. But to fulfill this role he must not relapse into the meek pedagogue: he must become once more the Socratic gadfly, stirring up a noble discontent, not merely providing the tools for change but awakening the desire for a life in which the cash nexus and the profit motive have been exchanged for a more co-operative bond and for a more humanly amenable goal.

Active participation in political life, at every level, then, is not merely becoming to the teacher: I should say that the failure to participate almost disables him from serving as a teacher, since to that extent he sets a feeble, unworthy example as the citizen of a democratic state. In his own professional association and union, in Parent-Teacher Associations, and in larger community enterprises the teacher must be ready to give the lead. I know the administrator's objection to such activities: that they are bound to arouse external opposition. But the answer to this is that conflict and opposition are an essential part of the social process. They are indeed a condition of social growth. It is by reason of tensions, difficulties, thrusting and resisting wills that situations develop both within the personality and within the group whose resolution sets free new energy and releases new meanings. Conflict must not be avoided. The only need is to discipline it, humanize it, translate it to higher levels, and above all keep from pressing the ultimate decision by a mere display of brute force.

If the transition to a more balanced economy and a more organic social order is to be effected, it will not be achieved without raising, again and again, a strong determined opposition on the part of those who cling, often vindictively, often irrationally, often with neurotic violence, to the culture that is in decay. Because frustration and fear are widespread, this kind of opposition exists in alarming amounts today. Such conflict will not always end happily for the teacher. Did not the greatest of teachers have to drink the cup of hemlock when he offended his fellow citizens by his challenge to their ancient beliefs?

That example brings out a fact I would further emphasize —the necessity to develop in the morale of the teacher today something closely approaching the heroic. For none of the changes that are necessary, if our society is to be saved from degrading violence, will be possible without the daily exercise of a soldierly discipline and an heroic perseverance on the side of those who represent the rational, the organic, the human. Unless we are willing to give up our lives in the defense of civilization, we shall probably lose both our lives and our civilization.

Timid people, slack-willed people, cagey people—let us confess it freely among ourselves—we have lured too many such people into the school system and have made their way too easy. Indeed we have even placed a premium upon their disabilities by masking them as valuable academic virtues. But the willingness to face dangers, to take risks, to endure hardships is something we cannot leave to gangsters and gunmen, to fascists and their armed agents of repression. The need of the present hour is to place people of steely will and unalterable courage in all those key positions against which barbarism and irrational violence make their earliest assault . . . and first of all, therefore, in our schools and colleges, upon whose untrammeled functioning the very hope of a peaceful transition to a post-capitalistic, post-militaristic, post-nationalistic era must be based.

## 8. THE TASK BEFORE US

Let me briefly sum up. The teacher, to accept his social responsibilities in the world today, must understand the nature of the present crisis. He must assist in the transformation of a social order based upon expansion, power, profit, one-sided private initiative, into a social order based upon symbiosis: a co-operative sharing of the means of life, toward the fullest possible development of both personality and community. Understanding the pressing need for balance and integration in this symbiotic order, those responsible for teacher education must introduce the concept of wholeness, many-sidedness, interrelatedness in every part of the teacher's curriculum and discipline. The restoration of manual effort and of the expressive arts, as an integral part of both a renewed social life and a revised curriculum, becomes imperative; for society is not merely a fact to be studied, but a medium for living. And the aim of teaching, therefore, is not to produce systematic sociologists but representative social men: political animals in the fullest sense of Aristotle's word. Such social discipline places the teacher in the very forefront of the effort to combat the irrational forces that are now, from within and without, threatening civilization. Through the focusing of this many-sided social experience, through confident invention in the social arts, comes the hope of creating a balanced society, capable of maintaining and renewing itself, capable of enriching and deepening man's common heritage. In achieving this order, I say again, our critical choice is that between the dictator and the educator. And this again depends upon whether the teacher is as eager for social responsibility as the dictator is eager for political conquest and personal power. Safety for the teacher does not lie in evading the choice: safety and service lie in his willingness to play his social part and to follow it through in all its ramifications.

# EDUCATION FOR WAR AND PEACE

[This address was given before the annual meeting of the
Bay Region Teachers' Association, held in the San Francisco Auditorium in December, 1942. Though the United
States had been in the war for a whole year, the country
was still far from having thrown itself with its whole
weight into the military effort; each institution, each
group, was still trying to hang on for as long as possible
to its peacetime ways, and even in the Army and Navy
the day of the routineer was not yet over. By holding
back from participation too long, our schools and colleges eventually lost much that they should have retained.]

## 1. THE MODERN TEMPER

My theme is a very simple one; and I can put it in a few
sentences. First: all that was valuable in our education in
peacetime is still valuable in war. To the extent that our education has produced active, disciplined, creative personalities, at home in every part of the modern environment, it has
done well, and we need more, not less of this spirit in our
actual military effort. Mathematics, physics, and chemistry,
and a knowledge of machines, though they may be essential
to the soldier, cannot perform acts of magic: well-tempered
men are as essential as well-run machines.

Second: all that has proved valuable in war itself, the
hard discipline, the facing of unpleasant tasks, the sense of
comradeship, the willingness to serve one's country to the
limit and give one's all to a human cause whose fulfillment

167

one may not live to see—all this will remain as an essential contribution to our education for the post-war world; and we shall need more, not less, of this stern sense of reality as we approach the future. To these two statements I should perhaps add a third; and this is that our entire scheme of living and learning must be drastically overhauled in order to meet the great tasks that lie before us. Those who see only the losses and miseries brought on by the war must realize that there is a more positive side to the struggle; for it is only through the efforts and sacrifices that the war has invoked that we shall get the courage to initiate a new epoch in civilization, an age in which our multiplied powers will be directed, not toward the conquest of nature or the exploitation of other men, but to a wider co-operation, a deeper understanding, a fuller development for all the peoples of the world.

The tragic period we are now witnessing and living through must have, for those of us who can think and feel at all, something of the same cathartic effect that Aristotle attributed to high drama. It enables us to see our own littleness and insufficiency in true perspective; it forces us to put first things first; and it gives us an opportunity to recover a sense of major human purposes and values, more directly oriented to the ultimate issues of life and death, which will help us put our own affairs in order.

Unfortunately, many people have lost the sense of tragedy, and having lost it, they are unable to understand the drama that is being enacted before them, and they are unable to extract any lesson from it. For such people, the fate that has befallen civilized man throughout the world is a grotesque and entirely meaningless accident; and it therefore calls for no revisions in their own routines or their own values. They want to get the war over quickly, not as any sane person does, in order to shorten the appalling miseries that each day imposes upon hundreds of millions of our fellow men, but merely in order to get back as quickly as possible to business as usual, to the familiar pleasures, the familiar tasks, the familiar cup of coffee with the pre-war quota of sugar, the familiar motor ride with four new tires and the latest set of gadgets on the instrument panel.

But the point about a tragedy is that it is not brought on solely by external circumstances, by avertible miscalculations and practical misjudgments: it is brought on likewise by our own very natures, by our own false ambitions, by our own failure to reckon with the essential nature of things. Not one of us, young or old, can escape some measure of blame for the tidal wave of barbarism that has been sweeping over the world; for if our own philosophy of life had not been wanting, if we ourselves had not denied the real values of civilization by our practical neglect of them, by our failure to renew them and realize them, we should not have let the barbarism of the Axis powers get the upper hand. On the contrary, we should have actively led the counter-attack on behalf of civilization long before our enemies were ready to strike us. Our doubts, our evasions, our wishful misinterpretations of our enemies' declared intentions, plainly showed we lacked any deep-seated belief in the essential mission of civilization—which is to preserve and renew and further the humanization of man in society.

The only thing that made the present war inevitable, then, was the paralysis of the more civilized people whose initiative might have kept the inevitable from happening. Now that the inevitable is here, many people seek to throw the blame on some particular organization or institution; they think that a scapegoat will relieve them of the burden of their own sins and do away with the necessity for re-examining their familiar mode of life. One of the favorite targets at the present moment is the educational system, and in particular, what is called modern education. Usually the critics are not very clear as to what they mean by this term; some of them have even curiously confused it with the noble wisdom that Socrates preached and practiced, as if we who live today are worthy either to be praised for Socrates' virtues or even to share the blame for his possible shortcomings.

But let us not take comfort too easily in the errors of current criticism. We must not make the mistake of thinking that, because many of our critics are wrong on specific points, we can give ourselves a clean bill of health or go on applying methods and repeating formulas that have made our schools and colleges what they now are. That would be a disastrous mistake; for though education does not deserve to be singled out as the one institution that has failed modern society, there is no doubt that our whole civilization itself has miscarried in many essential respects, that parts of it have been actively disintegrating; and that all our legitimate hopes for creating a better world must rest upon our ability to detect our weaknesses before they undermine us further, and to repair the damage that has been done by a determined creative effort.

The fact is that the war has found us all out. It has disclosed the weakness of our current philosophy of life, which has set the pleasure principle above the reality principle, and has made people loath to face the truth if it threatens to upset their comfortable habits or divert them from their familiar goals. The war has shown us many empty spots in our boasted culture. Some of our writers and teachers have so persistently debunked false virtues and dishonest pretensions that they have lost sight of real human values and entirely honest achievements: having no standard for distinguishing between good and bad, except as a matter of individual taste, they have lost any clear notion as to their real existence, and are unable to identify evil, even when it has reached mountainous proportions. The war has shown further that many of the achievements we were proudest of, like the machine and its products, have made us incapable of adapting ourselves swiftly to emergencies.* So far, as a people, we have tried to baby ourselves through this war: we have been more worried about preserving our comforts than preserving our freedom.

The war has not produced these weaknesses: it has simply revealed them. In times of peace, we had become more interested in the slick, cellophane-wrapped package than in the quality of the product it contained; and we were more interested in the machine as an abstract work of art, than we were in the human function it was supposed to serve. So, too, we were more interested in keeping our particular group, or our particular organization, running in the well-worn groove, with its usual budget, its usual complement of people, its usual program, than we were in responding to the world-wide catastrophe, which challenged all that we were, all that we habitually did, all that we could hope to see accomplished in our time. Educators and teachers have not been free from this sin.

* I must remind the reader that until 1943 our forces were compelled to fight with insufficient weapons—many of them obsolete and ineffective in comparison with those used by the Germans and Japanese. The vainglorious boasts of our publicity men in industry and the armed forces were particularly galling to our fighters, who knew the difference between prospectus and reality. The future historian will not appraise favorably the results of applying advertising methods to war; for self-deception never pays.

## 2. THE CALL TO RESPONSIBILITY

The war, I say, has found us all out. Our educational system has not proved better or worse than our industrial system or our political system. But the fact is that our schools have been part and parcel of our general scheme of life, and they have—if I may put it that way—adequately recorded its weaknesses. We live in a world that in less than fifty years has become mechanically unified by the radio, the airplane, the motor car; but morally and spiritually this world is more disrupted and confused and beset by conflict than it was at the beginning of the nineteenth century. We have created a civilization in which the machine has become a miracle of applied science and rational effort while men themselves have become the victims of misapplied science and irrational effort. Men have regimented machines only to become themselves the victims of that regimentation. Man's own culture has not grown in maturity to keep pace with the energies and materials he must now, at his own peril, control. Infantilism in many forms, in the form of superstition, wishful thinking, irresponsible frivolity, mass-sports and empty diversion, has reached gigantic proportions, at a moment when our democratic society needs the constant support and guidance of mature, responsible, active citizens in every part of the body politic.

Unfortunately our educational system, taking it in the large, has shown the same organic defects as the rest of our society. It has shared the current respect for large buildings and big operations; it has shared the businessman's love for organizing, routinizing, mechanizing, so that our organizations will turn out a relatively uniform product, to go on the market at about the same price. We have paid more attention to our physical plant, to our equipment, and to the superintendents who look after them than we have to the teaching personnel itself; and in line with the general tendency to seek security in this chaotic world, our teachers themselves have sought for economic safety without setting for themselves the problem that should go with security in one's vocation—responsibility for establishing a high standard of workmanship, with demotion for those who fail to meet it.

Within the field of pedagogy there has been the same over-elaboration of empty technique, the same loving refinement of superfluities, that there has been in the manufacture of motor cars; there has been the same fake attempt to stream-line stationary objects in plans of co-ordination that work out only on paper, since no real attention is paid to the human personalities whose interests must be aroused and whose aptitudes must be re-directed. This is not the whole picture of our education any more than it is the whole picture of our business and industrial world: there are a few Kaisers in our schools as well as in our shipyards. But we must judge our schools by their product; and there the war has already found us wanting.

You know the story of the man who went to the doctor and complained that he had a bad cough, a pain in his back, and that he could not sleep nights. The doctor asked him if anything else was wrong; and the patient replied: Yes, speaking personally, he didn't feel very well. Speaking personally, our educational system has fallen short in the main because it does not create a sufficient number of responsible, self-acting, self-directing young men and women: with all our concern for adjustment we have trained only smooth people who have learned to fit accommodatingly into smooth situations, and it has become increasingly clear that we have not produced people who are equal to all the emergencies of life, who are as capable of self-sacrifice as self-indulgence, people who can face difficult tasks cheerfully, people who exercise initiative, choice, discrimination, and self-control.*

In assuming that interest and positive enjoyment in a task will tend to create discipline, we have forgotten that an athletic discipline of the will is in turn necessary to tide one over the periods when interest flags and when enjoyment has reached the vanishing point. Ask the people who are most familiar with creative work. No good artist, no good writer, is ever under the illusion that the highest creative effort can dispense with sheer routine and drudgery.

Now one of the first things a young soldier or sailor learns is that certain tasks must be done whether he likes them or not; and this knowledge, bred on stiff route marches when he feels like dropping in his tracks, or cleaning equipment at the end of a tough day when he wants to relax, has a tonic effect in giving the soldier self-confidence and self-mastery. All of us have seen the wholesome effect of this on most of the young people we know; for the first time, an aimless, slack-willed, easily bored generation has a sense of a purpose and a goal and a new confidence in its own powers to bear up under whatever circumstances it may have to face. That is a precious asset. We should not have had to wait for the war to discover it. In reaction against the meaningless formalities of the old-fashioned drill school, in reaction against an almost sadistic discipline within the school, we had swung too far in the other direction, forgetting that there is such a thing as purposeful hardship and meaningful drill: forgetting that we learn, quite literally, by taking pains as

* Our superb achievement in war has not proved that our education system was adequate: what it has proved is that, by adding army discipline, comradely co-operation, and combat it *became* adequate.

well as by pursuing immediately pleasurable objects. In all this we have much to learn from the military forces; and we must hold fast to that lesson when the active demands of war have ceased.

## 3. THE FURTHER LESSONS OF WAR

There is still another lesson that our country must learn from the war itself, and apply to later peacetime education; and this is that citizenship in a democracy is not something that can be taught solely from textbooks; it is not even something that can be inculcated by class visits to the city hall or the municipal garbage plant. Citizenship must be incorporated in the school program, as an actual period of service and responsible work for the whole community, day by day, week by week, month by month. War demands a readiness to give up one's life for one's country. *But a democratic society, though it sometimes must make that hard demand, must not confine itself to the extreme case: it must ask a goodly share of its citizens' thought and labor and love every day of their lives.* That is the real price of our survival as a democratic people. Here the school must accept the responsibility for initiating and organizing the student's public activities and tasks; and some of the misplaced emotionality which now gathers unhealthily around football and basketball games must be drawn into more important duties. Fourier's old dream of youth's peace armies, revived by William James in his conception of a moral equivalent for war, and by Rosenstock-Huessy and others in their plans for work-camps, has now become a necessity of educational statesmanship, to meet the pressing needs for a responsible citizenship in the postwar world.

These are the real lessons to be drawn from the war, and

from the practice of military discipline even in its most limited forms. But there are other lessons that must be learned, lessons as important for our military success as for our postwar tasks; and one of these lessons is that one cannot build a unified co-operative world order with fragmentary, partly developed, one-sided and parochial personalities. We have too readily taken for granted the notion that the minute specialization of knowledge and labor, which has taken place in industry during the past two centuries, is a final process: that a method that has been so useful in creating powerful machines must be equally useful in creating the people who are to run them. As a result, we have created a kind of man, in every walk of life, who is incapable of rising out of the limitations of his job, his group, his class, his local community; and as his field becomes smaller and more specialized, his knowledge of the relationships and activities that lie beyond this field has grown thinner and emptier. The penalty for this one-sided development is inability to function in the real world. The curse of unrelated and fragmentary knowledge, no matter how accurate, is that, outside the narrowest of contexts, it ceases to be true, precisely because it is unattached to the total picture.

## 4. THE NEED FOR WHOLENESS

The need for a common background, a common set of experiences, a common body of values and interests, is more necessary in an age of intensive specialization than it is under any other circumstances. Every advance in analysis must be counterbalanced by a deliberate effort of synthesis. The wider the circumference of our horizon is, the more important it is for all of us to start from a common center, and to return, from time to time, to the starting point, in order that we should not lose touch with the common ties that bind men together and with the common language which they must master and speak if they are to remain in close co-operation. We have accepted too readily the fragmentation of knowledge and skill; and we have attempted to rectify this in too simple a fashion, by adding to our curricula a few extra courses that deal in generalities, which in turn only become another specialism. What we need, at every stage in education, is rather a common background which will correct for all the distortions and partialities of our vocational preparation— not to replace our vocational education, but to save it from imbecility. Education, if it avails at all, is an attempt to give to individual men what belongs to Man; and just as all men need air to breathe and food to eat and exercise for their bodies, so there are certain essential kinds of knowledge and discipline that they also must have in common, if they are to develop symmetrically into unified personalities.

To the notion of the specialized man, fitted adequately to his narrow daily task, we must now oppose quite a different ideal, that of the balanced man, capable of facing life on many fronts, ready for any emergency, moving freely from one sphere of activity to another, as our pioneer ancestors moved from one environment to another, not content with the limited horizon of his vocation or his local community, but eager to take part in a larger world. If we are to use creatively the vast energies we now command, we will need a new race of pioneers, ready to dream, to plan, to build, and to cultivate on a scale that will dwarf the best efforts of the nineteenth century.

Already the war is giving people a taste of the real versatility and initiative that will be needed to meet the post-war tasks: bookkeepers are handling machine guns and farmers' boys are flying bombing planes above distant rice-paddies.

They have given up the feeble timid dream of security perhaps but they have rediscovered the old virtue of self-reliance, combined with a reliance on comrades who have undergone the same experiences and now pursue the same objectives.

Precisely because the great task of the post-war world is to establish a dynamic equilibrium in our political and economic systems, we must found that equilibrium, not on a servile specialism and a hardened division of labor, but upon the balanced and many-sided cultivation of both the community and the individual personality. Citizenship, workmanship, and fellowship are the three sides of the balanced man: and the greatest of these is that ideal fellowship, which makes him a partner of all mankind in all that advances the spirit of man.

## 5. OBSTACLES TO IMPROVEMENT

One must not minimize the effort that will be necessary to create this new type of personality. The school can do much toward that end when it becomes conscious of this need— there are already schools in California that *have* done much; but most of our organizations and institutions have been ready to sacrifice the whole man in order to arrive more swiftly at more limited objectives.

Many devices and methods that have been introduced into education during the past generation have added to the evils of over-specialization and departmentalization: there has been the same over-refinement of techniques, the same over-emphasis on the mechanism of production and the same indifference to the quality or the distribution of the product that has prevailed in the world outside the school. We are engulfed in needless paper work; we are smothered by mani-

folding devices; we are tied to elaborate systems of accountancy which reveal little that is worth knowing; and there is
no indication whatever that, as organization becomes more
complicated, education becomes more adequate. Quite the
contrary: for the greater the emphasis that is laid upon the
educational machine, *as* a machine, the smaller the chance
there is for the teacher or the administrator to register in it,
as a full person. A refined pedagogy cannot take the place of
an active, developing, self-conscious man or woman, bringing
to the subject that is taught the interest and passion and wonder and discipline of a well-poised human being. Pedagogues
can teach subjects: but only men can teach men.

The over-elaboration of our external organization is
matched by the over-specialization and fragmentariness of
our typical curricula, despite many brave efforts to bring
together the separated fields of knowledge. One of my colleagues was once asked by a student whether he would be
marked wrong on an examination paper for using knowledge
he had acquired in another classroom on a different subject.
The question may appear comic; but it must painfully recall
to all of us the chaos of unrelated specialized items to which
much of our current education has perversely reduced itself.

It is time to realize that the progressive subdivision of
knowledge and experience is actually a phase of desiccation
and barbarism, not an advance: that the educated person, in
contrast to the ill-bred one, is a person whose knowledge is
always sufficiently generalized to be of use in more than one
small compartment. The old-fashioned classicist was wrong,
perhaps, in insisting that, given an extensive mastery of Latin
and Greek, a man was capable of handling any situation in
life; but if he was wrong in confining this ability to a single
means, he was not wrong in his ideal: for the aim of all education worth the name is not to stock the mind with bare facts,

so that the pupils will get prizes on Radio Quiz Programs, but to establish a set of values, a method, a point of view, that will bring reason and imagination to bear upon every situation. If one teaches English with intelligence, for example, there is only one kind of English to teach: as soon as one attempts to divide the subject into academic English, business English, engineering English, scientific English, and even—I believe the feat has been attempted—into *Hotel* English, one merely inculcates and perpetuates bad tricks that should be corrected, not reinforced.

This generalization applies to many other subjects. One cannot group together all the specialized items that have found their way into school curricula and call the result a balanced education, or the person produced by it a balanced person. It is no more a balanced education than the stale leftovers that go into hash are a balanced diet. If our whole educational system has accepted too complacently the notions of specialization and fragmentation of subject matter, it has also accepted too readily the current division that exists between knowledge and emotion and action. At the risk of a little obvious extravagance one may say that those who know, feel not, those who feel, act not, and those who act, know not. And if our knowledge and our actions are superficially orderly, indeed, often regimented and automatic, our emotions, which are an important source of our moral sentiments and our esthetic evaluations, live in a chaotic no-man's land, a dim confused underworld, of their own. In terms of our mechanical routine, emotions and feelings are unreal; and instead of being cultivated and disciplined, by art and morality and religion, they are either ruthlessly repressed, or allowed to come forth in their crudest form, without any intellectual or moral associations.

The emotional life of modern man has not ceased to exist;

as long as he lives it must take some form; but it has become degraded. Our emotions are attached to trivial objects, or they become enmeshed in regressive impulses which if they do not take the form of outright sadism, such as the Nazis practice, assume the shape current in our own country—an indecent interest in murder, crime, violence, sexual brutality. The art of misapplying emotion to irrelevant objects is daily practiced by the advertiser and the radio announcer; so much so that we are conditioned to believe that this is the normal function of the emotions, to deceive us, to lead us astray, to make the worse appear the better reason. As an outcome of this practice, people are afraid of their emotions and try to protect themselves against any manifestation: at length they are unable to have an honest emotional reaction to a situation that demands it.

## 6. EMOTIONS AND VALUES

Few things about our civilization are more sinister than the emotional paralysis that attended the oncoming and the first actual fighting of the war. Even now we have hardly yet thrown off our sense of unreality. The other day one of the heroes of the Solomon Islands naval engagements, a leader of unassailable skill and courage, was trying to explain to a newspaper reporter the quality of the effort there demanded. How did he bring it home to his listener? He tried to make the training, the co-ordination, the discipline, the struggle itself real—in terms of a football game. And why? Because these *mock*-struggles of the gridiron seem real to a generation that has wasted its energies on trivial pursuits and purposeless living; while the acts of war, infinitely more serious, infinitely more dangerous, infinitely more important to mankind, still remained incapable of summoning forth on their own merits the response demanded. There has still been no popular manifestation of interest in the gallant deeds of our army and navy, comparable to the spontaneous, ecstatic demonstration the hysterical inhabitants of Brooklyn gave to the home team, when it won the championship a few years ago. Let us not mistake this lack of emotional response for level-headedness, coolness, or self-control. Those are all admirable qualities; but our failure to have an emotional response to the moral issues of the war is not due to their operation.

Our psychologists have begun to tell us that our soldiers would make better fighters if they hated the enemy; they have even started to think up devices for warming up our soldiers to the proper degree of hate. *But why should there be any need for such prodding?* If our moral values were sufficiently developed, if pity and sympathy and love were on tap, if we were sensitive to the difference between evil and good, we would not need any further provocation to maintain a deep and abiding anger against the forces of evil we are now at last fighting: what the Nazis and their collaborators have done to the maimed peoples of Europe, what the Japanese have done to the Chinese and the Koreans, is deeply hateful to all the values and beliefs that make men truly human; and we should not need any extra synthetic hate to carry us through the ordeal of battle. Unless we hate evil we shall not be strong enough to rectify evil, nor shall we have the determination to see that justice is done at the end of the war.

One of the great problems for the educator today is to understand why our education has left the mass of men, in all civilized countries, so irresponsive to danger, so impassive to human suffering, so inert to the challenge of evil. Have we become automatons? Are we blocks, stones, worse than senseless things? I am afraid that the answer is that many of us have indeed become automatons, or nihilists, who passively deny the human values that the Axis powers, more dynamically, more energetically, trample upon.

Now the school, which has taken over so many of the functions performed by other institutions, including the Church and the Home, has shrunk from dealing with values and emotions: it has handled these subjects only when there was some intellectual potholder available to keep the teacher from getting burnt. It has studied, not the emotions of the poets, as revealed in poetry, but their lesser actions, as revealed in biography; it has studied, not the ideals of the saints and philosophers, but their historical relationships; when indeed it has studied them at all. Though the body and spirit are in organic association, we have covertly given precedence to the body and to the physical environment, as somehow more real than emotions and ideals: hence courage and temperance and justice and love and pity have ceased to stand for vital realities and have been reduced to the rank of "mere" words— as if words themselves were not significant and important.

If we are to create balanced human beings, capable of entering into world-wide co-operation with all other men of good will—and that is the supreme task of our generation, and the foundation of all its other potential achievements— we must give as much weight to the arousal of the emotions and to the expression of moral and esthetic values as we now give to science, to invention, to practical organization. One without the other is impotent. And values do not come ready-made: they are achieved by a resolute attempt to square the facts of one's own experience with the historic patterns formed in the past by those who devoted their whole lives to achieving and expressing values. If we are to express the love in our own hearts, we must also understand what love meant to Socrates and Saint Francis, to Dante and Shakespeare, to Emily Dickinson and Christina Rossetti, to the explorer Shackleton and to the intrepid physicians who deliberately exposed themselves to yellow fever. These historic manifestations of love are not recorded in the day's newspaper or the current radio program: they are hidden to people who possess only fashionable minds. Virtue is not a chemical product, as Taine once described it: it is a historic product, like language and literature; and this means that if we cease to care about it, cease to cultivate it, cease to transmit its funded values, a large part of it will become meaningless, like a dead language to which we have lost the key. That, I submit, is what has happened within our own lifetime.

Here, plainly, education has a large task on its hands; perhaps a larger one than it should be called on, by itself, to perform. But the recovery of values is an essential prelude to laying the foundations for our post-war world: those of us who think that the sole problems that need be dealt with are those of politics, economics, diplomacy, who fancy that the only kinds of value that need be spread through the world are cash values have no real grasp of the situation. The machine does not automatically produce the values that are necessary for running it justly and co-operatively. Our world-wide systems of communication and transport do not automatically endow people with the common language, the common background, the common moral impulses and the common goals that will be necessary to make the United Nations an actual achievement and not a pious dream. To create and transmit these common symbols is one of the great functions of modern education.

The fact is we are now at a critical moment of history, when mankind may either sink back into barbarism or lay the foundations for a new epoch in culture, which will place man, throughout the world, on a higher level than he has ever achieved before. To move toward the higher level we must constantly keep the concrete goal before us: the humanization, not the mechanization of man; the fullest utilization of every favorable aspect of the human personality and every resource in the community.

Our civilization has already passed through a lengthy period of disruption. The present war is the catastrophic fifth act of a drama that has reached its natural terminus: the drama of power, the drama of world conquest, the drama of mechanical organization, of salvation by machinery, to which Western man dedicated himself for the better part of four centuries. The period that is passing away before our eyes was one of the great epochs of human history. Much that it created, the methodical discipline of the merchant and soldier, the imaginativeness of the inventor, the systematic methodology of the experimental scientist, left a precious legacy to the human spirit: one that we must endeavor to maintain and transmit. But we can preserve the machine and all the values that derive from it only by recovering our own humanness. To hold what was precious in the past we must now transcend it; and in our education we must stress precisely those insights and values and purposes which were left out of the program of mechanization and material progress. We must return once more to the human scale; and we must justify all that we say or do and teach in terms of a new ideal of human life—that of a balanced personality, living within a universal society, aiming at the best life possible. The most essential act in the present war against barbarism is for us, the civilized men and women of the United Nations, to recover our own humanity.

In this world-wide process of revaluation and reorientation each one of us has a part to play. If we take our role seriously enough, the epilogue of the age that is passing may turn into the prologue of a greater drama, in which man, instead of being the subject of the machines he has created, will become their master. But if we would conquer the hell that now threatens to engulf us, we must not seek merely for a little less hell, we must not content ourselves with a sort of modified hell, with the brimstone deodorized and the heat made tolerable to us by a little asbestos insulation. Those who have conditioned themselves to hell do not, alas! realize that, no matter how many small improvements may be made in its accommodations, it is the place itself that is objectionable. No: only those who are capable of seeking boldly for the Kingdom of Heaven will be able to establish even the outlines of the post-war civilization.

The time-servers have served their time, and their departure is now overdue. We must now ask ourselves, not what we can get, but first, what is worth having. Once our values are established, once our goals are set, a large part of our present meaningless routine will fall away. And now the mission of education today becomes plain; it is nothing less than this: to prepare men and women who will be worthy of the great duties of worldwide co-operation and fellowship upon whose performance the fate of our whole civilization depends. That is a task worthy of our utmost efforts; and nothing less than our utmost efforts will be equal to the task.

# THE UNIFIED APPROACH TO KNOWLEDGE AND LIFE

[This paper was presented at the Fiftieth Anniversary Celebration of the founding of Stanford University, in June, 1941. It was published with the other papers given at that meeting in a book called The University and the Future of America, Stanford University Press, 1941. In view of the essay on the atomic bomb, which closes Book One, it is perhaps interesting to recall that one of the other papers given at this celebration was that by Professor Ernest Orlando Lawrence, called The New Frontiers in the Atom.]

## 1. THE END OF A PHASE

In 1910 Henry Adams predicted that the civilization of the Western world would, by 1917 or thereabouts, pass into a new phase. Mankind would enter into possession of almost unlimited powers and might, perhaps because of these very powers, be overtaken by catastrophe. "Bombs educate vigorously," observed Adams, "and even wireless telegraphy or airships might require the reconstruction of society." In 1918 Oswald Spengler predicted that the period of liberalism and humanitarianism and social progress was coming to an end. He foresaw the rise and rule of Caesarism: a ruthless exploitation of men and machines for the purpose of exercising power, devoid of further human purpose.

One need not accept the dubious premises upon which these two predictions were based. But it is plain by now that their intuitive conclusions were mainly correct: the worst has almost happened. Our Western society is now in the midst of a possibly catastrophic change whose dimensions even the most unflinching observers scarcely dare to measure or describe. We face not merely the overthrow of this or that government or the conquest of this or that country: we are threatened rather by the forcible extermination of the very principles and beliefs upon which a co-operative world order has been slowly shaping itself.

The certainties upon which men's lives seemed founded during the nineteenth century, above all the certainty that this civilization would continue in the path of development men had then laid down, have crumbled. Today mankind finds itself trapped, as in an earthquake, and the very instruments upon which we justly prided ourselves—our sciences, our technics, our administrative organization—now only add to our dangers. Like the crumbling walls and falling roofs and bursting water mains in a shaken city, our technical achievements complete the ruin caused by the upheaval itself. All the arts that seemed once to guarantee the co-operative union of mankind have become, in the hands of the new barbarian, a means of extending the domain of insensate power.

What has brought this situation about? By what mustering of mankind's latent resources can this civilization be rescued? By what changes in our beliefs and purposes and activities can we stay the processes of disintegration and establish the conditions that will favor the processes of life and growth in society? How shall we start our Western culture on a fresh cycle of development?

These questions, I submit, must underlie every rational discussion of the future of education. We can no more ignore them than St. Augustine could ignore the moral and political failures of the great Roman imperium when, on its wreckage, he attempted to lay down the foundations of the City of God. Nor must we make the mistake of blaming this vast secular change upon the errors and sins we have committed in the recent past: upon the first World War, upon the Treaty of Versailles, upon the recent unemployment and economic paralysis, upon the lethal unimaginativeness of the politicians and soldiers who governed the nontotalitarian countries. Those weaknesses were but symptoms. And it is only by examining the shaken foundations of our whole social structure, and by referring to a much wider span of time, that we can understand why the so-called Century of Progress now threatens to usher in an era of regression.

There is something arbitrary, in the nature of things, in any summary statement of the character of the epoch that is now drawing to an end. But I think it can be described, without too great a distortion, as a period dominated by mechanism, militarism, and mammonism: a period during which the motives of domination and acquisition came gradually to displace other human interests or reduce their capacity for effective expression. By means of a superior technical equipment—the magnetic compass, the three-masted sailing ship, muskets and cannon, astronomical knowledge and maps—Western man originally conquered and colonized the planet as a whole. In an amazing outburst of physical energy and spiritual audacity, he expanded the area of arable land, appropriated the practical culture of primitive peoples, multiplied the stock of usable natural resources, utilized the machine to magnify human productivity, and in a single century tripled his own population.

This whole phase of Western civilization may be characterized as an era of expansion. Most of the new institutions of our society were founded on the premise of expansion and keyed to the need for expansion. In every field of activity men left their neighbors behind them and set forth boldly, more or less at random, to discover new territory, to stake out a claim to unearthed treasures, to blaze a new trail through the wilderness, to push forward toward a remoter horizon.

During this era of expansion, which lasted roughly from the sixteenth to the twentieth century, Western civilization became mechanically unified and socially disintegrated: it multiplied the new physical means of living and lost sight of the purposes and ends that make those means significant. The pursuit of power ceased to be a means of adding to the security and variety of human life: it became an end in itself, attached to a disengaged fragment of the human personality. But because the power principle, pushing into every department of existence, seemed for a time to spread order and well-being on a scale man had never known before, the social and moral bases of this society were taken for granted.

This oversight was all the easier for the reason that the survivals and mutations of other cultures long remained active in the power economy. Not merely did the institutions of medieval society maintain their hold on large parts of daily life, but the heritage of a remoter classic past had been recovered; and during the eighteenth century a new humanitarian impulse, deeply akin to that which nurtured Christianity, temporarily softened the asperities of the machine. Furthermore, there was a deep-seated confusion, not confined to the popular mind, between mechanical improvements and social improvements. The optimism of the Victorian Age was based on the belief that the first in some sense guaranteed the second: the perfection of machines and the ennoblement of man seemed parts of a single process. . . . Though mechanical invention did not always prove as beneficent to the workers, at first, as the utilitarians had proclaimed it, no one doubted that in time it would fulfill the rosiest predictions that its apologists had made.

Even for those who did not look upon the educative process as automatic, the prescription, in effect, was simple. If machines could be improved so easily, why not men? Indeed, why should man not be improved by the same methods—by disregarding as unreal, as inoperative, the human feelings and emotions, human sentiments and purposes and ideals: by treating man as a self-operating automaton? To create this paragon of the mechanical age, it was necessary only to cast off the historic and social elements in his culture: to turn him loose from his home, to emancipate him from religion, to make him indifferent to art, to translate his dreams into stuff that could be fashioned by a machine, and instead of sublimating or etherealizing his exorbitant animal needs, to do just the opposite, that is, to materialize every manifestation of spirit. The crippled, lopsided creature that was left could then be hailed as "man almost at his full stature at last."

By a series of almost involuntary renunciations, the cult of the machine led to a disparagement of the rest of human culture. Labor-saving devices were treated as if they were, by nature, life-creating instruments. If only man improved machines, machines would inevitably improve man. So many people thought; and so many more acted, even when they did not think.

Superficially, this power culture conquered the world: conquered it and mechanically unified it. Throughout the planet, men spoke through the same kind of telephone; they read by the same kind of electric light; they shared the same news, sent over the same cables; and they viewed with pleasure the same black and white images on the motion-picture screen. Moreover, till the first World War, the white peoples traveled and migrated freely over the earth. But this unity was not a

genuinely inclusive one. Culturally, it was based on the dominance of Western man and Western modes of thought. But
even within that framework it covered only those parts of life
that submitted to mechanical routine or mechanical formula-
tion. The intellectual understanding, the moral consensus, the
scheme of values that were necessary, in human terms, to
complete this mechanical conquest remained in a primitive
stage; indeed, in certain departments the means of social
co-operation were poorer in the twentieth century than in the
seventeenth.

Take the matter of communication. For the last five centuries there has been a succession of bold mechanical improvements: the printed book, the universal postal service,
the telegraph, the radio. But in the seventeenth century Latin,
the common language of learned men, began to fall out of
fashion; and though in the eighteenth century statesmen could
still address each other in a common tongue, French, by the
end of the nineteenth century even that vehicle of intercourse
had dropped out of circulation. Precisely at the point where
mechanical communication had become instantaneous, translation, with all its delays and misconceptions, took the place
of direct intercourse. That blockage proved serious: the Babel
of tongues now matches the older Babel of theological creeds.
But unfortunately it is fairly typical. By mechanical invention the earth has been made one; but in human terms that
unity has proved a barefaced fiction.

In other words, the real work of carrying our mechanical
co-operations onto the human level still remains to be accomplished. This can be done only by an age that no longer looks
upon the machine as an automatic instrument of salvation.
Such an age must be ready to abandon the power-principle as
the chief motive of existence and deliberately set itself to
develop a balanced human culture.

Looking back upon the development of the machine, we can now see that there is both an inner reason and an outer cause for the crisis in which Western civilization now finds itself. The inner reason is due to the fact that the one-sided concentration on power has disrupted the human personality and has undernourished or paralyzed a large number of activities that are essential to the healthy development of the community. On the educational conclusions to be drawn from this fact and on the further steps we must take to overcome it, I propose to dwell at length in this paper. But the outer conditions must not be overlooked; for they make the crisis more grave and our search for a balanced culture more pressing. The great underlying economic and social fact of our time is that the era of expansion is rapidly coming to an end; and we can no longer continue life on the old basis or hope to prosper by holding doggedly to institutions that were geared for expansion.

The facts about the tapering off of the era of expansion should be fairly obvious by now; but except for a remarkable prophetic analysis by John Stuart Mill, in Volume II of his Principles of Political Economy, their implications have not been sufficiently appraised, and I regret that I can make only the sketchiest reference to them here. In brief, the expansion of Western man has had three aspects: an expansion of his territory, an expansion of the area of industrialism, and an expansion of population. The land surface of the globe has now been staked out and occupied: to achieve a better utilization of the land, a more harmonious distribution of groups and nations, the whole method of exploitation must be radically altered. The gross inequalities between continents, between peoples, between social classes, upon which our entire economic scheme was based, cannot now be maintained except by terrorism and brute force. If industries are to find

new customers, it will not be by adding to the numbers of
poor and backward peoples; by fostering the growth of an
external or an internal proletariat: it can come about only
by lifting the common living standard in every area. This
means a shift from a producer's and exploiter's economy to
a consumer's economy and, along with it, a readiness to diminish and even to forego profits for the sake of social security and well-being. We must prepare for the time when both
population and industry will be mainly on a replacement
basis: when the principle of continuous yield, as applied in
agriculture and forestry, will supplant the reckless mining
economy of the period of expansion.

Because of our slowness in interpreting this change, we
have not yet developed rational means for meeting it. When
people are confronted with a situation that defies their understanding and puts unbearable pressure upon them, they often
seek to revert to a more primitive pattern. In the case of the
totalitarian states, they have met the challenge of stabilization
by reinstating the original terms of our conquest: by the complete mechanization and militarization of their polities for
the purpose, once more, of unlimited expansion. To meet a
world that has become intellectually incomprehensible, the
totalitarians have a simple formula: they deny the value of
rationality and put their faith in a magical system of salvation, under a leader who is also a god. Stabilization by regression is their neurotic response to the present crisis: to solve
the social dilemmas of a power culture, the totalitarians propose simply to make power more unqualified. But we must
remember Lord Acton's great generalization: All power corrupts, and absolute power corrupts absolutely. This applies
to our civilization as a whole. The present reinstatement of
the power theme by the Nazis may be interpreted, perhaps,
as the last paroxysm of a dying civilization.

What, then, is the rational alternative? The rational alternative is for us to lay down the foundations for a new
culture: one based upon the primacy of the human personality and the human community; the substitution of life-
values for those of a power and profit economy; the reorganization of society as a whole toward the achievement of the
best life possible. The guiding themes for the coming era
cannot be derived from the needs and hopes of the era of
expansion: we have to frame a whole new set of objectives
in terms of balance, equilibrium, co-ordination, and cultivation, a many-sided organic development: above all, in terms
of human balance, human co-ordination, human development.
Power has become unruly because power alone has ruled.
Many of the great individual advances of the past era remain
to be done over again: this time, not for individual glory or
gain, but for the benefit of the whole community. Many of our
past dogmas must be abandoned; many of our past beliefs
have become irrelevant; all of what is sound in our culture
up to the present must be reworked into a more comprehensive and organic pattern. And the first place to start in
this new instauration is the realm of knowledge. Let us consider our historic weaknesses here, before we formulate a
regimen for education designed to correct them.

## 2. FROM UNITY TO UNIFORMITY

Now the first great change that marked the development of
the power culture was that which led from the quest for unity
to that for uniformity. In the Summa Theologia, the high
point of the medieval synthesis, Thomas Aquinas had succeeded in the task that had for long constituted the principal
effort of the Christian Church: to bring together in a single
structure the disparate and often contradictory elements that

had entered into the Christian order. The sources themselves were diverse; and the task of selection extremely difficult. Stoic law had to be accepted without stoic fatalism, Jewish morals without Jewish tribalism, Graeco-Arabic science without destroying the primacy of theology.

Such unities are never final, even when at the moment of achievement they seem inclusive; for they can be prolonged only by accepting their very relativity and incompleteness, and by continuing to add new elements while judiciously modifying or discarding the old. In other words, every synthesis must remain open or else, by the very fact of closing up, it will cease to unify the experience that has still to be included: if it remains outside history it will shortly become false to the new totality or, what is almost as bad, irrelevant. At no point is it possible to call a halt or say that a particular unification is final: one might as well try to preserve the shape of a fountain by freezing the water in mid-air and turning off the further supply. The guardians of medieval culture made precisely this mistake: they failed to keep their system open or to formulate a method for orderly change. As a result, new perceptions, new insights, new generalizations were made outside the established provinces and were never successfully attached to the main structure.

The growth of capitalism and political absolutism in Western Europe brought to an end the efforts of an Aquinas or a Dante. The search for a common basis for thought and feeling and action, for a common medium that would unite the temporal with the eternal, the particular with the universal, gave way to the demand for external uniformity. Outwardly, the practice of uniformity has many points in common with the achievement of unity; and in relation to inner need they both spring out of man's essential demand for law and order as a prerequisite for all other significant human activity. But, in practice, one is almost the diametric opposite of the other; for a unity is no real unity unless it is based on rational methods and free agreement, unless it recognizes and harmonizes and composes real differences: unless it retains within its order the variety and richness of life itself. Uniformity, in contrast, carries an element of compulsion: for the sake of an outward order, it will repress differences, or at all events, agree to ignore them.

By definition, the uniform is that which can be duplicated, multiplied, indefinitely repeated once the unit itself is established. In social life, uniformities first made their way into the Western scheme of life in the strict daily regimen of the monasteries; then in the growing demand for uniform coins, for uniform weights and measures, for uniform laws based on the Roman codes, for uniform military costumes. From the time of Frederick II of Sicily onward, the growth of despotism in Europe was accompanied by a strengthening of the cult of uniformity. There is no question about the efficacy of this principle in economizing energy: coins that are uniformly assayed and stamped are much easier to exchange than irregular bits of gold of uncertain quality, which must be weighed in each transaction; soldiers whose reflexes have been stiffened by drill are usually more reliable in action than more happy-go-lucky fellows whose behavior is less mechanical. Attention to uniformities had an enormous practical value in social life; and this was no less true in the realm of thought; for it was by paying attention to uniformities in the movements of the planets that the natural sciences acquired a method which reduced the complex welter of naive experience to aspects and dimensions that could be measured. Within its restricted sphere, uniformity performs a human service, provided its restrictions are taken for what they really are: practical devices of the human intelligence, not the ultimate revelations of the absolute.

But there is something arbitrary and procrustean in this kind of efficiency; almost always it is purchased at a price. The uniformities of the despotic national state were achieved at the price of eliminating, not only local laws, but local customs and local liberties, whose cultivation had given a special local savor and tang to the landscape, the architecture, and the human personality in every region of Europe. Similarly, the uniformities of science were purchased by a disregard for man's complex, many-sided experience: by a contempt for his historic heritage, by a readiness to disparage, as purely subjective, that which could not be reduced to measure, and then to dismiss the subjective itself as unreal. Poetry, music, religion, painting, philosophy, all remained in existence; but they were steadily segregated, as disorderly, indeed as disreputable elements, in a sort of red-light district of the mind: a reminder of human infirmity rather than of human wisdom. Treated as social outcasts, these realms of the personality rapidly lost self-respect and responsibility; and they had relatively little influence, accordingly, over the workaday activities of decent citizens.

Though in the seventeenth century, and even later, a few philosophers still strove mightily for unity, the dominant fact of Western life was a continued fragmentation of activities, and a progressive widening of subjective differences, under the loose rule of tolerance. Following Descartes, the search for unity almost ceased; for he split the human personality into an automaton governed by the same physical laws that prevailed in the rest of nature and a soul that fell under the exclusive care of the Church, to whom all its historic and transcendental attributes were committed. That dualism was fatal, and especially fatal to education. Both in content and in method education ceased in the end to care for the human personality as a whole. Large areas of historic experience, like those of religion and ethics, dropped out of the secular curriculum, and the gap that they left was, as Newman predicted, divided up among economics, politics, and anthropology. Only in secluded spots, still under the tutelage of the Church—the University of Oxford, for instance—did the cultivation of the whole personality remain, preserving in an archaic form, with an obsolescent context, the old tradition of unity.

## 3. REACTION AGAINST UNIFORMITY

Against the dominant cult of uniformity, there were various strong reactions; but unfortunately they tended to take a backward path. Romanticism, in all its many phases, was a protest against uniformity: as protestantism in religion, as nationalism in politics, as land-pioneering and colonization in economic life, as anarchism, Bohemianism, or nihilism in individual relations. But romanticism, while it properly attempted to reinstate neglected parts of the personality and discarded elements in the human tradition, made the mistake of condemning out of hand the order and discipline and efficiency that had in fact been made possible by the widening conquests of the physical sciences and the machine technics. In revenge for his being an outcast in the new mechanical world, the romantic sought to make the exponents of uniformity equally despised in his private world of passion, impulse, and fantasy. This only increased the gap between the two sides of the personality that were involved: it made it harder for them to come together in a common world. Instead of pursuing the search for unity along his own more organic lines, the romantic contented himself with evading the common social and intellectual obligations. Under the hardening crust of uniformity, romanticism presented the molten lava of the irrational and the irresponsible, seeking a fissure through which it might burst.

In the realm of education, the minor victories of romanticism, from Rousseau onward, were annulled by the radical changes that took place in the whole structure of knowledge. The most important of these was the rapidly increasing subdivision of the processes of intellectual production. This must be distinguished from the simple division of labor. Such a division, based on aptitudes and interests, is of course a necessary condition of human society: perhaps man's ancestors became human, among other reasons, precisely because of variations in native capacity that favored such a division. But the rational division of labor always assumes an underlying social objective and an intelligible common basis for action; and it is this basis and this objective that have increasingly disappeared.

The excuse usually offered for the minute subdivision of the processes of higher learning is that our knowledge today is too vast to be produced or absorbed by a single mind. But this has always been true. Even Aristotle, that prince of professors, did not command the entire body of his culture, though he added vastly to its domains. To make up for the increasing bulk of factual material, science in particular provides a system of shorthand notation, in the form of laws, or in the form of symbolic devices, like maps in geography. In other realms of experience, the same kind of condensation is performed by philosophic systems and works of art. Thanks to these notations and symbols, those familiar with their use can see the view from the mountaintop without having to climb every foot of the way; thanks to works of art, the experience of a multitude of lives can be utilized within a single lifetime. These processes of condensation, generalization, and sampling must be counted as man's supreme labor-saving device.

Why, then, have we renounced the search for a unified approach to knowledge and life? Is it not because we have looked for unity in the wrong place? Once we give up the quest for unity at the center, in the activities of the personality and the community, we must plainly abandon all hope for unity, even of the loosest kind, at the periphery, where facts and observations are overwhelming in their multiplicity, even if we restrict our search to the merest subdivision of any special field. What we need is not some all-embracing encyclopedia, which will be out of date at many points before it is even published: we require, rather, the invention of conceptual devices, and the perfection of a discipline, which will progressively transform our unrelated fragments of experience into an intelligible whole. The working out of these devices and the perfection of this discipline was the major preoccupation of the thinker from whom the underlying idea of this paper stems—Patrick Geddes. Others have been at work in the same domain. All these efforts must now be critically appraised, put to the test of daily use, and revised, modified, and elaborated.

The problem of unification is hopeless, then, only if one begins with a multitude of separate facts and separate academic disciplines. We cannot hope to create a coherent pattern of thought by laboriously picking up each fact and putting it into place: no lifetime is long enough to accomplish more than an infinitesimal part of the task and, if it could be performed, such a static arrangement would be valueless. What we need, rather, is a magnetic field at the center which will continuously polarize every fragment that enters into the field: which will keep each part in dynamic relationship with the whole, because at the center, in the human agent himself, there is a conceptual core where all the aspects of experience draw together into a significant pattern. A magnet can perform in a moment, with a million particles of iron dust, what the most ant-like patience would not achieve in a month. The human personality, properly organized, properly disciplined, properly equipped, works in a similar fashion. For the fragmentary man the world outside the narrow domain he has mastered is a shifting chaos of fragments: for the whole man every part of experience has a place; even what is unknown or undiscovered, or what lies beyond his personal compass, exists in an orderly relationship, like the undiscovered elements in Mendeleyev's original Periodic Table.

Now it happens that there is a close historic connection between the unrelated production of knowledge and the unrelated production of material goods: the present crisis in our civilization arises partly out of serious maladjustments in both departments. Both exhibit a growing rationalization within the process of production and a growing irrationality, marked by moral irresponsibility and social ineffectiveness, in the disposition of the product. Fundamentally, the factory and the university have accepted the same premise: the belief that fragments of mechanical production or fragments of knowledge, are real, are significant, and are valuable in themselves: to produce them and accumulate them is a profitable life occupation. This is the bias of an acquisitive society: a natural compensation, perhaps, for long centuries of intellectual sterility and material want. Filled with admiration for the new technical processes of production, we have, however, lost sight of the social destination of the goods themselves. When a factory goes on producing without finding an outlet, the result is a surplus of undisposable stock: a prelude to unemployment and perhaps bankruptcy. This has a parallel in our intellectual life. There is the same failure to translate technical advances into social values, and orderly methods of production into a planful and purposive scheme of living.

To sum up: the age of expansion widened the area of objective uniformities, both in the sciences and in many departments of social life; and by so doing it put almost immeasurable powers into the hands of modern man. But by concentrating on this element of power, we lost connections with other important human needs; so that beneath the surface uniformities there was an increasing area of subjective disruption, and beneath the surface manifestations of power there were, from the standpoint of the whole personality, indications of disorientation and rebellious conflict. The split personality, rational in its special field, open to irrationality in other departments, disciplined on the mechanical side but undisciplined and emotionally underdeveloped, became the characteristic human product of this culture. Partly because of the failure to make a synthesis of our growing body of knowledge and a unity of our lives, we are threatened with further disintegration.

## 4. TOWARD A NEW UNITY

At this point, we must not make the mistake of believing that our difficulties will be solved by more education: that the cry of the masses for salvation will be attained by inducing larger numbers to remain in high school or to pass through college, or by elaborating our physical plant and equipment and adding to the number of laboratories and libraries and courses. For more education of the kind we have laboriously perfected during the last seventy-five years will only widen the area of our difficulties. With a few struggling exceptions, our schools and universities are mirrors of the very condition

we must overcome. For fear of losing authority, the specialist
dares not step out of his narrow compartment; for fear of
being challenged on unfamiliar territory, he refuses to break
down the boundary lines that habit and convenience have
erected between various realms of discourse; for fear of losing time on his own job, he refuses to concern himself with
the difficult task of coupling and interconnection. Nor is there
merit solely in the suggestion for a holiday in the physical
sciences and mechanical invention: that is a crude empirical
scheme for temporarily overcoming the inherent lack of balance and relationship between the various spheres of organized knowledge.*

What is needed is a far more radical change: a change in
method, direction, tempo, and purpose. Our problem is not,
as some educators once thought, to adjust our education to the
needs of a changing world: the problem is equally that of
adjusting a changing world to the basic needs of education:
meaning by education the harmonious cultivation of the entire
personality, operating within the medium of a common culture, and within the frame of a going community. In short,
we must think out a rational alternative to the incoherent uniformities of the past. We must provide a progressive and
humane alternative to the regimentation that offers its so-
called "new order" today. In conceiving "the scope and nature of university education" in the days to come, we must
hold that "its matter must not be admitted into the mind
passively, as so much acquirement, but must be mastered and
appropriated as a system consisting of parts, related one to
the other, and interpretative of one another and the unity of a
whole." Our aim will be that which Leibnitz thought he
discerned in the universe itself: the achievement of the maxi-

* In view of the catastrophic disintegration that has taken place since,
I have altered this view: see Program for Survival.

mum variety compatible with the maintenance of order. This, at least, must be our aim if we recognize the imminent end of the period of unlimited power, unlimited acquisition, and unlimited expansion; and if we seek to lay the foundations for a more organic order, capable of more fully sustaining the life of the personality and the community.

Now beneath every system of education there are certain metaphysical assumptions as to the nature of the universe and the condition of man. Some of those who have talked in recent years about the need for a unified approach to knowledge have coupled this with a tacit demand to return to a defunct social structure and to a metaphysics that would deny the validity of historic experience. Since I do not share those views, without many strict reservations, I must make more explicit the underlying beliefs upon which the present outline rests.

The first of these is a reversal of the conventional order of modern thought, which looks upon the physical universe as basic and ultimate, and the facts of human society as entirely derivative. This metaphysics arose in the sixteenth century, through the fact that uniformities and mathematical certainties were first established in the physical sciences and gave man a vivid new world picture, which displaced that in which Heaven and God had been at the center. But man is not born into a bare physical universe; that is an abstraction which was first achieved, perhaps, by the Ionian philosophers. Man is born into a world of human values, human purposes, and human instruments: these values, purposes, and instruments condition all his other experiences; indeed without them he would live only on the level of brute sense and appetite. Every attempt to describe a world without human society presupposes the artifacts of human society as an integral part of the description.

By social artifice man has created a life that is not strictly dependent upon his biological state or his immediate environment. This is the realm of history, if one means by history, not simply the succession of recorded events, but the entire sum of man's available cultural heritage. We can approach nature only through the medium of human culture: not alone through our practical tools, but through language and logic and number. In the development of all these social instrumentalities our bodily processes and our organic aptitudes and our organized social responses to the challenges of life itself have played a part. The accumulations of culture form the topsoil and humus in which the higher life of man, distinguished here from all other brute creation, has flourished. Let the historic roots of our culture be plowed up, let the dust-storms scatter the loose soil, and what is left is a bare surface of nonhistoric experience which will not sustain human life or thought.

The metaphysics which put the physical universe first avoided reference to the natural history of the self and society. Hence it denied the importance of time except as a succession of physical events: there was no place in its scheme for the accumulations of time, for a past enregistered in memory and so constantly present, preserved for the community at large in its institutions. The isolated body, the abstracted piece of matter, was supposed, as Whitehead has put it, "to be conceived fully and adequately within the present moment." If we begin our inquiry with the facts of society, we find that memory, in all its biological and social and personal forms, is what chiefly distinguishes man from a well-contrived automaton. For a metaphysics that puts society first, history is the groundwork of specifically human activity. Unless one treats the making of history as the essential process of human life, no single event or action makes sense. In human terms purpose is what gives time its direction; while time is the condition under which goals are realized. History brings about a social partnership in time which complements and completes the manifold co-operations in space by means of which society flourishes.

Here, then, are my two fundamental assumptions: first, the facts of personality and the institutions of society are basic to all other human experience; and, second, man is a history-making animal, who lives in the three-dimensional world of the past, the present, and the possible, or, if you will, in a world of the real, the realizing, and the realizable.

## 5. COMMUNITY AND PERSONALITY

What follows should be fairly plain: the deliberate culture of the personality and the community is basic to every other kind of study; and the revitalization of history becomes accordingly an essential task of education. Let me deal with the second matter first. This is not simply a matter of adding history, as a prefatory calendar of events, to the existing body of knowledge, though history as organized record of course has a place in every curriculum. But it is more emphatically a matter of searching for the relevant past in every department of learning as the necessary context of an understandable present. The watchword of the political revolutionaries of the eighteenth century was: The past has nothing to teach us; history is the record of superstitions, frauds, and lies. But the actions of these sanguine reformers were usually more benign than their slogans. They were not so innocent of historic example as to deny that honesty was better than fraud. Only in our age have the final consequences of their anti-historic nihilism shown themselves.

Many of us remember the time when, in the name of the

so-called New History, it became fashionable to say that only modern history was important. Out of date was out of mind. Never was a shallower notion propounded to the world. For no generation can begin from scratch; when it does, it becomes a victim of the immediate past, and in the very act of throwing off history it submits with helpless docility to a small segment of it. Had our contemporaries carried with them a living consciousness of the Graeco-Roman world they would not have been so unprepared to understand the symptoms of their own disintegration; had our post-war interpreters of politics and diplomacy related their findings to the centuries-old background of the first World War, they would not have foisted on our generation the juvenile belief that all our difficulties began with the Treaty of Versailles.

What has been weak, in fact, in the development of human culture has been the imperfection of our instruments of record and interpretation. The destructive forces of nature and man tend blindly to wipe out a great part of the heritage before it has been assimilated in adequate symbolic form. So far from being overwhelmed by the accumulations of history, the fact is that mankind as a whole has never carried enough of its history along with it, in forms that permitted reflective criticism, rational selection, and renewed employment. By lengthening one's historical perspective one becomes able to throw off the partialities and relativities of one's immediate society: likewise, by facing the totality of human experience, one includes elements that the fashion or habit of a particular period may have arbitrarily rejected: archaic elements, primitive elements, irrational elements, that are often overlooked by the wise in their too narrow wisdom. Did not modern medicine drastically revise its practice in part through the recovery of Hippocrates? Did not Freud receive a special impetus from the dream book of Artemidorus

Daldianus, which preserved a form of human lore transmitted otherwise only through superstitious peasants and ignorant servant girls? In this sense history is a reservoir of human creativeness. And without the perpetual rediscovery and re-interpretation of history, without free access to that reservoir, human life would be but a trickle of brackish water in a desert. That is why a burning of the books, in modern Germany as in ancient China, is the first major act of the barbarians' attack on civilization.

But history has another side, which is usually neglected: it is the domain of the possible, the starting point of the ideal. Since Aristotle, the concept of the ideal has largely dropped out of scientific discourse, and because of the general influence of our practical and technical culture, it has dropped equally out of human life. When social scientists, for example, approach the future, they do so circumspectly in appearance—but in fact far too rashly—with the aid of statistical charts, in which a broken line, carrying forward the curve of past tendencies, is supposed to indicate the future path of development. But this statistical future, though often useful for limited practical guidance, has only a limited bearing. The real future is no mechanical continuation of the present: from moment to moment the line of the past may be altered by new factors operating from both inside and outside the human personality. It is a product of purpose.

For every potentiality that matures in the individual a score of others must be neglected. But at any time, under the influence of need or desire or memory, one or another fresh element may be brought into play. It is the same in society at large. The selection of potentialities and the projection of ideal goals, is, with reference to the future, the counterpart of an intelligent commerce with the past. No life is veritably purposive unless it exhibits prospective reference as a constant factor in its behavior. The neglect of the ideal leads only to the covert practice of giving to the present an ideal significance which it does not possess.

By means of history and utopia, then, the human personality partly transcends the limitations of its time, its place, and its social order. Through them, the potential and the actual constantly interplay.

This doctrine takes us a long way from current fashions. In the recent past, we have shied away from the normative aspects of education; and our failure here has not merely brought about a distrust of the imagination on almost every plane but has in turn lessened our capacity to anticipate or to control the future. Lacking an articulate system of ideals, our choices are inevitably chaotic, or unprincipled, to use an old-fashioned word that needs to be restored to an honorable post; that is, without direction and without ultimate moral and social reference. One of the remedies for this situation is a systematic renewal of the fields of esthetics, ethics, and religion, the great domains of ideal values. Their cultivation at every level, in reflection and in practice, in doctrine and in action, is essential to the balanced development of the human personality. An individual who has not yet entered into these realms has not yet reached the full human estate. Such cultivation, moreover, apart from its valuable inner discipline, will perhaps help bring back into our practical activities the powers of vision, of imaginative anticipation, and of ideal reference often so conspicuously absent.

Though the personal and the communal are primary, in the metaphysics I have been roughly outlining, one must assume that there is no break in continuity between the social, the biological, and the physical aspects of existence: they are organically related, and can be separated only as a convenience of thought. The doctrine of emergence, as developed by

Lloyd Morgan, is sufficient to account for the radical qualitative difference that may be observed as one passes from one
aspect of existence or experience to another. No matter at
what level of abstraction one may approach a particular
event, the meaningful context involves ultimately every other
level. A partial report may of course be true as far as it goes:
limitations of time and practice often make it imperative to
let the part stand for the whole. But truths, as Leibnitz well
observed, have degrees of adequacy as well as degrees of certainty; and only a method of thinking that acknowledges the
interrelatedness of all the fields of thought and experience
can give an adequate orientation to any part. The ground plan
of the whole must modify the structure of the individual
truth.

## 6. DOCTRINE OF THE WHOLE

This doctrine daily becomes more plain in practice, even
though it is still too much neglected in theory. For the physician who pursues his medicine far enough will eventually
come face to face with problems of psychology, social organization, economics, and even religion; while the engineer who
sees behind his slide rule and his drafting table will eventually intersect the path of the physician. So with every other
well-developed interest. The great creative efflorescence of
painting during the Renaissance was associated with the systematic research, by artists, into the physical laws of perspective and the anatomy of the human body, with increased devotion to the problems of mechanical invention and architec-
tural construction. In our day, professional training has dis-
couraged this deliberate ramification of knowledge and experience. Success has come mainly to the specialist, trained like
a race horse with blinkers, ridden to victory on condition that

he follows his lane on the track and pays no attention to what takes place on either side of him. This performance may win trophies and prizes; it may give intense satisfaction to the horse, the rider, the owner, the spectators; but it takes for granted the merits of the sport itself. And it is the merits of the sport, with respect either to adequate truth or effective social use, that I make bold here and now to challenge.

What I suggest is that specialized knowledge must be treated as only a part of organized human experience and that it must be directly related, from the start, to every other aspect of the human personality. Instead of overstressing subject matter and forgetting relationships, we must stress orientation, and make it possible for the student to find his way from any given starting point to every other relevant part of human experience. There have always been a few inspired teachers who have been at home in every part of their world and who have been as fully aware of their historic relationships and their social responsibilities as of their immediate professional quests: Joseph Henry in physics and William Osler in medicine were classic examples. But we can no longer leave to such accidental aids the processes of unification and interrelation; we can no longer leave to random pressure and interests matters that call for discipline, plan, and rational organization.

To define and articulate the common world of experience, shared by each and all of the arts and sciences, is one of the central tasks of philosophy; and to be familiar, in greater or less degree, with every part of it, so that one may pass freely back and forth between the objective and the subjective aspects, between the sciences and the ideologies, between active participation and contemplative withdrawal, is the essential characteristic of the fully educated man. One must understand the whole circle of experience if one is to cultivate properly any part of it. There is, I believe, only one effective means by which these ends can be accomplished; and that is by the institution of a common curriculum. One need not overlook the fact that intense interests must be recognized, special talents encouraged, and exacting professional requirements adequately met; but as both the prelude and accompaniment to these modes of emphasis, it is important to reinstate the humanistic notion of a common subject matter and a common discipline, at every stage in the educational program.

The psychological reasons for this common curriculum are no less significant than its social grounds. Dr. C. G. Jung has wisely suggested that it is important, in the interests of personal balance, to cultivate one's weaker aptitudes. This means that the contemplative man should have some share of practical responsibility, that the imaginative artist should be familiar with the scientific method, that the future organizer of great enterprises should familiarize himself with the theological conception of the special sinfulness of pride. In the past phase of culture the cultivation of personality and community was regarded as secondary and left to the end: human values remained as survivals of nonmechanical cultures or as accidental by-products of the machine itself. For us, on the other hand, the problem of personality has become central: as important to our society as it was to the disintegrating classic world. Our common subject matter must be human life, in all its historic manifestations: our common goal will be a maturing human personality, at home in a developing community.

Though for the sake of clarity I have emphasized the role of organized knowledge in this new orientation, I should be untrue to the philosophy I have been expounding if I assigned the entire task of integration to the realm of formal education. Far from it. Dr. Robert Maynard Hutchins has well observed that it is a modern heresy to hold "that all education is formal education and that formal education must assume the total responsibility for the full development of the individual." The Greek notion, he adds, "that the city educates the man, has been forgotten." Unfortunately, the Greek notion seems also to be forgotten by Dr. Hutchins himself; for it is obvious that our cities, as at present constituted, are incapable of furthering a well-balanced life, at every stage of human growth. Hence the reordering of the city and the region become an essential part of the unified approach to knowledge and life. While we must not expect the school to take the place of the community, it must nevertheless contain, in symbolic form, all that constitutes a community; so that the passage from reflection to practice, from experiment to action, may be clear and direct. So, too, the dynamic equilibrium we seek to establish within the personality can be maintained only through widening the processes of organic planning and development in every part of the body politic. It is only by establishing an outer order that an inner order can be fully confirmed and adequately perpetuated.

Above all, we must avoid the temptation, which would be fatal to our efforts, to confine the task of synthesis to the field of rational knowledge alone. Our feelings, our passions, our evaluations, our fantasies, our ideals are no less concerned in the effort for unity than our scientific and practical procedures. For an objective order that attempts to exclude subjective elements as unreal or irrelevant inevitably ends, as ours has in fact done, by leaving the field open to an addled subjectivity; and under the rule of tolerance it permits conflicts and irrationalities to multiply to a point that disintegrates the personality and puts the community itself beyond the possibility of rational treatment. We must meet this disorder at the beginning. In an age that calls for integration we can no longer admit the widening of the breach between the objective and the subjective aspects of the personality; nor can we permit the present raw contrast between our public and our private worlds. That way lies stultification and paralysis. Not merely do the subjective elements of the personality belong to the public world, in the form of arts and symbols that are shared by all the members of the community. But it is equally important, of course, that rational knowledge should penetrate every nook and cranny of the private world, disciplining uncontrolled fantasy, disinfecting superstition, and destroying infantile survivals. Intercourse, co-operation, and, when necessary, rational conflict must take place between these now separated realms of the personality; it is better that differences should be openly expressed, than that indifference should permit them to harden into permanent obstacles to co-operation.

## 7. THE ECOLOGY OF CULTURE

Fortunately, the search for an interrelated system of knowledge, for a balance of activities, for a unification of knowing, feeling, and acting, for an integrated community, is now going on in many different departments. That search is visible in the arts, no less than in the more ecological sciences; it has been partly embodied, for instance, in the work of engineers, architects, and community planners, like those who are still planning the many-sided development of the Tennessee Valley. The very ideas of social planning, industrial planning, community planning, and regional planning presuppose not only an orderly body of knowledge and a common method of communication and co-operation; they rest on an acknowledgment of common values and purposes. If the work still has social limitations, it is because the values are only partly formulated and because the process of unification is still incomplete. But in the concrete expressions of architecture and land-sculpture, there is already visible in the Tennessee Valley, in complete esthetic form, a sample of an environment completely ordered to embody and sustain every aspect of the common life. This is a true parallel to the Greek Cities of the fifth century; and in such an environment we can reasonably hope that Nature and the City will both complete the formal education of man. One must put such premonitory achievements, which are equally notable in their esthetic and their practical aspects, alongside the similar efforts in the world of thought. Here it is enough to mention the philosophies of Patrick Geddes, Victor Branford, Lloyd Morgan, A. N. Whitehead, and Karl Mannheim, or, in another department, the admirable essay toward unity in the field of personology presided over by Dr. Henry A. Murray.* These are but samples. Without this growing evidence of both the need and the response, however, the present paper would have only a remote speculative value.

Let me sum up. Our civilization is now passing from an era of expansion to an era that must achieve stabilization, cultivation, and balance, as the very price of continued survival. In our attempt to control the disintegrating forces that are at work in our society, we must resume the search for unity; and to this end, we must begin with the personality and the community in all their richness, variety, complication, and historic depth, as both the means and the end of our effort. As the process of unification widens in the mind, as it multiplies the interconnections and the social co-operations between fragments of the personality now distant or insu-

* See also L. L. Whyte: The Next Development of Man. London: 1944.

lated, we may expect to see a similar unification, a similar dynamic balance of forces and activities, a similar displacement of the one-sided power-impulse by an integrated life-impulse take place in the world at large. Such is the problem that confronts the organization of the American university in the opening future; and along some such lines as those indicated, I humbly believe, must be laid the foundations of our new education.

# THE MAKING OF MEN

*"Of the making of books there is no end."*

[This paper was presented on 8 May 1943, at the First
Annual Conference held by the Stanford School of Hu-
manities, to discuss The Humanities in the War and Post-
War World; and it was printed in the symposium called
The Humanities Look Ahead, Stanford University Press,
1943.]

## 1. THE PLIGHT OF THE HUMANITIES

The generation that has spanned the last thirty years has
demonstrated the need for a radical reorientation in its guiding ideas: such a change in heart and mind as only a world
catastrophe could bring about and carry through. For this
generation was characterized by two deep-seated failures.
One of these was the flight from reality, fostered by the impulse to live according to the pleasure principle, on the pattern of the Do-as-you-likes in Charles Kingsley's fable. The
other failure was a disbelief in the higher life of man: a disbelief so widespread, so corrosive, that even those who still
kept their faith in man's transcendental interests nevertheless
thought it necessary to justify them in terms of jobs created,
mechanical comforts invented, or amusements offered to fill
in the empty moments of the day.

What was a commonplace for every thinker in the sixteenth
century, namely, that man's memory, his imagination, his
feelings, his dreams, his rational conceptions are, as Jean

218

Calvin said, "certain proofs of the divinity of man," had become a heresy with which even the avowed exponents of the humanities hesitated to ally themselves. Divinity? Who would look for it in man, or who would utter Dante's words of gratitude to his teacher, Brunetto Latini, because he had taught him how man makes himself eternal? The machine had become our deity, and we had made the fatal error, indeed we had committed the mortal sin, of worshiping the created good and forgetting its creator. In order to effect our proud conquest of the external world, we had surrendered the inner kingdom of man, and by that surrender we had robbed our truly great achievements in science and technics of half the value they might have had for man's higher life. The open fascist revolt against civilization, long ago described by Dostoyevsky in The Possessed, is only the malignant and mortal form of a disease that has been slowly eating into the healthy tissues of our democratic culture.

One of the hardest things for the common man to understand about the present catastrophe is the extent to which it has been conceived and nourished by the very civilization whose achievements stand so high in his own estimate. The war seems to him an aberration; but the society that produced it in no wise seems an aberration. He is willing, when driven to it, to make many sacrifices in order to save this civilization; but few, as yet, are willing to make the hardest sacrifice of all, and that is to discard their illusions about it. Most of the current plans for establishing a better post-war world assume too easily that the major changes needed are in the realm of political and economic organization alone, and that we can produce a new world without creating a philosophy and a religion that will be capable of giving it unity and purpose. People who think in this way forget that before we can conquer the fascist we must conquer all those weaknesses in

our own scheme of thinking and living that have permitted
this formidable race of Calibans to come into existence. To
remove this lower form of life, in all its cancerous vitality,
we must nourish a higher form in ourselves.

When I say that the common man fails to understand this
task I am talking about all those who have not reflected seriously upon the nature and dimensions of the present crisis;
and in this group I must place a large number, perhaps a
majority, of our intelligentsia or, to bring the argument even
nearer home, of the exponents of the humanities. These people are conscious of little troubles and they are looking for
little remedies: they are like sailors who would worry about
a leak in the plumbing when their ship had a hole torn in its
side and their compass was out of order and their steering
gear failed to work. Such people take too easily for granted
the essential soundness of the world in which they have grown
up and to which they are adapted. If they see weaknesses outside their college and university, they do not identify those
same weaknesses within their familiar territory—though they
are in fact just as gross and just as formidable, if masked
under a more tranquil routine. Not having any sufficient sense
of the peril that envelops our whole world, the world of
thought and the world of action alike, many of us find it hard
even dimly to conceive the bold and decisive steps, the hard
and heroic steps, that will be necessary to save it.

Now the plight in which the humanities find themselves is
not something that we can separate from the vast secular
changes that have been taking place during the last three
centuries, or from the whole Thirty Years' War in which our
particular generation has found itself so helplessly involved.
And we should be foolish indeed if we thought that short-
sighted decisions by the leaders of our military forces, or the
inexorable draining away of men and minds by the war itself,

is responsible for the present state of the humanities, so that a change in the present military directives would effect a real reprieve and give us a fitting part to play in the educational life of our country. The case is not so easy as that. For the humanities are not self-sustaining disciplines: they are bound up with the fate of humanity itself: not by a mere play on words, but by the fact that the humanities, when they are worthy of the name, are concerned with man thinking, man feeling, man in expression, and man in action; and if they are not needed in wartime it is because they did not themselves understand their task and did not make their power felt during the period that preceded the war.

In the School of Humanities here at Stanford we sometimes receive letters from presumably poor and certainly often illiterate people, who put before us their own difficulties in living and their own desire for justice or enlightenment. They turn to us for advice and comfort in the way that those who are vexed in matrimony turn to the appropriate column of their favorite newspaper. It is easy to smile a supercilious and yet slightly embarrassed smile at the belief of some poor ranchman in Wyoming or housewife in Utah that the School of Humanities would by its nature have some word of guidance for them in their daily living. But as one reflects a little on this pathetic confidence, it becomes plain that there is more wisdom in this ignorance, more understanding in this misunderstanding, than first meets the eye. What indeed are the humanities for—if they are not to serve humanity? Why should there be such a gap between the teaching of literature, art, or philosophy and the daily needs of ordinary men and women? How does it come about, indeed, that the humanities have forgotten humanity, and that we think of saving ourselves or our precious subjects without being primarily concerned with the salvation of the world? I submit that we must not only ask these questions but struggle to answer them.

## 2. PLATO'S DILEMMA

The crisis we now face has had parallels in other cultures; and we can gain some insight into our own position, it seems to me, if we interpret correctly the situation in which Plato found himself, as a representative Athenian, at the end of the Peloponnesian War. Both his insight and his blindness, his achievements and his failures, are instructive.

Plato, nearer to the high fifth-century culture than Aristotle, was profoundly molded by it: in both his thought and his personality it received living form, though the Athenian polity, while momentarily recovering from the Rule of the Thirty, was already on the down grade, exhausted by the great plague, undermined by war, tempted by the facile, false solutions of dictatorship, tempted even more by those flesh-pots which had played such a small role in the fifth-century scheme. Plato's whole life was in effect an effort to find a means to restore order and purpose into a life that was becoming progressively disorganized, banal, and purposeless: in which the divine was succumbing to the all-too-human. He sought to conceive a man and a commonwealth that could survive in a disintegrating world; and to this end he united the virtues of the Athenian and the Spartan: the pliant individualist culture of the first with the self-abnegating public discipline of the second.

Not the least significant thing about Plato's utopias, however, was that he did not go to any pains to restore the arts and humanities to the place they had occupied in fifth-century Athens: he sought rather to subordinate them, to regulate them, even to banish some of them from his ideal commonwealth. Was this a perverse judgment on Plato's part? To generations of later humanists it has often seemed so. But what forced Plato to this hard choice? The answer should be plain: Athens needed men, and the humanities by themselves did not produce them. Indeed, for lack of political discipline and moral responsibility, the teachers of the humanities hindered rather than aided the making of whole men: they were producing facile rhetoricians, glib orators, clever teachers, connoisseurs, not men capable of living robustly on every plane of existence. Citizens who would serve in the law courts or on the battlefield as readily as they would write a poem or pursue an abstract truth, men of the stature of Sophocles and Socrates, were no longer being created. Plato, the artist, was ready to reduce the scope and influence of the arts in order to save the civilization that had created them. Was he wrong?

Plato's prescription did not save Hellenic civilization: I need hardly remind you of that; nor need I go into the shortcomings of the platonic concern for a static and changeless reality in which a conceptual perfection became a substitute for the struggles, the mischances, the ordeals, and the triumphs of growth. Plato's thought did not bequeath to Demosthenes an Athens where men were ready to unite private needs with public duties and in which they attended to their affairs with some true regard for their relative worth and significance: we know rather that the money which should have gone into the rebuilding of the Athenian navy was frittered away on lavish public festivals which now celebrated an increasingly hollow and archaic way of life. Why did Plato fail so completely in his civic mission? Some of you may insist that it was *because* he neglected the role of the humanities; but the fact is that those disciplines we value so highly never flourished better than in the decadent Athens of the

fourth century, the century of Plato, Aristotle, Epicurus,
Zeno. What undermined Plato's philosophy, what undermined the Greeks, was their failure to embrace humanity:
their failure to be concerned with the development of the
whole life of man and with every member of human society,
to address the soldier, the sailor, the craftsman, the farmer,
and to give hope and faith to the common man. Plato's message was addressed solely to his class and his culture: it
called for a radical reorientation of life, and yet it left the
chief sacred cows of his world, slavery and class rule, con-
tentedly chewing their cud.

When Christianity laid new ideological foundations under
the crumbling structure of Hellenistic life, it worked through
simple people, credulous, limited, no doubt often illiterate,
who despised the cities and academies of this world, who had
little respect for the arts and the humanities, but who were
concerned, concerned overwhelmingly, with the salvation of
mankind. Those who sought to save the humanities, to further
the intellectual pursuit of truth and beauty and goodness,
forgot to save man; and therefore, quite deliberately, those
who saved man neglected to save the humanities and in fact
despised them: for how, as Saint Jerome said, could Horace
go with the Psalter, Virgil with the Gospels, Cicero with the
Apostle?

We today must not repeat Plato's fatal mistake; nor must
we confuse that mistake with the important truth for which
he properly stands—namely, that the highest end of pure
thought is to realize justice, to embody order and significance
and purpose, within the human community. We can have no
prosperity in the humanities without cultivating a firm sense
of political responsibility and without promoting an affection-
ate concern for the salvation of the common man. Our task
is to help make human life meaningful and valuable.

## 3. STARVATION OF VALUES

Since humanistic education ceased to be concerned with the training and discipline of the gentleman—a limited and snobbish ideal, but good as far is it went—the humanities have lost their preoccupation with the forming of men: they have even succumbed to the very vocationalism their adherents sometimes so eloquently despise: they turn out professional humanists. One has only to read the many wails and complaints that broke out among the professors of the humanities when the war closed in on them to realize how shadowy, how painfully modest, were their claims to be considered an essential part of our educational system. Did not too many of our colleagues confess that their subjects were desirable in peace but useless in war, that they enriched the life of the individual but did nothing to promote the life of the community? Did not some of them hope that the war would treat their departments as cold weather treats the hibernating animals, so that, when the struggle was over, they could emerge again, slightly emaciated perhaps, to nibble like so many voracious rabbits on the tender, succulent greens that had survived the winter?

In the very act of asking for consideration some of our colleagues, I humbly submit, forfeited the right to be considered: for the real justification of the humanities in the program of training a fighting generation is not that they are by nature above the battle, a rainbow to give hope after the storm, but that, truly interpreted and responsibly taught, the humanities are an integral part of the life of man, precisely that which he requires in order to be fully human: that they give the student an insight into the rational purposes, the significant goods, and the ultimate ends of human life—into all the things that are worth living for, struggling for, fighting for, and, if need be, dying for, so that those who come after us shall continue to possess man's full inheritance. He who knows his Plato and his Aeschylus, his Lao-Tse and his Isaiah, his Demosthenes and his Cicero, his Paul and his Augustine, his Aquinas and his Spinoza, his Shakespeare and his Molière, his Cervantes and his Tolstoy is twice armed: prepared for the eventualities of defeat or victory, frustration or fulfillment, death or life.

If the exponents of the humanities had been faithfully dealing with these essentials for man's development, no war department would have dared to drop the humanities from its training curriculum: for the authorities would have understood that they were indispensable to the morale and self-confidence of the men who do the fighting.

The valid reason for urging a more intense dedication to the humanities during the war is not merely so that we can live better after the war but so that we can fight better now, when we need fighters, both on the battlefield and in government, who can bring to the effort the cool-headed skill and unyielding vigilance of a Socrates at Potidaea. Our interest is not merely to save something that belongs to our past which is precious to us, but to make ourselves ready to create something in the future which will turn out to be equally precious. A challenge that is honestly met and wholeheartedly lived through brings a special reward which no smooth, peaceful, easy life ever earns: the reward that came to the Greeks after the Persian War and to the Elizabethans after the Great Armada had been defeated. The humanities are not by nature confined to the hours of leisure or the smiling Sunday afternoons of peace: far from it. We condemn a large part of our humanistic studies if we give to them such a minor ornamental role.

The function of the humanities is to focus and intensify the possibilities of life, by creating, on the basis of the natural order, a world in which nothing is irrational, nothing is unintelligible, nothing is trivial, insignificant, or purposeless. When such a world is formed in the mind, every daily activity, even the humblest, even the hardest, falls into place and acquires a special significance: the time, the place, the scenery, the action, the dialogue, even the work of the unseen stagehands and electricians then unite to form a great collective work of art. When the humanities fail in their function, when no common world has been created in the mind, when no common standards are accepted and no common goals pursued, then even the most imposing fragment of culture and each special activity, no longer contributing to the whole and no longer supported by the whole, loses its proper meaning and value. During the last generation the humanities have failed us. A fragmentation, a purposeless proliferation, has been going on in the humanities as it has been going on in every other part of our civilization. And what has been the result? We, too, have been starving in the midst of plenty: our very intellectual productivity has undermined our ability to evaluate, to select, to direct all our minute special activities to the advantage of the human personality and the community in which men live and move and have their being. Not merely have we lost the power of positive choice, but a negative selection has taken its place: when we choose at all we have a tendency to prefer the inessentials; and we had rather see a minor work of research done perfectly than countenance the occasional weaknesses and lapses that are inevitable in any major task. This has been true for a long while: De Sanctis' masterly study of Italian literature was long neglected because of a handful of minor errors it contained, while Burckhardt, a truly great spirit in his field, met a similar fate at the hands of the specialist. Is it a wonder that by now a De Sanctis or a Burckhardt is far to seek?

Our starvation has become chronic because we have over-valued intellectual certitude and have undervalued every other aspect of the spirit. We have treated the humanities as if it were more important to create teachers, museum cura-tors, critics, and other professional expositors of the humani-ties than to create men and women. Mark you: I hold no brief against curators and critics, any more than I hold a brief against philosophers, artists, and poets. Quite the contrary: I maintain not merely that we need a plentiful supply of creators, but that to encourage them and discipline them we also need those who apply to the acts of creative expression the tests of a critical and searching intellect, a sensitive, well-schooled taste, and a stable scheme of values. The aims of all these special vocations are valid: provided we do not for-get the Vocation of Man. They are valid, that is, only if they are subordinated to a still higher aim, which is the under-standing, the development, and the perfection of the human spirit. If we truly understand the functions of the humanities, we will insist that they belong in every part of the curricu-lum: in the education of the scientist as well as the artist, in the professional school no less than in the liberal arts college, in the education of the common man no less than in the prepa-ration of the elite. It is by their forgetfulness of the vocation of man that the humanities have lost their grip upon their own special subject matter and have condemned much of it to triviality.

## 4. MISSION OF THE HUMANITIES

I come back then to the central theme of this paper: namely, that the humanities must be concerned with the en-

tire life of man and accept all the responsibilities of that life
if they are to exert the directive power that is needed to bring
the political, the moral, and the intellectual spheres into a
harmonious working order. In other words, the humanities
must educate for action as well as for contemplation: they
must develop the citizen and the responsible leader no less
than the connoisseur and the scholar: indeed, their highest
aim is to create a balanced and unified personality capable
of meeting the challenges of life on every front. We today
face the same dilemma that Plato faced; but we should bring
to our answer a deeper understanding of the nature and mission of the humanities, which will keep us from seeking for
either the static perfection sought by the Greeks or the "pneu-
matic bliss" which is promised us by the shallow Bounder-
bys and Gradgrinds who rule our industrial civilization.

The cultivation of the humanities means a cultivation of a
keener sense of reality than our venal, mechanical, utilitarian
culture has produced. We seek beauty and truth; but we also
know the chill of disaster and the ugliness of error. Though
man must now abolish the institution of war as he once abolished cannibalism, he does so in order to promote "saner,
life-giving wars," as Whitman called them. Conflict, struggle,
accident, sin, malice, and death—all these are constants in
human life: constants that the poetic vision transforms, sub-
limates, transcends, but never leaves altogether behind, any
more than it can leave behind our primitive animal inheritance. From the Odyssey to Moby Dick, from Isaiah to Dante,
the great masters of reality have cultivated the tragic sense
of life and have enabled men to survive, with courage and
faith, even in a crumbling world. That faith, that courage,
will stand us in stead today, provided we hold to the core of
our own tradition and are not swept away by a fashionable

opportunism. Life is on our side—if only we view it unflinchingly and act our manful part in it.

If the humanities had continued to perform their task adequately in our generation, our students would not have been
as bewildered and unprepared as they were when the forces
of evil broke out again: they would not have been so skep-
tical as to the extent of the fascist menace or so empty of the
very values they were supposed to uphold. Did I say our
students? I should have said all the educated classes, not
least of all the so-called practical men, whose shallow optimism was reflected in so much of our teaching. One of our
students at Stanford said to me the other day: "We have de-
cided that the main trouble with our education is that our
parents and teachers fed us with fairy tales; they taught us
that we lived in a world where everyone had a right to be
happy, and where he would certainly achieve happiness if he
managed to get a sufficient income. That kind of philosophy
isn't very useful to us now, when we have to say good-bye to
our lovers or our husbands whom we have just married and
may never see again. We suspect that this fairy tale kind of
happiness never was real in the first place; now it seems a
cheap five-and-ten-cent-store substitute for something harder
and better, harder to get and better worth keeping."

The point of view of this student is not an exception. Indeed, if I can tell the story without becoming embarrassed at
my own immodesty, I would like to back it up with still another one, associated with the first basic course we gave in
the new humanities program, a course on "The Nature of
Man." That course is a philosophical exposition of the nature of man as revealed in both the sciences and the humanities; it seeks to embrace both the objective and the subjective
aspects of man's existence, the external and the internal, the
empirical and the transcendental. The first lecture discussed

the nature of the present crisis and pointed out the dismaying evidences of disintegration in our present-day culture: symptoms that remind us of fourth century B.C. in Athens or second century A.D. in Rome. The last ten lectures, which concentrated on the nature of man as revealed in art, philosophy, and religion, wound up with a presentation of the type of personality needed to enable us to overcome the present crisis and unify all the chaotic fragments of our life. I will not pretend that the course my colleagues and I gave corresponded to our platonic ideal of such a course: far from it; no one could be more critical of our actual achievement than the present lecturer, whose weaknesses in scholarship were pitilessly revealed by his very ambitions. But for all that our time was certainly not wasted; and I cherish one student's testimony as a proof of this.

This student came to me when the first course was over and said she would have to leave, because she was married and expected to have a baby in a few months more. "Before I came here to study," she said, "I was a disheartened and cynical girl; I could not see any meaning in the war and I couldn't see any meaning in life, either. I even resented the fact that I was going to have a baby, for my husband was going to be torn from me in a few months—he is a lieutenant in the Navy and he might never see me or the child again. He had a fine career in business before him when we married; and I hated the war for breaking that up, too. Now," she went on, "I don't feel that way any more: this course has made me understand what we are fighting for. At last, life has some meaning for me, and you ought to hear me argue with the officers and wives back at the station, trying to make them understand some of the things the humanities have made me see so clearly. My husband is on my side now; the others have a long way to go. But I haven't told you the best thing

I got out of the course: I am *glad* I am going to have my baby, whether my husband comes back from the war or not. I have something to give the child now, and if my man dies he won't die in vain."

Some of you will perhaps say in your hearts, if you are too polite to utter your words openly, that no academic institution can hope to be faithful to the great tradition of the university, the disinterested pursuit of knowledge, if the proudest boast of its new Professor of Humanities is that he has made a young wife ready to accept the responsibilities of motherhood. So I hasten to add that the contents of the course had nothing specifically to do with the prenatal mental care of mothers or the morale of soldiers' and sailors' wives. But who can study the nature of man in all its manifestations, its animal inheritance, its social connections, its personal developments, man as the fashioner of symbols, man as the interpreter of meanings, man as the inventor of machines, as the builder of cities, as the fabricator of laws and moral codes and ethical standards, without having a better grasp on his own life, a better insight into his own duties and purposes?

One proviso alone I would add: if one is interpreting the whole nature of man, one must employ the whole nature of man in order to make this teaching effectual. The one bold departure this course made was to lay as much stress upon feelings, emotions, evaluations as upon factual knowledge and intellectual discriminations. I did not carry this method as far as I should like to, as far as I intend to in future; there was perhaps too much reading and too little reflection, though not a few of our students were bewildered and even aggrieved because we put reflection ahead of undigested factual knowledge. And if there was too little reflection, there was also too little positive discipline—too little experimental re-ordering of the student's personal habits and aims. Nevertheless, some

of the students did begin to acquire the kind of self-knowledge, a self-knowledge for the sake of both self-development
and fuller social responsibility, which is one of the most
precious fruits of an education in the humanities. With such
an inner reorientation, the student should be able to face life
at both its best and its worst, life on the childbed or the battlefield, as well as in the library, the art gallery, or the study.
What he learns will be a moving and operative part of his
life; not a skimpy academic costume, but flesh and blood and
bone.

In short, with respect to the humanities, I should emphasize
the point that Milton makes in the matter of church doctrine,
namely, that preaching avails nothing unless backed by discipline, as diagnosis in medicine avails nothing without a regimen for the patient. Here an ounce of example is worth a
pound of careful exposition. That unity, that wholeness which
we need in our intellectual life, will not avail unless we can
carry it into every part of the student's existence, and so
finally into every part of society. Our work in teaching
Shakespeare is partly lost if the student can go back to the
drivel of a radio program without a profound feeling of disgust; our work in teaching ethics is lost if the student continues to live the automatic, drifting, choiceless, self-indulgent existence that so often prevailed before the war presented a counter-challenge. But to say this is to admit that our
colleges and universities, in their *present* form, cannot hope
effectively to revive the humanities; for their intellectual
overspecialization needs to be balanced off on the side of
emotion and action and practice. That is a hard saying, but
I would hold to it. Our mistake consists in thinking that there
is anything final or absolute in the present form and traditional methods of the university, and in not seeing that if only
a profound change in all our cultural habits will save our

civilization, we must plan and effect that change. Our decisions about the future of the humanities are forced upon us by a crisis that has already injured and impaired no small part of our civilization. We will be saved not by homeopathic medicine but by surgery: by surgery and blood transfusions, and a rigorous diet.

## 5. THE HUMAN TRANSFORMATION

The transformation we must contemplate—and effect—is perhaps as great as the change from the municipal universities of Rome to the monasteries established by Benedict of Nursia. If such a comparison shocks you, it is, I think, because you do not yet realize how strenuous must be our efforts to control the forces that threaten to wreck our civilization. Do not, I pray, misunderstand the illustration: I do not advocate a return to the Benedictine monastery, but a fresh effort at discipline and organization which will be comparable, in its many bold departures, to those which supplanted the Roman lecture system with the Benedictine Rule.

The present world catastrophe overtook us as it might overtake the passengers on a streamliner, rushing through the night at ninety miles an hour, proud of their speed, comfortable in their well-designed cars, and secure in the thought of the signal system that protected the train—but unconscious of the fact that the engineer had just rushed past the red signal light because, as it happened, he was color blind. Everything about the train and the railroad system might seem in order; but the safety of the passengers depended upon the human capacity of the engineer to distinguish between red and green. This color blindness must stand as a brief symbol of our failure to recognize qualitative differences in every phase of life: our inability to distinguish between good and evil, our inability to distinguish between mechanical order and organic order, our inability to realize that the emotions and feelings of men are as primary, as much in need of discipline and cultivation, as important in every situation, as the purely intellectual operations in which we take so much proper pride. All these weaknesses crept into the teaching of the humanities. And they were aggravated by the fact that while the area of humane studies was becoming wider, like the spreading dormitories of a modern metropolis, the central core, the preparatory disciplines, were deserted: a veritable blighted area.

How indeed can we even perform the intellectual functions in the humanities properly—and that is only a part of the whole task—if we do not encourage inquiries into the nature of meaning, form, value, and end: if we allow linguistics, semantics, esthetics, ethics, and religion to be taught only to specialists, and do not even make sure that they are taught systematically to them? For lack of any sufficient cultivation of these fields, too much of our work in the humanities has been haphazard and impressionistic, and too much of our material has been considered only as an object of historical investigation, in a timid effort to avoid those very judgments as to significance and value which make a particular historic moment important. Mrs. Susanne K. Langer's recent brilliant book, Philosophy in a New Key, indicates how a penetrating study of the semantic and esthetic problems, in their interactions, opens up vistas on nearly every part of our higher culture and establishes, not only the fundamental value of the symbolic functions, but also the relative autonomy of all man's higher activities. If we took our preparation in the humanities as seriously as the engineer or the physical scien-

tist takes his preparation, we should understand that semantics, esthetics, logic, philosophy, and religion were as essential to us as algebra, geometry, and calculus are in the analysis of nature. These normative studies provide a key for
understanding the arts and the humanities. In practice, we
try to open too many doors for the student without giving him
this key, whereas if he spent sufficient time on the key, we
could leave it to the student himself to open more doors than
we can ever hope even to hold ajar for him.

Let us not pretend to ourselves, then, that the humanities,
as they are now conceived and presented, can accomplish
even the purely intellectual task of synthesis and integration,
of reconciliation and unification, that lies before us. Let us
not make believe that any reshuffling of existing courses, any
facile method of conference between the existing specialisms,
formed for another time and limited by that time, formed for
another purpose and limited by that purpose, will bring about
the change that is needed. Many of us are indeed ready for
that kind of effort and are willing to facilitate it verbally with
that blessed American catchword, co-operation; but I fear
that those who will go no farther than this are only raking up
dead leaves under the impression that they are planting fresh
seed. No; something much more difficult must be done. This
is a time for stripping down to essentials, a time when, to
achieve unity, to recapture meaning and value, we must be
ready to give up many things we once lazily supposed were
essential but are not really so, many courses that were charm-
ing bypaths in the humanities but led nowhere in particular,
many courses that remained like sorry monuments to mark
even sorrier battlefields, filled with dead bones. We cannot
do what is essential in the humanities without rigorously cur-
tailing all that has become merely honorific and therefore

picayune. This applies to many courses in contemporary aspects of the humanities, not less than to more antiquarian learning.

I have time, I fear, for only one illustration of the kind of reorientation that will be needed in every department of the humanities; and I choose this because it relates directly to the pressing need for tying the future of the humanities into the future of humanity itself. What is the largest task of the post-war world? The largest and most important task, perhaps, is that of creating the world-wide political and cultural co-operations that mankind needs in order to give a more solid basis for international law and order and peace. Vainly, this last century, we have hoped that these co-operations would be established by purely physical instruments; we have deluded ourselves with the belief that the steamship, the airplane, the motion picture, the radio, would automatically make mankind one, and turn enemies into brothers. That was a false hope: the machine is pathetically unable by itself to accomplish purposes that rest on the will and imagination and moral discipline of men. We must now carry the unifying processes in our culture a stage further; and this immediately brings to the fore the contribution of the humanities. But here we must transcend the limitations of our own humanist tradition: for the first step toward world co-operation must rest on our realization that the humanities are not a special creation of Western civilization and that our particular forms of art, metaphysics, and religion do not provide an eternal norm for the rest of the world. One of our pressing tasks as humanists, a task most of us have faced too belatedly, is to understand and interpret the non-European cultures—not only the sophisticated cultures of the East but the more primitive cultures of the South Seas and Africa and

South America. Unless we are humble enough to learn from all these sources, we will never be strong enough to teach them, still less to work in fruitful political partnership.

In short, we must study these remoter cultures as eagerly as Emerson and Thoreau studied the East in the middle of the last century; and it will be well if we succeed in studying them to such good purpose. I need hardly emphasize that this change cannot come about without grave occupational readjustments: most of us will have to bestir ourselves with our own re-education if we are to have a part in it. But if sober examination shows that the need is a valid one, we must not shrink from it. At a moment when many of our soldiers, for wholly practical purposes, are working long hours every day to master the lore of the Japanese, the Javanese, or the Malay cultures, it little becomes the scholar to shrink from such a duty to the humanities.

This is but a brief sample of the far-reaching changes that will revivify our studies, extend our influence, and make the work of the humanities essential once more both in war and in peace. We have a new world to explore, to conquer, and to cultivate: the world of man's higher self, with all its myths and symbols, a new world which is also an old world: today a jungle which tomorrow we must transform into park, garden, and city. Once the humanities address themselves to the essential life of man, once they are truly concerned with his fate and destiny, not as frigid spectators, but as willing participants, they will not have to ask for special privileges in wartime or regret the fact that their claims are neglected. There is nothing to prevent the humanities from carving out a much larger and much more significant place for themselves than they have ever occupied before: nothing to stop us except our blindness, our lack of courage, our unwillingness to make sacrifices, our stiff-necked pride of intellect, and the

blight of our own smug indifference. All those weaknesses can
be overcome. And in the light of the world's needs they *must*
be overcome if our society is to resume its age-long pursuit
of a never-attainable but always beckoning goal: its effort to
build that City of Man which draws ever closer in design to
the City of God.

# BOOK THREE:

# LETTERS TO GERMANS

Man is composed of faith;
he is indeed as that wherein
he has faith.

BHAGAVAD-GITA: LESSON XVII

# LETTERS TO GERMANS

[Shortly after the defeat of Germany, the Office of War Information asked me to write a short book addressed to the Germans, to give them some insight into the way an American looks upon the career of Nazism and the crimes that were committed in the name of Germany. This task proved a difficult one as long as I confined myself to the letter of my directive, and appealed to the anonymous mass of Germans. I could not imagine any German reading three pages of what I had to say: the psychological distance between us was too great. That is what led me to adopt the form of the letter, addressed either to a real person, or to a composite person based upon actual acquaintances and friends in pre-war Germany. This method has its limitations, chiefly because it has confined me to people of my own generation; but that limitation has a certain advantage, in that it enables me to deal with weaknesses that were not specifically National Socialist in origin. It is important for both Germans and Americans to realize how deep the roots of German Nazism lie; let us not make the mistake of thinking again that we have destroyed the tree when we have only cut it back to the main trunk.

Obviously, the transformation of Germany must be accomplished by the Germans themselves. All that the sternest of conquerors could do would be to encourage them in this process. Meanwhile we have much to change in our own philosophy and our own way of life, in order not to contribute, out of callous thoughtlessness, if not out of pride and greed, to the annihilation of mankind. If I have spoken with unsparing candor about the sins of the Germans, I have perhaps partly earned the right to speak freely, because throughout a lifetime of writing I have addressed myself, in no less unsparing terms, to the sins I share with my own countrymen.]

# 1. TO FRAU MARIA Z. IN LÜBECK

. . . You have been often in my mind, dear Frau Z., these last fourteen years, ever since you brought a bouquet of sweet peas to the station, where you said good-bye to my wife and me. For both of us you were the essence of all that we loved in Germany; and yet, but for the modeling of your head, which was so much like one of the elder Lucas Cranach's Venuses, how little you represented your nation, even then. You belonged to a Germany that had still to be born; a Germany which, the world hopes, will not have to wait as long for its birth as Barbarossa for his awakening.

If I knew what had become of you, dear Frau Z., and if I knew what you felt and thought, I should have a clearer picture of Germany's future. Are you more alone than ever, more conspicuous for your differences than you were in Lübeck in 1932; or have others like you begun to rise, by the dozens and by the scores—I dare not say by the hundreds—from the filth and folly of the Third Reich?

Very possibly, you are not alive. It was with great misgivings that I wrote to you in March, 1933, after the Nazis finally came to power, to tell you what you already knew: how shocked every intelligent American friend of Germany was by that final betrayal of the Republic. I never heard from you again.

Even in the summer of 1932, the National Socialists visibly dominated Lübeck: when I came back in August that year, after the order against the wearing of uniforms had been repealed, their Brown Shirts were conspicuous everywhere, as they strutted and marched about, in two's and three's, pushing the non-uniformed out of their path. Did the old Frau Senator, your mother-in-law, protect you against the Nazi regime; or did she turn against you and betray you to her fanatical friends, as dyed-in-the-wool Nazis even broke the oath of blood-brotherhood and turned over to the Gestapo their sworn comrades of the battlefield when they opposed, even by word, the new defenders of German "honor"?

The very letter I wrote you may have been used as evidence of your hostility to all that the Nazis stood for; perhaps it was your passport to a concentration camp, from which you returned, in a month or a year, broken in health if not in spirit, but fiercely clinging to life in order to interpose your body between the Nazi hyenas and your own children. Or did they apply torture to you: torture so humiliating that only in suicide could your proud spirit vindicate itself? Are you dead and am I writing to a ghost? That is very possible; yet even if it is true I will continue to write you this, my first letter to Germany since 1939, feeling that in addressing you I am talking to the ghost of a better Germany. If you are dead, you are still more alive than the Third Reich was at any moment of its existence.

I wish there were more ghosts like you, to awaken the German soul from its deadness, to deliver your countrymen from their self-chosen enslavement to death. Has your gallant spirit passed over to Kurt and Gerhart and Else; and if so, how did they behave during these last dozen years and what fate has befallen them? I confess that, though I strain my imagination, I cannot picture to myself what has happened to any of you; and perhaps the reason that I cannot do so is that I do not see how you or your children could have been true to yourselves and have remained alive, still less how you could have kept loyal to Nazi Germany and have remained alive. In either event you had a bitter choice:

no active path to life remained open to you except through exile or through participation in an almost non-existent and powerless underground.

It is easier for me to picture what happened to Rosa Bitberg, that lovely sixteen-year-old Jewess, who was Else's friend: she who was your house guest and who played all sorts of silly parlor games with us that last night in Lübeck, as plump as a well-ripened peach, as friendly and innocent as a kitten. I can picture Rosa's fate because I know what your countrymen did to millions of Rosas all over Europe. Very likely she was defiled before she was tortured in even more bestial fashion; and then perhaps she was sent in a tightly packed boxcar in the dead of winter to a Polish extermination camp, before she was stripped of her last belongings and buried alive or gassed. Wrapped in the security she enjoyed in your household, finding out too late that the people she had called her fellow-countrymen had transformed themselves into Hitler's trained beasts, criminally obedient to his every command, Rosa probably did not escape.

Even the friendly living room of your villa outside Lübeck, with its gray porcelain stove, its Bechstein piano, and the painting by Carl Hofer on the wall, held a hint during that gay evening of what was in store for Rosa. For you had another guest, a clever sharp-tongued man, polished and worldly, the editor of *Der Querschnitt:* a man very much at ease in the cosmopolitan world of Paris, London, and New York, was he not? He was a man full of salty stories and poisonous opinions. Something that I said about politics started him, to my surprise, upon a long tirade against the Jews: a tirade as violent as it was prejudiced and untruthful, and no deference to you or your Jewish guest caused him to soften his opinions or to curb his tongue. Finally you could bear it no longer: you turned to him and under your breath said indignantly, "Shameful!" Presently you found some excuse to interrupt him; perhaps it was then that we began to play charades.

At the time, my wife and I were still too innocent of the forces working below the surface of German life to attach to this incident the significance it actually had. But in the years that followed it dramatized all that was happening to Germany, and all that set it off, step by step, act by act, from the rest of the world. The rudeness and the mocking brutality of the editor of *Der Querschnitt* was not a reflection of the state of mind of the down-and-outs who followed Hitler for the sake of a handout: it was the cultivated deformity of an otherwise keen and active intelligence.

Every country has a "lunatic fringe": people filled with irrational hatred for any idea or any way of life but their own; people who, because of their ignorance, their frustration, or their mental enfeeblement boil over with prejudices against other races, or other nations. We have such people in America; but except in a few backward areas they remain at the periphery of our political life and our culture. One did not expect to find such opinions and attitudes as the editor of *Der Querschnitt* expressed in a person of his general culture. You had made me forget, dear Frau Z., by your own warm humanity and your own clarity of mind, how deeply this strain of irrationality went all through German life.

When the Nazis came into power, the avowed prophet of barbarism, Oswald Spengler, scornfully observed: "This was no victory: there was no opposition." Remembering that evening, I know what he meant: those who should have formed an impregnable buttress against all that National Socialism stood for, already belonged in its camp. The offense of the editor in the friendly confines of your drawing room was precisely of the same order as Himmler's well-contrived sadism. Rosa's humiliation, Rosa's death sentence, Rosa's unspeakable future, already appeared as menacing shadows on the walls of your own house.

Yes: the editor's words were shameful; but infinitely more shameful were the deeds that followed them. If Macbeth's sole murder of Duncan could "the multitudinous seas incarnadine" what shall one say of the systematic torture and organized extermination your countrymen practiced? What shall one say of the broken minds, the rattling, mutilated bodies, the piles of human ashes which marked their temporary conquest of their European neighbors? In your countrymen the ogres that had once merely existed in the German unconscious, represented in the fairy stories collected by the Brothers Grimm, became creatures of flesh and blood. You had no part in that terrible transformation; I am sure of that. Yet you were present, and whether you wished to or not, you witnessed it, even as against your will you listened to the editor's tirade and put up with his insufferable rudeness. Did you close your eyes when the police came for your communist neighbor, who lived in that little allotment Siedlung near-by? That was not enough: surely you heard the screams that came from the concentration camp? Perhaps you closed your ears, too; but could you also close your mind? Did you keep from spiritual suffocation? Until I learn differently, I shall still hope that your spirit remained sound and free, that the core of you kept its integrity. If this did not happen in you, then the redemption of Germany may take centuries.

About your husband's fate, I am not so sure. He was a very intelligent man and we got on famously together; we met in the train from Bremen and he came over to the Stadt Hamburg the first day and showed me around the city. I could not have wished for a better guide. We drank porter together at the Schnabelhaus, for even in 1932, I like to recall, the old Hansa connections with England were maintained and porter and rum were as common as beer in Lübeck or Hamburg; he took me through the Marienkirche, showed me the organ Buxtehude, Bach's master, had played; and pointed out the garden of the old burgher house, now a museum, where he had courted his first sweetheart. Through his eyes I saw the old Lübeck from the inside: our tour became a sort of postscript to Buddenbrooks, just as my staying at the Stadt Hamburg, in a room facing the garden, established a private connection with Tonio Kröger. But even that summer, though your husband still called himself a Social Democrat, it was obvious that he lacked any militant faith in democracy, no matter how he still felt about socialism. In the train he had shown me a copy of *Die Tat* and commended its politics to me. Those were very authoritarian politics: *Die Tat* stood for making permanent the kind of dictatorship that Bruening had in fact accustomed his countrymen to: a sort of Nazism without the Nazis: the politics of the General Staff.

In other words, Herr Z. believed in democracy in the way your great "liberal" sociologist, Max Weber, believed in it, as reported in his interview with Ludendorff: the election of an authoritarian regime, which would then put an end to further public interference in the affairs of state. That is merely a polite definition of a permanent dictatorship. It would not surprise me if your husband, even against your passionate protests, had slipped into active collaboration with the National Socialists. Part of the business of a lawyer is to find adequate legal justification for acts that may be morally reprehensible, to cover moldy bread, so to say, with fresh legal butter. Indeed, his very sense of order would put him on the side of established authority; for had not Hitler come into power by legal means? Your husband would have

wished the Nazis to be sensible and businesslike; but when
they proved to be otherwise, an old war veteran like him
would hardly challenge his military superiors. Respect for
army discipline, respect for law, respect for authority, would
all lead to the same conclusion: Heil Hitler! I hope I do not
do him an injustice. But there were millions like him in Germany. For them, democracy was a foreign affectation: indeed, a disease that threatened to undermine the military and
biological health of Germany. Perhaps the coming of the
Nazis created a domestic conflict, and your home fell apart.
That, indeed, would not surprise me. But I will be the first
to apologize to Herr Z. if it turns out that he became more
of a democrat after the Nazis took over than he was when
he propounded the theory that the German needs leadership,
rather than self-government.

As for Gerhart, that supercilious but lovable adolescent,
who was so surprised—in true German fashion! I must add—
when he found that a mere American could recite from memory the very English ballads he was learning at the Gymnasium, as for Gerhart I feel that the last dozen years must have
filled him with conflicts that only a neurosis could transform
or death could solve. Conflict between the mother in him and
the father in him: conflict between the Italy where he was
born and the Lübeck where he grew up: conflict between his
pride as a good European, who had been received as a student visitor in the home of an English clergyman and a Swed-
ish nobleman, and pride as a German and a Hansa citizen.

In a Germany that had remained part of the civilized
world, Gerhart could have become a useful citizen: indeed,
a model of that more universal culture which we must create
if we are not to become the helpless victims of the mechanical
instruments that have shattered time and space, and for lack
of political intelligence and harmony, may finally destroy the

civilization that created them. In Nazi Germany, Gerhart must have remained perpetually frustrated: his intellectual gifts rejected, since they were more humanistic than technical, and his emotional capacities thwarted, because they were human. Yes, Frau Z., Gerhart was your own son. His tact might keep him out of the concentration camp, but his sensitive intelligence may easily have driven him to the Hospital for Nervous Diseases. There is more than one way to evade an ugly reality.

I remember the anxiety in your eyes during that spring of 1932; I laid it then to some private worry or some personal frustration; but now I wonder how much you then felt premonitions of what was about to happen. We discussed D. H. Lawrence together, do you remember? You had seen him or had actually met him in Italy and had read some of his novels. As a prophet he had a certain advantage in his observations on Germany; for his wife was a von Richtofen, and he had visited Germany before 1914 as well as after the war. His Letter from Germany was written in 1924, though it was not published in the New Statesman in England till after the Third Reich had, by its final appearance, justified his intuitions. One year after he wrote that letter the Pact of Locarno was signed, and everyone took for granted that a new era of good feeling and understanding was under way: the year that your dishonest and disastrous inflation policy was brought to an end, having accomplished only half of what its German sponsors secretly sought to achieve, since while it canceled your internal debts it did not free you—as your reactionary politicians and financiers had hoped—from your reparation payments. All these facts only make Lawrence's prediction more remarkable.

Germany, this bit of Germany, is very different from what it was two and a half years ago, when I was here. Then it was still open to Europe. Then it still looked to Western Europe for a reunion, for a sort of reconciliation. Now that is over. The inevitable, mysterious barrier has fallen again, and the great leaning of the Germanic spirit is once more eastwards, towards Russia, towards Tartary. . . . At night you feel strange things stirring in the darkness, strange feelings stirring out of this still-unconquered Black Forest. There is a sense of danger. It isn't the people. They don't seem dangerous. Out of the very air comes a sense of danger, a queer, bristling feeling of uncanny danger.

Something has happened. Something has happened which has not yet eventuated. The old spell of the old world has broken, and the old, bristling, savage spirit has set in. The war did not break the old peace-and-production hope of the world, though it gave it a severe wrench. Yet the old peace-and-production hope still governs, at least the consciousness. Even in Germany it has not quite gone.

But it feels as if, virtually, it were gone. The last two years have done it. The hope in peace-and-production is broken. The old flow, the old adherence is ruptured. And a still older flow has set in. Back, back to the savage polarity of Tartary, and away from the polarity of civilised Christian Europe. This, it seems to me, has already happened. And it is a happening of far more profound import than any actual *event*. It is the father of the next phase of events. . . .

And it all looks as if the years were wheeling swiftly backwards, no more onwards. Like a spring that is broken, and whirls swiftly back, so time seems to be whirling with mysterious swiftness to a sort of death. Whirling to the ghost of the old Middle Ages of Germany, then to the Roman days, then to the days of the silent forest and the dangerous, lurking barbarians.*

All that Lawrence prophesied in that letter has come to pass in our time: indeed, it had begun before Lawrence observed it, for what the masses of men felt in their souls was already declared in the self-conscious doctrines of a Moeller van den Bruck or an Ernst Jünger or an Oswald Spengler, who provided new symbols for everything in the German soul that was dark, repressive, and alien to the life of the rest of the world. There were plenty of outward signs of this change

* Posthumous Papers of D. H. Lawrence, A Letter from Germany, 1924. In Phoenix. New York: 1936. The Viking Press.

before 1933 if one had the sense to pay attention to them. The election of Hindenburg as second President of the Republic in 1925 showed which way the wind was blowing: a symbol of a re-established continuity with all that was archaic and backward looking in Germany: its worship of the army, its obedience to the Junker caste, its gift for political Machiavellianism in the style of Frederick the Great. Did not this man who first betrayed the Monarchy find it no less easy to betray the Republic that had put him into power? Both times he had the supreme satisfaction of justifying his Judas-like career under the guise of duty.

Yes: your countrymen turned toward the primeval and the savage; that is, they turned back upon what bound them to the rest of the civilized world: they enslaved themselves, willingly, joyfully, in order that they might more effectively prepare for the enslavement of mankind. But it was only a Lawrence who felt in the political air of 1924 "a sense of danger, a queer, bristling feeling of uncanny danger." While we still thought of your Wandervögel as youths in rebellion against the old Germany, with its strictness, its harshness, its tyranny, he recognized this youth movement for what it was: an uprising, not against Germany, but against civilization. Your youngest child, dear Frau Z., with his pouting lips and his quick tears that too easily claimed your affection—I hardly dare to speculate what happened to him, only because I know what his joining the Hitler Jugend must have meant to you. You lost him, I have no doubt: maybe he even turned against you, because only by overt brutality could he tear out the roots of compassion and gentleness you had planted, out of your own love, in his heart.

Meanwhile, if you are alive, do you still live in Lübeck, that city whose Seven Spires once rose above the flat meadow-land and heath, reminding its burghers of the time when the

Hansa cities had not only been rich and powerful, but free; when they were not only self-governing cities, but cities in an economy and a polity that stretched from Bergen to the Holy Land? The towers of your beautiful city are no longer seven: the richest of your memorials has been bombed, an inevitable retribution for the forces of evil which your own fellow citizens in their stupidity, in their slavish folly, helped set in motion. It is the world's loss as well as your own. The Lübeck I once visited and lost my heart to I shall never see again. It has vanished for both of us as hundreds of other places and monuments have vanished, from Bath to Canterbury, Bayeux to Leningrad. Those terrible scars unite the victors and the vanquished.

Do you remember the walk we took along the Landstrasse toward Travemunde, that April afternoon, when the wind from the Baltic whipped against our faces and gave just a touch of color to the tip of your tip-tilted Cranach nose? We talked about the earthy humor of Ernst Barlach's sculptures, and how he had brought back into modern Germany the very spirit of the old Northern Gothic: the spirit of Brueghel, without the under-current of nightmare in some of Brueghel's works. And you said then: "The nightmare may still come. You know the Nazis hate him and they want to remove his war monument in Hamburg."

You were right. The nightmare came, and one of the first things the Nazis did, along with the burning of the books, was the removal of Barlach's tender monument of a mother and child, because, they said, it wasn't Aryan. By that they meant that its humanness was more visible than its Germanness; and in this they were right. That spirit of nihilism, which denied the human, that spirit which "worked for the extinction of mankind," as their Ludwig Klages said, has been successful; and in attempting to wipe out the human your leaders have also brought upon your fellow countrymen the fate they sought to visit upon others. That was inevitable. They reaped the whirlwind.

As you look upon these gaps in the center of your native city, what thoughts take possession of you? Or are you still too shocked to think? Is it anger or shame that you feel? If it is anger, if it is reproach, at whom are you angry and whom do you reproach? It is a sign of the dreadful abyss into which the world has sunk that I am not even sure what your answer to these questions will be now, as I would have been sure in 1932. Yet if *your* heart has not been touched to the quick by what Germany has done to the world, then certainly Germany, and possibly even the world, will be doomed; for neither the art of medicine nor the art of politics has given us any instruments for dealing with seventy million monsters, who still think of themselves as more sinned against by the rest of the world than sinning.

The servile smiles and the stony hatred with which your countrymen have greeted our American soldiers, our American newspaper correspondents, still leave me in doubt as to what expression I should find on your face. It would not be servile, and since you are no longer young, it would hardly attempt to be seductive: but it might be hostile. In that case, I should conclude that the war was not yet over. If I should find tears of humiliation in your eyes, I would have a little more hope for the immediate future.

# 2. TO DR. HERMANN K., ARCHITECT AND CITY PLANNER, IN HAMBURG

. . . We exchanged books in 1938. You sent me your autobiography in courteous reciprocity for The Culture of Cities: a book that could no longer be translated into German or even circulated in the English text, because of its uncompromising attacks upon fascism. Now, dear Dr. K., seven years have passed: seven years that might be seven centuries, because the Europe that surrounds you is as unlike the Europe the eye beheld in 1938 as the Europe of the twelfth century was unlike the Europe of the fifth century. Unfortunately, no robe of white churches now mantles Europe, as a symbol of its emergence from the Dark Ages: Europe's present garment is a shroud of blackened ruins: a sign that Europe—or at least Germany—has crept back into the Dark Ages.

Men of wisdom and light like yourself are happy now to find enough bread to keep their families alive, without hoping for the extra energy and time out of which creative thought arises. Everywhere life has been reduced to a primitive level: books cannot be printed because there is no paper; what has been printed cannot be circulated because traffic of all kinds is limited to the barest necessities. At the end of the last war chaos spread everywhere; but with it spread life, and even hope. For you they were years of great opportunity.

Totalitarian nihilism is one step beyond chaos. If you are alive you have already found this out. For you, this dismantling of modern civilization in Europe must indeed be a cruel blow. You were almost three score and ten in 1939, having retired in good season when the Nazis came into power; and sometimes I have hoped that Nature was kind to you and let you die in peace, before you saw the work of your lifetime, and the work of the generation before you, work that you deeply venerated, lying in ruins at your feet. You deserved that kindness, I think, if anyone in Germany did; for I have met very few people in my lifetime who had so completely welded together into a harmonious personality the traditional values of the past and the new values that science and the machine had created. I put your personality above your work; but of course your work was an expression of that personality, and unlike most of the men of your generation, you showed a remarkable capacity for remaining abreast of youth, because you, too, were growing, to the very end—or almost to the end.

You were indeed a master builder and you had left a mark on Hamburg comparable to that which Sir Christopher Wren had left on London: at almost any point in the city, one had only to raise one's eyes to see a school, a housing development, a museum, an office building, which you had created. Before the first World War your buildings were, with Tessenow's, perhaps the freshest expression of tradition: the old brick Gothic tradition of the Hansa towns. After the war, you learned to play freely with materials and with technical innovations; but your buildings, however *sachlich*, never lost the human touch: the most economical structure bore the imprint of your imagination. No one had a better opportunity than you had, as architect and planner, in the decade between 1923 and 1933; and no one made better use of it. When you retired in 1933 you were a man to be envied. Well might you say to yourself: *Consummatum est.* Well might you look forward to distant generations who would still walk the streets you had planned, still play in the parks, and remember the benign architect who had done so much to transform the slums of the nineteenth century port, slums as vile as Rotterdam's, or Liverpool's, or New York's, into a people's playground and a people's city.

Did you remain alive long enough to see your lifework tumble into a heap of rubble? Was your own house on the Alster bombed out of existence? Your last public building, before the Nazis took over, was a crematorium. That has proved to be an ominous symbol: innocently you furnished your new rulers with their ultimate weapon of vile barbarity. If any of your buildings are left standing, they must seem like a grim mockery; for they were part of a growing whole, and that whole has been destroyed. What is worse, the process of growth, so beautifully exemplified in your own intelligence and your own imagination, has come to an end. But do not think that the bombs dropped by British and American aviators were responsible for halting the processes of growth. The war came, the bombs fell, because your own countrymen worshiped death under the guise of power. It was they who first conceived and willed a war of annihilation.

You were the ripe fruit of an old tree. When you stepped out of office in 1933 your place was taken by people who talked sentimentally of *Heimatsarchitektur* and who built concentration camps, people who talked of freedom for the German people and planned to make the whole world a prison: rootless people who talked of blood and soil while they nourished plans for a synthetic barbarism, which would turn men into carnivores and uproot millions of good Europeans from the soil their families had cultivated for centuries. What happened visibly to Hamburg after 1941, actually already happened in 1933: your lifework then lay in ruins, because that part of the German heritage which was inimical to modern civilization became dominant.

Yes: your fate was visible even before 1933: it was written prophetically on the archaic-modern walls of the Böttchergasse in Bremen, where the architect had substituted Wotan for Jesus. The dregs of paganism, the dregs of feudalism, and the dregs of modern mechanism composed the poisonous brew of National Socialism: your countrymen drank this foul potion, as though it were the golden elixir of life, and like victims of the witch's enchantment in a fairy story, they were transformed by this drink into creatures of a lower order, patterned after the infantile Goering, the twisted dwarf Goebbels, the obscene Streicher, the faceless Hitler.

Once this change had taken place, *your* world was in ruins: the ideas your buildings had symbolized, humane ideas, had been replaced with another kind of ideology; and at the Ordnungschulen for the new elite, cruelty was inculcated as a virtue, and two thousand years of Christian culture were removed, while technics, whose virtues you so well defended against the blind criticism of Oswald Spengler, was reduced to an instrument for exterminating whatever stood in the way of the Third Reich and its leaders.

You did not understand this transformation, I fear; if you did, your silence can hardly be accounted for. Perhaps you did not see what was happening before your eyes because the *visible* world about you was still largely the world you yourself had helped to create. A few of your friends were in concentration camps perhaps; a few of your colleagues had gone into exile: otherwise the new regime was only the old regime of the army, with a lifetime's military service taking the place of the limited period that prevailed before. Did you assent to it in your heart because, after all, it was German and gave Germany world leadership once more?

I am judging your reaction to the Nazis by your silence. Perhaps I am also judging you by the letter you wrote me in thanking me for my book. It was a courteous and generous letter; but at the end of it you took exception to some of the things I had said against fascism, and pointed out what progress had been made under National Socialism in unified planning. Very possibly this eulogy of the Nazis was only a prudent effort to appease the censor, and to clear yourself, in case the Gestapo inquired into your correspondence with such a public enemy of fascism as myself; it was in that light that I originally took your observations.

But there was nothing perfunctory in your defense of the new regime: you pointed out that they had done things in a few years that you might have worked a whole lifetime to accomplish by the ordinary methods of republican government, with its divided responsibilities and its need for persuasion and consent. Re-reading that letter, I find something more than prudence: I find a failure to understand the importance of process and an over-evaluation of mere results. Such a failure of understanding I would not expect in a mind so well-seasoned as yours. Surely you should have seen in advance that the very quality that gave such a bright sheen of success to everything that the Nazis undertook would largely account for their ultimate failure. If you were deceived, too, if even despite your fine intelligence you found yourself admiring their "results," that would show that this weakness probably was at work all through German culture.

What is the radical mistake of all tyrannies? If any one characteristic can be singled out, it might be called the tendency to substitute power for time. In social change, if one shortens the time interval one must multiply the amount of power to be applied to produce the desired result. In those circumstances, compulsion, ever more arbitrary, takes the place of rational consent and voluntary co-operation.

Democracy, even in the form of parliamentary republicanism, has often been reproached for the fact that it consumes time: the members of Congress debate and argue and delay, before they come to conclusions which a single man might formulate after a few hours' consideration. This characterization is correct; but the criticism is far from damaging; for democracy limits its actions, except in times of great stress, to measures which have been formulated under debate, and it refrains from acting until the processes of persuasion have made it unnecessary to use force on those who have been in the opposition: for even if the latter have been defeated, they have still been respected and they have been heard.

Democracy pays a price for the freedom of consent: sometimes desirable measures are put through too slowly, and sometimes they cannot be put through at all. In times of war, democracy has often been placed in extreme danger by these habits of debate and delay: enemies who desire war can take the initiative, as Japan took the initiative in waging war upon the United States, catching us unprepared at Pearl Harbor, because, while perhaps the majority knew that there was no other way of meeting the danger of an Axis-dominated world, millions of Americans still waited for some miracle that would save them from the hard tasks and sacrifices of war.

But if we pay dearly for our slowness, how much more dearly have your countrymen paid, my dear Dr. K., for the speed you were prepared to admire: that speed which comes only through concentration of power. In the United States we used to have an ironical definition for a great business executive: we said he was someone who makes all his decisions instantly—and sometimes is right! By now your countrymen may well appreciate the truth of that jest. A series of swift decisions brought about the reoccupation of the Rhineland, the full rearmament of Germany, the occupation of Austria, the conquest of Czechoslovakia, decisions that fell like hammer blows upon the anvil of Europe and forged a new sword for further conquests. Swift were the decisions that led to the invasion of Poland and the wiping out of the center of Rotterdam: no second thoughts in the mind of your leaders, no vocal opposition to a war that might mean a world catastrophe, or to methods that would eventually bring about reprisals, delayed your countrymen for a split second. Your success was dazzling; but, in a short while, your own eyes were blinded by it and every later stroke, no matter how brilliant it seemed at first, from the invasion of Russia to the invention of your revenge weapons, was simply a further act of suicide.

From the time of Frederick II in Sicily, Europe had six hundred years' experience in the vices and miseries of tyrannical government. The rise of parliamentary government in England in the seventeenth century, in the United States and France in the eighteenth century, the rise of the more simple democracy of Switzerland even earlier, was due to the fact that absolutism had been tried and found wanting. In the long run, the inefficiencies of democracy were still more satisfactory than the merciless efficiencies of absolutism, which only a ruthless concentration of power made possible. Your countrymen never learned that lesson: the lesson that self-respecting free men taught themselves all over the world, spelling it out, letter by letter, when they formed a drinking society or a burial association, a masonic lodge or an insurance organization, a sports club or a co-operative grocery shop and transferred the lesson they had learned to the political state. What is that lesson? It is the essential discovery that good government is no substitute for self-government, and that no society can remain either efficient or secure if it deprives itself of the organs of criticism, the practice of free speech and free publication, or if it fails to rest its powers on the active consent of the governed.

In democracy, the co-operative process of arriving at the political result is as important as the result; for it is an education in self-discipline. Leadership and authority, the leadership based on actual ability, the authority that derives from special knowledge or special experience, must function within the general pattern of democratic control. Otherwise, the alternative is government by martial law: government with the aid of the secret police and the army, the official torturer and the official exterminator. Any fool can rule a nation by that method; but only a fool would mistake the process for government.

One of the most important theorems in government was expressed by the great Catholic liberal, Lord Acton: All power corrupts and absolute power corrupts absolutely. That is why every species of government, from that of a trade union to that of a great state, requires the watchful participation of its members; so that pride will not beget insolence, insolence will not beget irresponsibility, and irresponsibility will not beget further moral decay. Only when power is so controlled and so distributed can it be saved from corruption. Precisely because the power of National Socialism was absolute and unconditional, its corruption was also absolute and unconditional.

You probably do not remember the first time I met you; I called at your office in the Hochbauamt, in the company of a young Russian: your friend Frau Z., who like you was a citizen of Bremen, had arranged the meeting. You had just risen from your afternoon nap on the old-fashioned chaise-longue in your office, and I commented on the wisdom of this practice, as helping to account for the huge amount of work you and your small staff had accomplished in two short years. We talked about the abandonment of the Exhibition that had been planned to take place in Köln in 1933, the city whose inner quarters you had replanned. I told you how enthusiastic some of us in America had been over Dr. Ernest Jäckh's program for that Exhibition: how it made me feel personally that Germany, rising out of the defeat of the last war, had assumed the leadership in Western Civilization and was ready to bring together and fuse into an organic whole all the fragmentary aspects of the modern world.

That enthusiasm was, alas! misplaced; but in 1930, when the program was printed in *Die Form*, it was still possible to think that people like you and Jäckh and the leaders of the Deutscher Werkbund were truly representative of Germany; that you were its actual leaders, and not the polite disguise for quite another kind of leadership. When my friend Walter Curt Behrendt was still the editor of *Die Form*, I used to contribute to that paper; and I still have my old back numbers. Just the other day I refreshed my memory by re-reading the program of the Exposition. In one sense, its words are still fresh and meaningful; and nothing I could say will give you a better sense of the chasm your countrymen have created than to contrast the potentialities of 1930 with the actualities of 1945.

What does the idea of a "New Era" mean? [asked Dr. Jäckh] . . . The "New Era" is an organic result of the development of a century, the conscious experience of the continuity of the most decisive century of discoveries, inventions, and transformations of form. To represent the totality and unity of such a "New Era," to make it palpable, to develop it avowedly and credibly, is the aim of the International Exhibition of 1933, which points to the future. We are convinced that Max Scheler, the philosopher, was right when he characterized the epochal significance of our times as the beginning of a new era. "The geometric order, in which every extensive transformation of matter and man lies, at the beginning of which we are standing, can scarcely be overestimated. Impossible of comparison with any of the periods into which the historian divides the history of the so-called European modern era, it appears to me in depth and versatility to surpass even that total transformation which leads from the European Middle Ages to modern times; and we must go back to the origin of Christianity and the rise of the Germano-Roman peoples in order to have an approximate comparison of the depth of the transformation. It is not only a transformation of matter, circumstances, institutions, the fundamental ideas and forms of the arts and nearly all the sciences, it is a transformation of man himself, of the character of his inner construction, in body, instincts, soul and spirit; it is not only a transformation of his actual being, but also a transformation of his standards. . . ."

Unaware of how bitterly ironic these words would sound within a few short years, the General Commissioner of the Exhibition went on to describe all the forces in the modern world, from physics and biology to psychoanalysis, the cinema eye and the radio ear, which would alter the vision of the universe and benignly modify its ethics and its laws. His outline divided the Exposition into seven groups, beginning with a new vision of the universe and the new development of man, and going through the control of power and material, through city and regional planning, to the "establishment of a world order."

A new feeling towards the universe, in conjunction with the experience of universal economic interdependence and universal political confederation changes peoples and countries, creates a society of states which shall be a federation of their peoples, creates new bonds and new conceptions of freedom, new solidarities, and other sovereignties. "Consciousness of life and the universe in our day has taken a turn of at least 90 degrees." Such a life-unit includes . . . universal economic concerns and (for the first time in the history of the world) an international bank, a League of Nations and (also for the first time in the history of the world) an international, even an intercontinental agreement against war.

Time has made that brave program hollow and empty; but when those words were written they expressed the best hope of the world; and in that world Germany was still an active associate and partner, indeed, Germany had become by acclaim its accepted leader. In an effort to do justice to all that was fresh and creative in Germany, the other nations closed their eyes to the peculiar facts of Germany's history and unlearned the harsh lessons that the mailed fists of your rulers had again and again driven home. This desire to see only the best in Germany was a serious error on our part; but it was a magnanimous error, an error of generosity and love; and Germans like yourself made it easy for us to commit this mistake. Surely, we said to ourselves, the country that produced such as you would not follow the loutish Hitler. Surely the spiritual understanding which came so easily to us, the lack of barriers and frontiers between our minds, was the harbinger of an age when all men would share such sentiments and work together for a common good. We forgot that you had already followed Frederick the Great and Bismarck on the same path of violence; that under the Republic in 1927 Carl von Ossietsky had been imprisoned for revealing your actual rearmament; and that you were prepared to follow the General Staff anywhere they might lead—even into the arms of Hitler.

So the New Era did not come: the "New Order" took its place. Even before Hitler came into power the New Era Exhibition was abandoned and with Hitler's triumph the Nürnberg Festival, that purely German orgy of primitive solidarity and bravado and boastfulness and dramatized barbarism, filled the stage. At that moment the consciousness of German life indeed took a "turn of ninety degrees," but that radical change of direction was away from the Christian and the universal, back to the barbaric and the tribal: away from the new vision of the universe that has been taking shape through the co-operative endeavors of science and back to organized corruptions to which men who had once been trained as scientists now gave their sanction: the Rassenlehre of Günther and Rosenberg, the myth of the Herrenrasse, the claim to seize by force all that force can capture, and to subject the very forms of justice to the most barbarous instincts of the German people. )

Instead of guiding the world toward the promised land, your leaders led the world to a desert, a desert of moral nihilism and spiritual death, a desert in which your country-men became the victims of the mirages of power, wealth, and world-domination that your neurotic leaders had conjured up. Out of their deepest corruption your countrymen created a God and cast themselves at his feet, worshiping in him their own basest selves. *Eigenlob stinkt!* What then shall we say of the orgy of Germanic self-worship which brought the Nazis into power and endowed them with capacities for evil that scarcely Dostoyevsky himself could have conceived in his most demonic moments, even though he had outlined the very figure and form of Hitler in the boastful sniveler who writes his Letters from the Underworld. By making Hitler their leader, your countrymen all became denizens of the Under-world, or rather, you condemned yourselves to the lowest and slimiest pit of the Inferno, in whose depths you still struggle and writhe today.

The promise of the New Era vanished on the breath that spoke it; and it may be many generations will pass before that promise will be real again.

While still in your early sixties you retired from the scene gracefully, turning from building to writing, where your clear mind and disciplined feeling expressed themselves with equal poise. The Germany you represented also retired gracefully

—too gracefully in fact. Your study of modern architecture in Germany, your own autobiography, give no hint of your feelings toward the new regime; certainly they give no hint of criticism. To judge by your published words, before 1939, nothing serious had happened either to Germany or to the rest of the world. And that is why the work of your lifetime lies in ruins. You could only have saved it by sounding the alarm. You could only have saved your country if the class you had represented had devoted strenuous nights and days to undermining and fighting everything the Nazis only stood for. With all your virtues you did not do this. The books you published under the eyes of the Nazis were all the "Reflections of a Non-Political."

Too late, perhaps, you understood what had happened: too late you realized that the day of writing as well as of building was over: the anointed Terror had come and its purpose was Frederick the Great's purpose and Bismarck's purpose, to concentrate power and to utilize fraud in order to extend the rule of the German State. Today Germany: tomorrow the world!

Were you actually surprised that the war came so soon? I don't see how that was possible. If anything were needed to inform anyone as to Germany's purposes after 1933, the technical catalog of Boysen and Maasch in Hamburg—your own publishers—should have offered enough evidence to anyone who could read print. Before 1933 housing and city development shared a place with engineering. After that date military construction, military engineering, and books on arms and armies took their place. One did not have to read Mein Kampf afresh or to listen to Hitler's speeches to understand where Germany's destiny lay. I have gone back to your autobiography to find out what you thought about the last war. Politically, the pages are empty.

Perhaps you went through agonies of doubt and conflict as you found yourself more and more cut off from the outside world. Then came the moment when you realized that all the gates were closed, except the gate of death. An era of construction, the era that had built modern Germany, had established its leadership in technics, had transformed its cities and made them spacious, sanitary, orderly, and often beautiful, had come to an end: an era of unrestricted destruction supplanted it. You had been one of the great leaders in the first era; you were one of the victims of the second. Yet both eras had their sources in Germany.

What conclusions can anyone draw from this terrible catastrophe? The only rational conclusion that one can draw now, after German scientists have perfected the rocket weapon, is one that was already true in 1938; namely, that we live in an open world, and that unless mankind organizes its affairs throughout the planet on a basis of co-operation and reciprocity, rejecting all notions of one-sided domination, all notions of special privileges and special disabilities, all notions of racial inequality, it will be doomed by the very technical advances it has achieved. At the very moment civilization had achieved an unprecedented degree of unity, your countrymen sought to withdraw from it. At the moment when our life called for more complete co-operation, economic, social, political, than had ever before been achieved, they sought domination; and instead of perfecting the open world, they withdrew into a closed world, as closed as a prison, as insulated from reality as the mind of the insane.

Even if this letter reaches you, dear Dr. K., its message must be a sad one: it reminds you of a challenge that was not met, of an opportunity that was wasted, of a lifetime's effort that has fallen in ruins. I write you, not to reproach you, but to stir you to meditate upon what has happened during these years when we were cut off from each other; but even more I write in the hope that you will be led by that process of thought to review what happened in Germany in the years of your maturity and your ascendancy.

Something was wrong in your national life: what was it? What caused these repeated defeats; what caused this ultimate destruction? I have my own interpretations; but I do not propose to sit in judgment upon you: it is you who must do that. If not you, then your colleagues, your pupils: such of them as are left. Now is the time for self-criticism: that is the first step toward self-government. Unless you make that step the Germans will not be ready, even a century from now, for the responsibilities of freedom, and all your creative efforts will again be blasted away.

# 3. TO ALFONS F.,
## A GERMAN WRITER IN AUSTRIA

. . . Five or six years ago, dear Alfons, I heard you had come to the United States by way of Russia and Japan; I even heard rumors that with your reputation as a playwright you had settled down in Hollywood. Then I learned that the person who had informed me had somehow mixed you up with Carl Zuckmayer, who came over a year or two before and who hated Hollywood: so I should not be surprised if by now you have left Zürich and have already gone back to your chalet in the Zillertal, deep among the fir trees, with the milky glacier water boiling among the stones of the riverbed below.

The Zillertal was the first bond between us, when we met in Zürich in 1925. Chance plumped us down together at the same table in Sprüngli's. You had absentmindedly said "Grüss' Gott" as you took the other place at table and some indefinable swagger of the mountaineer about your heavy shoulders and your trim waist had made me reply with: "Heil!"—capping your greeting with the salute mountain climbers give when they approach the snow line. In five minutes I was telling you about my experiences in the Zillertal in 1922, when my wife and I went camping there with a party of English schoolmarms; and you had drawn a map on the tablecloth to show me exactly where your Alpenhütte lay, a half hour's climb above Mayrhofen.

I have not looked to see which army now controls your part of the Tyrol; nevertheless, I can see the old life going on pretty much as it did when we visited it in 1922, in the midst of the inflation. The old women still climb tirelessly with their baskets on their backs, to gather the hay on some alp, six or seven thousand feet above sea level, a straight thousand above their own barns; the goat bells still tinkle about the Edelweisshütte as the goats come into the yard to be milked; the eggs are again scarce and the pancakes are a little thin and tough; the Ersatz coffee has only its blackness to remind one of the drink it pretends to be. But the essential life remains what it always was: work, prayer, love, babies, illness, death. If any part of Europe looks the way it did in 1922, it is probably this very valley. Here the traditional and the primitive endure.

I would not disturb your peace, dear Alfons, by reminding you how different the world actually is; your own writer's imagination must constantly conjure up terrible images that cannot be suppressed. But I fear that your refuge in the Zillertal may become for you another Magic Mountain, and you, who look so strong, may prove to be one of life's delicate children, unable to face the consequences of your own life and work, and therefore incapable of bringing about any transformation of either your own self or that of your countrymen. I have read two of those curious novels you wrote in Switzerland during the last dozen years; novels that were almost poems in prose, peopled with characters that might have been created by Wilhelm Busch and then transposed into Dresden china, so delicately colored and glazed were all the faces of your peasants, even the comic ones. You would have nothing to do with the new regime, you told me, the last time we met; you would never go back to Germany until all these Hanswursts were thrown on the manure pile; you rejected the overtures that the Chamber of Writers had made to you, as the foremost representative of the Blood and Soil tradition in German literature, indignantly repudiating all that the co-ordinated writers, headed by Hauptmann, that Hindenburg of German letters, now stood for.

Physically, you kept yourself apart. But the books that you wrote continued to circulate in Germany: one of them was even a best-seller there; and you lamented rather bitterly, in the last letter you wrote me, that any third-rate writer who was a refugee could get his books translated into English, if he described for the twentieth time how he had made his escape, whilst you, who were a creative spirit, no longer were sought by foreign publishers. "After all the German public's taste has not been entirely debauched by the Austrian paper-hanger," you wrote me; "so long as they continue to read books like mine there will be hope for my country. Let Hitler beware! Every book of mine that circulates in Germany is a Trojan horse."

Forgive me for deflating your boast, dear Alfons. But your books differed from the Trojan horse that the Greeks built: there were no armed men in the new kind of horse—it was empty! You were an asset to the Nazis, not a liability; in the humorously sentimental vein you cultivated, with your gothic woodcarvings and your Meissen-ware eroticism you made it seem as if the Germany of Hitler were as innocent of evil purposes as, I was about to say, the Germany of Lessing, forgetting for the moment that the Germany of Lessing was also the Germany of Frederick the Great—that is, with a Prussia that spent ten times as much on its Army, in proportion to its size and wealth, as any other state in Europe.

When I challenged your position at the time, you answered, sulkily, that you were a creative writer—*ein Dichter*—and not a politician. Have you lived to regret that attitude and those words; or have you gone back to the Zillertal so that you may nourish and fatten the illusions that have turned you, with all your fine capacities, into—forgive the candor of an old friend—such a trivial writer? True: your last play was written in 1931: in its social intransigence it even got the better of your esthetic principles. It infuriated the reactionary because it took Wagner's Rheingold legend and showed the heroes engaged in acts of chicane and dishonesty, very much like those that became a public scandal in connection with the scheme for the Junker landowners' Osthilfe: your German audiences didn't like the fact that the only honest and loyal character in the piece was a Social Democrat and a Jew.

That was a double-barreled satire: it not merely hit the evils of the present but it also sent a shaft into the great Wagner himself, the reactionary and the anti-Semitic Wagner. It is strange that a man who could write a satire of this order has taken to writing idylls of an irrecoverable past, a past which never existed in the first place, during the last dozen years. Now, admittedly it is too late for satire. Only tragic themes are left to you. Unfortunately, only those who have been in the battle for freedom and have faced death, like Sophocles, can write such tragedies as would purge the soul of the Germans today. Perhaps the concentration camp might have taught you the nature of your task as a writer. You will not find in your high mountain retreat the materials for leadership. That you could find only in the depths.

The time we met in Paris in 1932 we had many talks about art and about the mission of the writer and about the response of his audience: whether he wrote as a "pure" writer, or whether, when he wrote, he was also a citizen and a moralist. You held the view that art was autonomous; that it knew no other laws than those of its own nature and that it acknowledged no other responsibility than that of being true to itself, to have made the most, through the perfection of its technical means, of the materials that the artist shaped. A work of art, you said, is as innocent of morality as an isosceles triangle. You quoted Croce; you quoted Goethe. The artist, you said, is a non-political animal. Indeed, you laid your opposition to the Nazis to the fact that Hitler wrote and spoke such abominable German prose. That was only a facetious self-exaggeration of your general position.

At that time we agreed on many things; on the shallowness of the French surrealists and on the importance of intelligibility and communicability, on the over-inflated reputation of James Joyce and on the perfection of Rilke's lyrics. But we were divided about the political responsibilities of the artist; and you set down my views as puritanical and provincial. Today we are probably more divided than ever. I have been waiting to hear from Germany the voice of a Milton, the voice of a Victor Hugo, the voice of a Whitman speaking to the German people with the tongue of an ancient prophet, indicting them in words more terrible to hear, more stern, more inexorable, than the words of their avowed enemies and conquerors. Yes: I have been waiting for an "enemy of the people" to arise in Germany, who would proclaim that truth and freedom, not lies and slavery, were the eternal Pillars of Society: for one who would dare to look into his own mirror and tell the Germans the truth he had already told himself: that the Germans had only one enemy—themselves. . . . And what an enemy!

Perhaps the saddest misfortune of Germany is that the German lacks the capacity for self-criticism. When Nietzsche had the courage to stand aside and comment upon your weaknesses, he was canny enough to pose as a Pole. But even he selected as his targets the bourgeois failings that you shared with the rest of Western Civilization; so that he never turned upon his own Germanic assumptions and his own Germanic idols. The worship of power, the cult of the supermen, the

denial of mercy, peace, and pity and the affirmation of brutality and hardness—what were all these Nietzschean slogans
but adulation of the Prussian tradition: self-adulation of the
most sentimental order: a self-adulation that reached its natural climax in the writings and speeches of Adolf Hitler. For
all his boasted courage, Nietzsche never wrote such an in-
dictment of specifically *German* weaknesses as the mild-
mannered Arnold wrote of British weaknesses in Culture and
Anarchy. He failed, because he lacked perspective and intellectual distance, because he was incapable of being hard with
himself: indeed because he accepted your traditional barbarism as a proof of your spiritual strength—so different
from the "Modern Ideas" of the English and the French,
which he despised.

Is it not strange that your philosophy and your literature,
so rich in other respects, should be so impoverished in the
literature of self-criticism? What have you to put alongside
Milton's The Tenure of Kings and Magistrates, alongside
Thomas Paine's Common Sense, alongside Thoreau's Essay
on Civil Disobedience, alongside Carlyle's Past and Present?
Who among your men of letters has indicted your social system, your historic tradition, as soberly and as unflinchingly
as Walt Whitman, the prophet of democracy, indicted his
own country in Democratic Vistas? During the last century
two writers stand out, among a bare handful one might name:
Heinrich Heine and Heinrich Mann. These men dared to challenge Germany. When they attacked they did not graze a few
hairs: they aimed at the fatty tissue around the heart. I wonder if you recall that it was Heinrich Mann that you yourself
used as a symbol of the impure artist, whose work was un-
pleasantly discolored by his democratic political opinions?

You had the advantage of me at this point. At the time I
had not read Heinrich Mann; I somehow had even escaped

*Der Untertan,* though it had been translated into English shortly after the first World War, under the title, The Patrioteer.*

There are novels and plays that tell one more about the character of a nation than more systematic works. If one wants to know the essence of England, one must read Shaw's Pygmalion; it is a clue both to the oligarchical structure of English society and to its democratic foundations. If you want to know the heart of America, read Sinclair Lewis's Main Street; it is a caricature of our life and it treats of the small country town rather than the city; yet the caricature tells something important about the kind of community and the kinds of personality we have developed here: while he winces at the picture, every American recognizes its truth. You in Germany have such a modern novel: it is a piece of merciless criticism, coarse in its outlines, with few qualifying touches: certainly, dear Alfons, it is very plainly colored—I would not use your word dis-colored—by the writer's political opinions, his hatred of caste, servility, militarism, cold deceit, and brutality: his outrage at all the traits and habits that have made democracy impossible in Germany. But in *Der Untertan* Heinrich Mann touched precisely those aspects of your character as a people that are hardest for a foreigner to describe without seeming prejudiced: indeed, if a foreigner painted a similar portrait today you would accuse him of malignant Vansittartism. Obviously, it is hard for you to dissociate yourself from the crawling, materialistic, decadent Germany that Mann presented. It was easier to dissociate yourself from Mann, by saying that he was not a pure artist.

* First published in translation in The European Library (J. E. Spingarn, Editor). New York: Harcourt, Brace & Co. 1921. Republished as Little Superman (Ernest Boyd, Translator). New York: Creative Age Press. 1945.

Yet if your countrymen had taken that novel seriously, that is, if they had been capable of Heinrich Mann's kind of self-criticism, their entire life after the defeat of 1918 might have taken a different course. If the rest of the world had understood its essential truth, they would have remained on guard, and would never have indulgently over-looked the re-arming of Germany, which took place even under the Republic. For remember: the Germany Mann described was not Nazi Germany: it was the "good" and "enlightened" Germany of the eighteen-nineties, when German music, German philosophy, and German science were at the height of their reputation if not of their power. Diederich, the "hero" of the book, lacked only one qualification for being a Nazi: a brown shirt. *Everything else was there.* Diederich's cringing fear of his father is only equaled by his masochistic love of being beaten by him; as he grows up he becomes an informer, just as Hitler was in the days before the Beer Hall Putsch; and Diederich's mixture of sadism and sentiment prepares one's mind for equally revolting spectacles in our own day—the entrance to one of your extermination camps, *neatly gardened,* or the sign on the walls of one of your human abattoirs, reminding attendants, in the interest of health, to keep their hands clean.

Here is an answer to the old question, so often discussed in Germany, *What is German?* Do you dare now to admit the terrible answer? *Diederich* is German: what *Diederich did* was German. The life he led in his student union needed only to be organized on a wholesale scale, covering the whole country, to become the life of storm troopers and SS men and the bureaucracy and the Wehrmacht. The brutality, the servile loyalty to the leader, his absolute devotion (in theory) to war, were all of the same order. In its plot, the book was prophetic. Anyone who read *Der Untertan* in 1918, when it came out, would have been fully prepared for all that happened in 1933, including the gullibility and the paralysis of the Social Democrats. He would have been prepared, provided he accepted Heinrich Mann's satire as the expression of an essential truth—admittedly not the whole truth or the best truth—about German society. You were not prepared, dear Alfons: you attributed to Heinrich Mann's political philosophy the discoloration that actually existed on the face of Germany. All that Hitler changed was to enable his followers to do openly, boastfully, shamelessly the same things that the Diederich of the Second Reich did slyly and underhandedly. Even there the change was not of a radical nature: for did not Diederich beat up a Jewish classmate with the tacit approval of his teachers?

Your attitude has remained that of the non-political artist: in that respect, up to 1935, it kept closer to Heinrich Mann's more famous brother, Thomas. Perhaps indeed you were influenced by the book that Thomas Mann wrote in the midst of the first World War, Reflections of a Non-Political Man. If so, you again had the advantage of me; for I had the American's tendency, immediately after the last war, to look upon that whole conflict as a disgraceful episode, accidental and meaningless, an interruption to the normal life of man; and I turned away from the all-too-revealing books your great writers and scholars had put forth during that period, hastening to forget them, so that I might the more easily forgive their nation.

This unwillingness to remember was a sign of the political callowness and the ethical superficiality of my generation: we actually showed more pity for the "unfortunate Germans" than we showed for the peoples whose lands you had invaded and sacked, whose cities you had destroyed, whose mines you had deliberately flooded and whose factories you had blown up, to lessen the number of your post-war competitors. But I have sought to atone for the folly of my generation by taking belated account of those writings, since I know that if we had followed up and completed the lesson we had only half-learned when we joined the fight against Germany, my own son, and tens of thousands like him, would not be lying in a soldier's grave on foreign soil.

Many of your countrymen who have found refuge in the United States and England, dear Alfons, talk about Germany as if it had been unaccountably captured by a gang of foreign bandits in 1933. They profess to have nothing in common with the National Socialists, and they have a way of saying: Help us to get rid of those foreign monsters, the Nazi dogs, and then return Germany to us! There was a touch of that plea in the last letter you wrote me in 1940. I wonder if you are ignorant—or if you are relying upon a foreigner's ignorance—of the real Germany: or were you merely forgetful of something you preferred not to remember?

If there was a single representative writer among the younger group in 1914 it was surely Thomas Mann; and if there was any German who could also be called a "good European" it was the author of Death in Venice (1911). But what was the essential theme of Mann's Reflections of a Non-Political Man? It was nothing less than a hymn of praise to the essential Germanism of Germany: praise of its militarism, its cult of war, its authoritarianism, its anti-democratic spirit. There was plenty of politics in these non-political reflections; but it was authoritarian politics. Between Mann's sentiments in 1915 and those of the National Socialists there was a far smaller gap than there was between him and, say, Woodrow Wilson. If Wilson had, indeed, been a close student of German institutions he would never have made the blunder of hanging the guilt on Germany's rulers alone and absolving the German people. In all his irrational premises, Mann was already almost as much of a National Socialist as Schacht and Hugenberg and von Rundstedt, not to say Hess, Rosenberg, and Hitler.

For Thomas Mann, "militarism is modernism;" while what he understood by "civilization," the state valued by the Allied powers, was the opposite, namely, "security and sleepiness." Mann's words throughout this remarkable book could have been intoned at a Nürnberg celebration or delivered to the puppet Reichstag by Hitler himself. I will not heap up the citations; the book is still probably in your personal library; but I cannot resist a final quotation from Mann, for it completely demolishes the "foreign bandit" theory of National Socialism.

No [he says on page 186], it is not the peace of national-international democracy that Europe needs: that is impossible and it would be no peace, but only perpetuated anarchy. The peace of Europe must not be national but supernational; not a democratic peace but a German peace. The peace of Europe can rest only on the victory and the might of a supernational people, a people that calls its own the highest universal traditions, the richest cosmopolitan endowments, the deepest feeling of European responsibility.

At their worst, the Nazis could add nothing to this program: was that not essentially what they meant by the new order?

Were Thomas Mann's sentiments exceptional? The pages of the enlightened *Neue Rundschau,* all through the first World War, show that he was a true representative, not merely of his country but of his class: it was not Mann alone but 92 other intellectuals who signed the declaration backing up the German government and the German army at the outset of the war, proclaiming the innocence of Germany at the same moment that even "pacifists" like Maximilian Harden were rejoicing that the war had finally come, and proclaiming that Germany had willed it. Even the purest of your writers, dear Alfons, shared these sentiments, at least during the first wave of emotion. It was doubtless an accident that Rilke's poem to his ancestor, Cornet Christopher Rilke, swept him into popularity when the war broke out. But what was it that caused this pure sensitive spirit, who had suffered so bitterly at Military School, this cosmopolitan who said that Russia was his spiritual fatherland, and who served as Rodin's secretary and established himself as his friend—what was it that made Rilke, too, write five hymns of exultant praise to the god of war?

No, dear Alfons, this taste for war, this adulation of power, this belief in German supremacy, and in peace only if it is a German peace—these are not the private characteristics of a small group of corrupt or demented men: these are the common postulates of Germanism, so common that few Germans have even dreamt of examining them. The chief difference between your militarists and your more democratic groups is that the latter would prefer to achieve the same results without fighting. You need not accept my word for it, the word of a foreigner: I refer you to the best of authorities, to Thomas Mann himself. After the first World War, Thomas Mann underwent a slow but thorough change; first he allied himself with the social democratic cause; finally, during the thirties, he became one of the spiritual leaders of world democracy. That inner development, toward citizenship, toward responsibility, toward a universal morality, required courage and insight of the highest order. Had your countrymen undergone a similar change, they would not have plunged into a career of collective terrorism and totalitarian war.

Unlike so many of his fellow refugees, even many who have called themselves democrats for a far longer time, Mann understands the gap that exists between Germany and the rest of the Western world; and he does not attribute this gap to the Nazis: he attributes it to Germanism.

A little while ago Dr. Mann delivered an address at the Library of Congress in Washington on Germany and the Germans: the address of a highly courageous and honorable man, because it was in effect a public confession, made by one who, in achieving self-knowledge, has become deeply aware of his own weaknesses and his own sins. This address had the profound self-knowledge, the brave humility, of Saint Augustine's Confessions. With the skill of a surgeon making a post-mortem autopsy, he opened up the mind of Germany and, revealing layer upon layer, organ after organ, he disclosed the morbid developments that accompanied the growth of protestantism, romanticism, naturalism, nationalism in Germany. No one, not even Heine, has given such an unsparing revelation of the German nature, the German character, its mixture of the rational and the demonic, of the progressive and the primitive.

Wherever arrogance of the intellect mates with the spiritually obsolete and archaic [Dr. Mann said], there is the Devil's domain; and the Devil, Luther's Devil, Faust's Devil, strikes me as a very German figure; and the pact with him, the Satanic covenant, to win all treasures and power on earth for a time at the cost of the soul's salvation, strikes me as something exceedingly typical of German nature. A lonely thinker and searcher, a theologian and philosopher in his cell, who, in his desire for world enjoyment and world domination barters his soul to the Devil—isn't this the right moment to see Germany in this picture, the moment in which Germany is literally being carried off by the Devil?

The outcome of Mann's analysis is to show how deeply the German people, low and high, ignorant and intelligent, not least such people as he himself, who stood at the very pinnacle of European culture, have been involved in Germany's present downfall. At seventy, rich in years and honors and works, Thomas Mann nevertheless at last understands the elements in his own life and thought that made the triumph of National Socialism, not an accident, a hideous accident, entirely foreign to the real spirit of Germany, but an inevitable culmination of its divided loyalties and its warped destiny. He identifies the evil that conquered Germany and led to its final debacle as the evil that was nourished by such a good German as he was, the evil that was present in Luther and Fichte, in Nietzsche and Wagner: the spirit whose ultimate heresy was to subordinate the human to the German.

This story [Thomas Mann concludes] should convince us of one thing: there are *not* two Germanys, a good one and a bad one, but only one, whose best turned into evil through devilish cunning. Wicked Germany is merely good Germany gone astray, good Germany in misfortune, in guilt, in ruin. For that reason it is quite impossible for one born there simply to renounce the wicked, guilty Germany and to declare: "I am the good, the noble, the just Germany in the white robe; I leave it to you to exterminate the wicked one."

Perhaps these last six years, dear Alfons, have caused such a thoroughgoing change in you as the last thirty years brought about in Thomas Mann. Perhaps they have turned the nonpolitical artist into the responsible citizen, capable of exerting moral leadership, as ready to acknowledge and root out the weaknesses in your own life and work as Thomas Mann has been. You are now only a little older than Mann was at the end of the last war. Admittedly, your task unfortunately is an even heavier one than his was: for he fought a losing fight in a country where his words could still be easily published and his voice heard: whereas you will speak like a prophet in the wilderness, to a people that has been debased by participating in evil plans, sullied by their victories, and embittered by their defeats. If you rise to your task, you will be more lonely in spirit than you would be in your Alpenhütte in wintertime when snow blocks the road down to the valley, even for the skier. For you, who tried so long to stay apart, perhaps especially for you, there is no easy road back. The snow will stay long upon the ground.

Unfortunately, my friend, there will be no peace for you, even in the Zillertal, until you break your covenant with the devil: the covenant whereby you gained riches and honor as an artist by closing your eyes to the political scene. If you are to live once more as a writer, you must first earn your right to live by proving yourself a man. Your country is still waiting for a man. It has been waiting for a long time.

# 4. TO J.E.F., A MANUFACTURER IN THE HARZ MOUNTAINS

. . . It is seven years since the last of your Christmas greetings came, this time only a card, with the traditional symbols of the feast and a printed greeting in heavy Gothic type. The last of your personal messages, indeed, came in 1934, along with that handsome little brochure in which you told the story of the tub and bucket industry, celebrating the history of your family's business enterprise, your family's fidelity to craftsmanship, your family's Saxon thoroughness. Those Christmas greetings were your link in memory with the outside world. By 1939, for all I know, your modest factory for making pails and tubs was already turning out shell cases or caterpillar treads.

We met in 1927 on your first and only trip to America; our friend Behrendt, who died last spring, an honored and respected professor at Dartmouth College, had given you an introduction; and when you sat down to supper in our very modest Long Island City apartment, you were innocently delighted to find in the meal the same sort of simplicity you had deliberately introduced in your own life, in defiance of the customs of your community. You told us about your wife and about your five children; your love of fruits and raw vegetables—foods that could be eaten without cooking, and your doing away with table linen and with elaborate forms of service, so as to make the family self-helping and self-sufficient. "People have been the slaves of their possessions!" you exclaimed. "Some of my friends think I am parsimonious because I do not live on the same scale as other people

285

with my income and my position in the community. But I tell them I am not saving money: I am saving my time and my life for better things."

Then you told us a little story which I shall always treasure, about a wealthy German family whose children had never played with their parents, or indeed had even seen much of them, before the inflation; but when the family lost their money, they went out for walks into the country for the first time together, and the children adored being with their parents, and sharing their life. As soon as the financial conditions were stabilized, the mother and father went back to their old ostentatious life: theaters, concerts, clubs, parties, and the children were inconsolable. "I don't want my children ever to long for another inflation period," you concluded, "so I have tried to arrange my life in accordance with the ideas of your great Emerson, in his essay on Domestic Life."

For me you were a new kind of industrialist, and even though I had known Germans well all my life, a new kind of German. Your freshness of mind, your eagerness to adventure, your willingness to break with old ways that no longer had any sound reason for existence, were mixed with a veneration for the traditional; and at the end of the evening you were matching folk songs with my wife, singing your German versions of a common theme, against my wife's English or Kentucky Mountain words and tunes. You were part of a traditional pre-industrial economy which was also, we agreed, far nearer to the requirements of a new economy, based on the needs of the human personality rather than on mere productivity, than were the great factory organizations of the big cities. Your family business was still on a scale small enough to permit you to know as a neighbor or a friend every person who worked for you; though your galvanized pails and tubs had a large market and you yourself had just made an addition to your plant, to enable you to make rust-less steel as well as galvanized iron utensils. "I am not afraid of the machine," you boasted, "so long as the Man remains in command of it."

We had so many ideas in common that it is not strange that we kept in touch with each other for a dozen years; yet I hardly know anything about your political opinions, except what you revealed that day we spent together in 1927. I remember particularly that you said: "I am much more of a Social Democrat than the people who work for me. So long as they have their sausages and their beer their belief in the upper classes is unqualified. There's only one old fellow, the son of a 'forty-eighter who was shot by the authorities, who understands why I should like my people to be free as well as happy. Most of the older men think I am a weakling because I don't swear at them in the same fashion as my grandfather did; and if I would only give them a few whacks on the behind occasionally they would be happier." That told me something about your workers, and I remember saying: "It's no wonder Germany has been unable to make a successful political revolution." But it gives me no key to what happened to you after 1930. Did you, too, swing all the way over to Nazism?

Certainly, there were elements in National Socialism that may have appealed to you, for the corrupt minds of the Nazis were cunning enough to mingle the good with the bad, in order to cloak their purposes and to profit by the weaknesses of the forces that opposed them. So the Nazis made much of the family, and they were violent in their opposition to the decrease in the German birthrate; similarly, they showed a special interest in rural life, and in the traditional arts of the countryside and the region; they even professed a special interest in small business enterprises and in family indus-

tries. On all these points you would hardly have been in opposition to them; on the contrary, you would be predisposed
in their favor, so much so that it might have closed your eyes
to the Nazis' real purposes, which soiled everything they
touched.

At first you might not have guessed that these lovers of the
family would advocate wholesale reproduction as a duty to
the State with as little concern for family sentiment itself as
a breeder of cattle. You would not have understood that the
children desired by the Nazis would be ruthlessly taken away
by the State, deliberately seduced, often by sexual means, and
even taught to denounce their own parents to the authorities
if they showed any disposition to challenge the authority of
the Nazi party. So, too, you might hardly have observed in
1930 or even in 1932 that these praisers of the traditional
outward forms of German life were spreading the cancer of
nihilism through every old German institution, so that nothing of your past would survive except that which was servile
and brutal by nature.

While your traditional relation to your workers was a
paternal one, the new principle of leadership was based upon
the power to terrorize and to inflict death; and when your
own industry was co-ordinated in the war production system
you found yourself, doubtless, taking orders from a party
leader in the bureaucracy, who may or may not have been
competent, who may or may not have been honest. Were you
forced to expand beyond the limits of your own ability to
ensure personal supervision of the plant and the working
force? Were your family holdings transferred to a new state-
managed cartel which made your own works a mere cog in
the machine of military production? If you actually embraced Nazism in the hope that it would preserve and extend
the traditional ways of life, you discovered, all too soon,

that you had deceived yourself. Their purposes were not your purposes. Your business picked up again even before the war contracts were signed: in the new Randsiedlungen your galvanized iron tubs, which could be filled in the kitchen, were more in demand than the porcelain bathtubs which the Republic had fostered. But long before 1939 you must have realized that you had been duped. Your profits were illusory and your property was no longer your own.

Perhaps your plant, nestling under a fold of the hills, by the side of the swift river that once turned your water mill and now runs your transformer, escaped the bombers. In the near-by fields, beets and turnips still are growing; there is rye on the hillsides; and the espaliers in your own garden still bear cherries and apricots in season. Nothing has changed about your house except that your four sons are no longer there; perhaps one of them died on the snowy steppes of Russia; another, the aviator, may be a prisoner in England, after being rescued from the sea; the other two have not been heard from in a long time; maybe they are undoing the damage they did in Russia or France.

Nothing has changed? Everything has changed. Every day the memory of the dead and the missing unites in silent suffering your wife and yourself. Your sorrow is not eased by any redeeming pride in the cause for which they suffered and died. By now you must know that they died for a lie. They died to make universal a corruption and a debasement far more terrible than the unrestrained savagery of a Genghis Khan. You have seen pictures of the starved and mangled corpses of Buchenwald and Belsen, where the living dead were forced to lie helplessly among the rotting corpses of their comrades. Your sons fought to extend the system that made such horrors possible. And whether you willed it or not, you, too, were a part of that system.

Everything has changed; and your country, which only a little while ago seemed the leader of modern civilization, has become instead the detested symbol of all the forces that are debasing and dehumanizing mankind: the symbol of organized superstition, organized barbarity, organized corruption. You have sunk far lower than you realize: collectively, the crimes you have committed against mankind are so great, the destruction and the bestiality has been pushed so far, that it will take generations, perhaps centuries, to erase from mankind the memory of your vileness. You have only one thing to be thankful for: the fact that you were finally overcome by your enemies.

What will become of your factory? What will become of the industries which Saxon thrift and Saxon stubbornness built up in the course of six centuries: those industries whose advanced technical facilities, so thoroughly described by your Luther's contemporary, Agricola, led the way for the rest of Europe; so that but for your initiative the railway, the water pump, and even air conditioning apparatus would not have played the part they have done. I am not a prophet, dear F., so I will not predict what will happen; my business as a philosopher presents an even more difficult task, to suggest what *should* be done; and here I find myself puzzled over what is both a political and a social problem. Your modest plant in the Erzgebirge is, in fact, a sort of touchstone to the problem.

In a world that could be sure of Germany's good intentions, your industry would survive. You produce the simplest of utensils; you control no patents that might block the industrial efficiency or the military readiness of any other nation; until 1935 you were not part of a national cartel for monopolizing and dominating the markets of neighboring countries; your modest products had a home market that absorbed your entire production and that of one or two other rivals. But

how can the United Nations be sure that the sort of re-arming
that was done after the last war is not carried on once more,
with the aid of just such modest plants, producing peaceful
utensils, as you direct? It was easier to keep track of the
concentrated productivity of the Ruhr district than to keep
an eye on a thousand little plants and workshops scattered
all over Germany; and yet, if your people maintain their
engineering and their scientific skill, if even a fragment of
your General Staff survives in hiding, it is not impossible to
think of your manufacturing parts of a V-3 or a V-4 weapon
in twenty different places, and assembling them in abandoned
mineshafts right under our very noses. Your launching sites
might be hidden in the earth instead of being mounted on a
conspicuous platform. The invention of the atomic bomb does
not lessen this anxiety, but adds to it a thousandfold.

Where there's a will there's a way, as the English proverb
says. If your countrymen still mean war, if they still harbor
thoughts of a third World War which will bring them ultimate
success, even if the rest of the world lies in ruins, then your
innocent workshop should be as completely dismantled as the
chemical factories of Frankfort or the electrical industries
of Berlin. Decentralized industry, with fine tools, electric
motors, and skilled craftsmanship is capable of turning out
far better weapons than the mass manufactures of Detroit: we
both know that! You would have the opportunity to make up
in quality and deadliness for any shortness of quantity; given
a little time indeed, while the world was lulled to sleep by
your apparent pacifism, or at least, your apparent docility,
you might amass a sufficient quantity of weapons for an attack
that would make the rocket bombing of England and Belgium
in the present war seem feeble.

Does this mean that your mining and smelting industries
are doomed, too: that in order to grant the world immunity

from your ever-growing desire for domination, you should be made to equip yourselves with only wooden tools and instruments? I wish the problem were as easy as that; but I am not at all sure that the replacement of steel and aluminum by wood and plastics and glass would be an insurance against war: science now has an armamentarium of materials and processes that might prove equally deadly to any that are now produced in metal. Until the world has had long and well-tried proof of Germany's good intentions, it might be well for the peace of the world to reduce it to an agricultural nation. A great hue and cry went up against this proposal, both in America and in Germany, at the time it was first suggested by an American official; but the opposition was based upon purely economic considerations, including the desire to salvage Germany as a possible market for other countries' trade, or it was based upon the notion that such a fate, that of an agricultural nation, was the equivalent of serfdom; and unbearable.

I wish that these were the only objections that could be brought against this plan, dear F.: if the peace of the world could be achieved only at the price of making Germany an agricultural country, that might be a cheap price to pay for it, and the Potsdam decisions would continue to have every reasonable man's approval. But the people who have broached this solution have not reckoned with the natural results of creating such a regime: namely, that Germany will under these conditions probably have a great increase in its population and it will be increasing its biological strength at a rate disproportionate to its neighbors, whose urban habits of living, whose standards of luxury, whose continued sterility, will—unless corrected—put them in an even more inferior position than they now find themselves. Such a Germany would be more under the control of your feudal magnates than ever; which means also that it would be more primitive in its mentality and more reactionary; for whatever opposition to Germanism existed in the past, came from the radical industrial workers of the big cities, not excluding Berlin. It would be ironic if your conquerors gave such generous support to the doctrine of blood and soil.

No: even if mechanical industry were moved out of Germany into the countries whose industries you have deliberately ruined by wrecking corps, even if Germany became a country of peasant proprietors, living on a subsistence level, the world would not be freed from the nightmare of your military resurrection, planned and executed by your General Staff. With no more facilities for production than might remain in the possession of your dentists and your isolated craftsmen, you would still be dangerous in your present state of mind. You menace your own future by idolizing your past conquests and dreaming of their restoration.

Whatever we do with your industry, whether we dismantle it completely or let you re-establish yourselves in certain branches of manufacture, nothing will suffice to absolve us from the necessity to occupy and inspect, under the authority of the United Nations, every part of your establishment, with the legal rights of search on mere suspicion, and of seizure of contraband. Nothing can make us safe again except a change in your plans and your purposes as a nation. The fate of your industry depends, in the last analysis, upon Germany's capacity for moral regeneration.

When I started to write you this letter and recalled the common interests that brought us together I found myself carried along on a wave of old friendliness: in bringing back those images of the past I also ran the risk of bringing back some of the feelings of self-reproach and even of guilt, that so many Americans and English, indeed, even French people had, when they compared the actual results of the last war with those universal hopes for peace and brotherhood that Woodrow Wilson had voiced for mankind. You profited as a people, during the years of compromise and appeasement that started with the Locarno Pact, by the fact that we attributed to you the same feelings, the same hopes for peace, the same desire to correct the egoisms and partialities of nationalism, as we representatives of the Western powers shared. No country had enjoyed so much unearned good will as Germany did during the twenties and even the thirties. Believe me: I feel no such friendly feelings now.

The most violent hatred of Germany during the first World War was better justified by the facts than the guileless feeling of forbearance and friendship that followed.

Even though I keep your image in front of me, even though I feel your plight as a human being, with a great part of his country in ruins, his family decimated, and his life work broken up, the original wave of friendliness has spent itself. For your own sufferings as a people cannot be put in the same category as the sufferings you inflicted upon Czechoslovakia, upon the Low Countries, upon Norway, France, Yugoslavia, and Greece: countries whose sole offense was that they stood in the way of your plans for aggression. These countries have an account to settle with you. Before you ask for mercy and sympathy, you would do well to show that you understand how little you deserve anything from other men but the strictest justice.

Your countrymen puzzle us, dear F., by their attitude toward both their onetime rulers and toward themselves. They reprove their leaders for having made blunders and errors; so that, because of these failures, they lost the war. Does this mean that you think you deserved to win? Does this mean that you think right was on your side? Does this mean that

you altogether lack any sense of sin and guilt for the crimes
that have been committed by the groups you voted into power
during the 1930's? If that is so with you, this letter is wasted.
You are the victims of a moral paralysis which not only made
your crimes possible but has made their redemption impossible.

The fact is that only one thing will save the German people
from a fate even worse than their present one: the ability to
accept their collective guilt and to meet their victims more
than half-way in an effort to redeem it. Tears will avail you
nothing; self-pity will avail you nothing; protests and threats
will bring you less than nothing. You still have to show that
you are capable of being moved by what you have done to
the rest of the human race and that you are willing to under-
take your own self-castigation and self-correction: not merely
helping to get rid of the more notorious butchers and sadists,
but willingly taking upon your own selves, however remote
and innocent your conduct may seem to yourselves, some part
of the punishment. It is not the Nazis alone who must atone
for their deeds: it is the Germans as a people, the Germans
who accepted their leadership and who fell in with their evil
purposes: the Germans who lacked the moral capacity to per-
ceive this evil or the civil courage to resist it.

There is a story by our American writer, Nathaniel Hawthorne, that portrays the present fate of Germany; you should
ponder it well; for it is a story of a modern Faust who goes
in search of the Unpardonable Sin and in the end finds it.
The story is called Ethan Brand. Brand began life, as Germany began it in the period of the Enlightenment, as a simple,
loving man; but in the course of his search a fatal change
came over him.

He remembered [says Hawthorne] with what tenderness, with
what love and sympathy for mankind, and with what pity for human

guilt and woe, he had first begun to contemplate those ideas which afterwards became the inspiration of his life; with what reverence he had then looked into the heart of man, viewing it as a temple originally divine, and however desecrated, still to be held sacred by a brother; with what awful fear he had deprecated the success of his pursuits and prayed that the Unpardonable Sin might never be revealed to him. Then ensued that vast intellectual development, which, in its progress, disturbed the counterpoise between his mind and heart.

(You and I agreed, dear F., that such a change had taken place in Germany after 1870; with your mass production of those imbecile specialists and bat-eyed technicians about whom Nietzsche had written in Thus Spake Zarathustra: "I have seen human beings to whom everything was lacking except that of one thing they had too much—men who are nothing more than a big eye or a big mouth, or a big belly, or something else big—reversed cripples I name such men." Everywhere these reversed cripples have become the "normal" men of our age; nowhere more so than in Germany. But I must not interrupt Hawthorne: without knowing it, he was prophesying the nature of the Beast in the modern Apocalypse. We Americans, too, have become the victims of these crippled minds.)

. . . So much for the intellect! But where was the heart! That, indeed, had withered,—had contracted,—had hardened,—had perished! It had ceased to partake of the universal throb. He had lost his hold on the magnetic chain of humanity. He was no longer a brother-man, opening the chambers or the dungeons of our common nature by the key of holy sympathy, which gave him a right to share in all its secrets; he was now a cold observer, looking on mankind as the subject of his experiment, and, at length, converting man and woman to be his puppets, and pulling the wires that moved them to such degrees of crime as were demanded for his study.

Thus Ethan Brand became a fiend. He began to be so from the moment that his moral nature had ceased to keep the pace of improvement with his intellect. And now, as his highest effort and inevitable development—as the bright and gorgeous flower, and rich, delicious fruit of his life's labor—he had produced the Unpardonable Sin.

So Ethan Brand takes his farewell of Mother Earth and of the mankind whose brotherhood he had cast off, whose great heart he had trampled beneath his feet, and he casts himself into the flames of his charcoal furnace.

Have your countrymen not lived through Ethan Brand's experience? Did they not lose their hold on the magnetic chain of humanity? Did they not permit political prisoners to be treated like rats in a medical laboratory, without even the anesthesia Western scientists use for their animal experiments; did they not kill unresisting Jews by the million as if they were exterminating vermin? Yes, my friend: you Germans have demonstrated what happens when the moral nature has ceased to keep pace with the improvement of the intellect. You committed the Unpardonable Sin. You cut yourselves off as a people from the standards and values of mankind: for you, whatever was German was good; whatever horror was committed by official command you obeyed—or at least you tolerated. This is what your generation must expiate before we will again clasp your hand and make it, once more, part of the magnetic chain of humanity.

# 5. TO E.A.T., A PROFESSOR
## OF PHILOSOPHY IN MUNICH

. . . It is just twenty years ago, dear Eduard, that we met at the School of International Studies in Geneva. That was your first visit outside Germany since the war; and although you were then almost thirty, there was still a touch of the Wandervogel in you, in the shorts you wore when we went climbing up the Salève, and your open-fronted shirt with flaring collar in the fashion of Schiller and Stefan George. You were one of the new youth, strangely different from my own generation in America: on principle, as well as out of economy, you did not smoke and you drank nothing stronger than lemonade. Our discussions would begin early in the morning, when we assembled at the Conservatoire for the morning's lectures, and sometimes they would go on, with breaks for swimming, for lunch at the Hotel Russie, for student conferences, until late at night.

Those were good days; perhaps they even seemed better at the time than they do now in retrospect; for we all believed that Europe was raising up its battered body out of the morass of war, and when we met at Geneva, it was as if the world were meeting and conversing in our persons, learning the way to peaceful understanding and to self-respecting co-operation. The sunlight of a perfect Geneva summer hung over our meetings; the green water of the lake, as icily refreshing as the North Sea, made our bodies tingle with vitality; and there was a gay sparkle of self-confidence in all the clashes of our minds, concentrated in the persons of the Five Musketeers as we then called ourselves. It seemed impossible that we would fall out of communication with each other as soon as we did.

Jules Matelot, Jules, the brilliant, the witty, product of Oxford and the Collège de France, Jules with his Egyptian-Jewish father and his French mother and his strange mixture of Zionism and Thomism, went the way of his master Bergson; indeed, he anticipated him and became a Dominican monk before five years had passed. Willem Kuypers, that shy and lovable Dutchman, became a member of the Foreign Service and was already near the top of the colonial bureaucracy when the Japanese invaded the Netherland Indies. That dry young Englishman whom we all spontaneously called Sherlock Holmes published a single volume of verse before committing suicide: the last thing any of us would have expected from that level, sensible mind, in the face of any provocation that life might have offered: in his case, the unexpected faithlessness and cynicism of his young wife. Our comradeship was broken up even before Europe's peace was corrupted and shattered: a personal foretaste of what was to come. It is now almost ten years since you wrote to me to explain why you did not propose to take advantage of my offer to help find you a post in an American college, at the same time that you begged me, in guarded language, to confine our correspondence to superficial matters.

I respected both your prudence and your resolution. Not least, your determination to sweat it out in Germany. I knew that this took courage on your part, for by 1935 you could have had no hope that the acquisition of power by the National Socialists and their collaborators would subject their hallucinations and their corrupt fantasies to the correction of your own philosophy, in spite of certain superficial points of contact between your own concept of the organic, which you took over from the biologist Driesch and the philosopher

Othmar Spann, and the parallel conceptions among the more literate followers of Hitler.

You probably kept on giving your lectures in Philosophy without deviating by a hair's breadth from any of your previous convictions: you gave your course on Greek Educational Ideals, your reconciliation of the Spartan and the Athenian, without altering a word of your praise for the belated effort of Demosthenes to restore the old Athenian democracy and bring into an effective political whole these two complementary ideals of life—though even before the National Socialists ruled Germany it had long been an academic heresy of the highest order to side with Demosthenes, rather than with the Bismarckian Philip of Macedon.

It likewise took a certain degree of independence to expound your own philosophy of the organic, and to emphasize the ways in which it differed from the Nazis, by making the National part of an organic whole that included humanity, as well as the ways in which it paralleled their views without accepting their pseudo-science and their nihilistic goals. If it was hard to be a refugee outside Germany, it was perhaps even harder to be a refugee inside Germany. So I respected your decision to stay. But during the years of our silence I sometimes found myself carrying on in my own mind those discussions between us that began in Geneva and recurred during that week I spent in your little villa outside Munich. For you expressed in your own person, in a very lovable fashion, an attitude that I found expressed by the Nazi fanatics in a repulsive fashion; and what you expressed is also something I find in all your representative philosophers from Kant onwards: an error which is often combined with many truths, a radical vice which is surrounded by virtues of the highest order.

What is this attitude? It is the worship of uncontrolled subjectivity. It is the belief, to paraphrase Schopenhauer, that the real world does not exist, apart from its representation in your thought. Subjective idealism is the technical name for this view. It seems like an innocent metaphysical doctrine, and it has certainly been held by many educated people who were not Germans; but in Germany it has percolated through your educational system and filtered into even the vulgarest mind, where it exists in a form so crude that you would naturally reject it: namely, whatever I believe is true, because truth is what I wish to believe; furthermore, as a German, my truth must be essentially different from, and therefore incomparable to, any other form of truth; and this is a mark of my superiority.

Subjective idealism reduces all reality to a communion between the Ego and Its Own. Even Goethe, in his youth at least, succumbed to this disease: one might call it the Werther complex. Once you accept its premises, you are driven to deny the existence of a common world which other men share, and which other men have helped to create. What you call reality is your own inviolable image. Thus you forget the ancient social nature of the very instruments of knowledge you use, the forms of language and the logic of thought, so that you finally attribute to the solitary private ego the whole experience of the human race. The element of truth in this doctrine —and unlike the positivists I do not deny this element—must always be balanced by its opposite, a common sense that binds us to other men, a humility, which accepts the infinite processes and powers that men call God.

Without this common sense and this humility you make it impossible to distinguish between realities and hallucinations, between truths and errors, because both truth and sanity rest upon the ability to co-operate with and understand other men. Always, when one pushes this philosophy of yours back to its ultimate premises, one finds that it is isolationist: to preserve its illusions of absolute truth it must never accept the check of other men's experiences or other men's judgments. Hence that hostility to British empiricism, to French rationalism, to American pragmatism that runs through your thought: you are afraid to be corrected, and to preserve your errors you are willing to cut yourselves off from the rest of the human race and even regard this as a definite mark of your own special virtue.

These are harsh words, dear Eduard, but I used them to your face long ago, and I have no hesitation in repeating the argument now, though it may seem so painful. Your deep tendency toward isolationism accounts for the fact that your countrymen are notoriously inept at understanding the psychology of any other people, and by the same token feel themselves grievously misunderstood by the rest of the world —indeed, believe that they are surrounded by a wall of hostile peoples even when, as in the 1920's, those nations were doing you homage and expressing a really amazing amount of good will.

In this subjectivism, Luther is the main German archetype.* But Oswald Spengler is as good an example as any other, because the very coarseness of his thought brings out, by carica-

---

* But not in his subjectivism alone. Anti-Semitism and tyranny both found an eloquent apologist in this great figure. Witness this passage from his screed "On the Jews and their Lies" (1542): "Beware of the Jews, for this book will show you that God's anger has delivered them over to the devil." To the Jews themselves he addresses these words: "That Bible only should you expose which lies concealed beneath the sow's tail; the letters that drop from it you are free to eat and drink." Here is lewd precedent for Hitler and Streicher. . . . In his discussion, "Whether Soldiers, too, can be saved," Luther says: "We cannot pipe much to the mob. It goes mad too quickly, and it is better to take ten ells from it than to allow to it a hand-breadth, nay a finger's breadth in such a case, and it is better that the tyrants do wrong a hundred times than that they once do wrong to tyrants."

ture, your essential error. By his peculiar interpretation of human cultures, Spengler reveals both aspects of your vice: first, he tries to show that each true culture is a self-contained unit, which possesses nothing belonging to another culture, so that, for him, the human race has no common history and therefore no common destiny; on the contrary, no culture can even understand the categories of thought or the forms of art created by another culture. Then Spengler completes this ingenious theory by writing a two volume interpretation in which the soul and essence of every other culture is, miraculously, revealed to the German mind! He does all this without even a passing smile of self-criticism; and he covers over his contradiction by proclaiming that Faustian culture alone possesses this power of passing into the soul of other cultures.

This profound error in your national philosophy, which arises out of a colossal case of narcissism, or self-admiration, has the effect of cutting the German off from the rest of the human race. For your countrymen what is not German is contemptible. What he cannot stamp with his own image he therefore seeks to destroy. Fichte exhibits this vanity and this arrogance with all the bravado of an adolescent youth; there are passages in his Talks to the German People that leave a non-German simply breathless with astonishment—or laughter. Your hatred of rationalism is not so much hatred for its inherent limitations, as hatred for the bounds which it properly would place upon your capacity for unlimited subjectivism. Rationalism pre-supposes a public world in which the rest of humanity can share: it calls for a public order of the mind like the public order of the democratic state, with its common sense and its common purpose. You refuse, at bottom, to admit that there may be a real world which is different from your German idea of it. You do not like the notion of a truth that is, as it were, a statistical average of a thousand observations by other men, dead, living, and still to be born: a truth not born directly of the German ego. For you, as for Schopenhauer, the subjective is timeless, and the ego, your own ego, the German ego, is the only full and complete source of truth. Only a people who had habitually consulted such a demented Oracle would have listened twice to the words of a Hitler.

With you, dear Eduard, I need hardly insist that philosophy has practical consequences. You would be the first to admit this truth; indeed, you used to boast that without Hegel there could have been no conquering Bismarck. But I would remind you that my interpretation of the latent evils in your national philosophy, the cult of the subjective, is not the result of my reactions to either the first or the second World Wars, for almost precisely a century before Hitler came into power, your exiled poet, Heine, predicted the practical consequences of your common philosophy. At the time, his intuitions seemed more subjective than the subject he was dealing with; but you and I have lived to see Heine's predictions come true: a proof of the depth and accuracy of his insight. Perhaps Heine is no longer on your bookshelves. Hence I take the liberty of quoting him at length. This passage comes from his essay on Religion and Philosophy in Germany; and its original date was 1834.

German philosophy is an important matter, of concern to the whole human race, and only our remotest descendants will be able to decide whether we are to be praised or blamed for having worked out our philosophy first and our revolution afterwards. It seems to me that a methodical nation like ours had to start with the Reformation and could only then take up philosophy, and was not until its completion allowed to pass on to the political revolution. . . . But do not worry, German republicans; the German revolution will not be milder and gentler because it was preceded by Kant's *Critique*, by Fichte's transcendental idealism, and even by the philosophy of nature.

These doctrines have developed revolutionary forces that wait only the day when they can erupt and fill the world with terror and admiration. There will be Kantians forthcoming who will hear nothing of piety in the visible world, either, and with sword and ax will mercilessly churn the soil of our European life, to exterminate the very last roots of the past. Armed Fichteans will enter the lists, whose fanaticism of will can be curbed neither by fear nor by self-interest; for they live in the spirit and defy matter, like the early Christians who were similarly impervious to physical pleasure. In fact, in a social revolution such transcendental idealists would be even more inflexible than the first Christians; for those bore earthly martyrdom in order thereby to attain heavenly bliss, while the transcendental idealist regards the torture itself as an idle delusion and remains inaccessible behind the ramparts of his own thoughts. But the most terrible of all would be natural philosophers taking an active part in a German revolution and identifying themselves with the work of destruction. For if the Kantian's hand strikes strongly and surely because his heart is moved by no traditional respect—if the Fichtean defies all danger because for him it does not really exist—the philosopher of nature will be fearful because he can join the primeval forces of nature, because he can call up the demoniac energies of ancient Germanic pantheism and because then there will awake in him that fighting folly that we find among the ancient Germans, that fights neither to kill nor to conquer, but simply to fight. Christianity has—and that is its fairest merit—somewhat mitigated the brutal German lust for battle. But it could not destroy it; and once the taming talisman, the Cross, is broken, the savagery of the old battlers will flare up again, the insane Berserk rage of which Nordic bards have so much to say and sing. That talisman is brittle. The day will come when it will pitiably collapse. Then the old stone gods will rise from forgotten rubble and rub the dust of a thousand years from their eyes; and Thor will leap up with his giant hammer and start smashing Gothic Cathedrals.*

Yes: we have seen the old stone gods rise up from their forgotten rubble. We have beheld the new gods walking the streets, hammer in hand, breaking the windows of Jewish-owned shops or smashing the fingers of prisoners held for

* In Works of Prose, by Heinrich Heine. Edited by Hermann Kesten. New York: 1943. L. B. Fischer.

questioning. (Even those warrior gods might have recoiled over your treatment of political prisoners and foreign slaves. Your scientific savagery would have caused them to retch.) Heine's terrible predictions have abundantly been confirmed. Within a generation the frenetic Nietzsche had proclaimed the overthrow of Christianity, and in his insanity even conceived himself as the anti-Christ; while within one further generation a whole party, indeed a whole people, turned its back upon two thousand years of Christian civilization, attacking its foundations in Judaism, in order that the structure might be all the more effectually brought to the ground. Were not Heine's long range predictions much closer to reality than the contemporary analyses of the political observers, the diplomats, the economists, before the Nazis came into power?

Heine was correct, my dear Eduard, because he realized that the errors of the subjective idealist were not simply the errors of a system or the aberrations of a few academic minds: he understood that these errors spring from the very roots of German psychology. Your philosophers merely provided a rational basis for your education in collective irrationality; they brought into the open and spread it more widely, so that ordinary men, who took it at fourth or fifth hand, eventually participated in the error, accentuated it and multiplied it. Every nation is subject to the same temptation: I grant that. Every nation tends to worship its own image and to attribute to its own efforts the millennial achievements of the human race as a whole. But universal ideals, like those of Christianity, universal methods, such as those of science, even universal practices, such as those of international commerce, tend to modify these gross examples of national pride and national self-worship.

You guarded against such a weakening of Germanism by undermining the human and the universal. First you attacked

Christianity and rejected its morality of disinterested co-
operation and good will as well as its theology; you even
created a new kind of monster, which you named German
science: a Nobel prize winner like the physicist Lennard
dared to talk gibbering nonsense about German physics, as
opposed to Jewish or even Western physics, just as your quack
anthropologists talked about an Aryan or a German race.
You even created a German god in your own image, whom
you called Hitler; and when your countrymen worshiped him
they worshiped all that was perverse, irrational, and destructive in themselves. Ultimately, dear Eduard, even you yourself had a part in creating this monster: you who used to tell
me, so earnestly and so unctuously, how impossible it was to
convey to an American the meaning of Gemeinschaft and
Brüderschaft in their true German sense. Your benign
dreams, I fear, were composed of the same elemental stuff as
the Nazi's nightmares.

Indeed your own life, seemingly so innocent, so virtuous,
was a prophecy of the days to come. The history of the movement with which, as a youth, you had identified yourself
should cause you some uneasiness and occasion no little critical self-examination. For consider the transformation that
took place in the German youth movement between 1924 and
1934. Who could have been better aware of this than yourself, who attended the original gathering on Hoher Meissner
in 1913, when you were still a student at the Gymnasium,
just sixteen years old. You described to me the torch proces-
sion on Midsummer Eve and the initiation of the naked
youths, by jumping through the fire: you contrasted it, favorably in 1925, with the watery baptism of Christianity. As you
pictured the original youth movement it was a revolt of the
young against their fathers: against the tyranny of the past,
against the stale ideals of the bourgeoisie, against a mealy-

mouthed and hypocritical Christian Church, against all the
customs and institutions that were opposed to what was spontaneous, free and healthy.

What could have seemed, on the face of it, more roman-
tically innocent than this movement? Did it not bring about
a transvaluation of values? Were you not able to escape from
the cities and cast your lot in with the peasant; did you not
sleep in barns, walk along the open road singing your folk
songs? What could seem more opposed in spirit to the cult
of the soldier and the bureaucrat, to the settled life of the
office, the machine, with its drab monotonous prospects and
its defilement of even animal faith and animal joy?

But alas! your belief in the folk was an irrational one: it
bound you to an archaic and ingrown past. The same unfet-
tered youth who repeated the old pagan fire ceremony became
the disciples of the motheaten hero, Ludendorff, he who had
run away like the proverbial rat from a sinking ship when his
armies were being driven back by the Allies. How quickly it
turned out that free German youth and fettered German age
worshiped the same gods! You threw off your commonplace
fathers and embraced—Hitler. What did your people exchange for the discipline of your prisonlike schools? The
Sturmabteilung and the Wehrmacht. What did you exchange
for the theology of the Christian Church? The crude myth of
Wotan, or even worse, the deification of the psychopath,
Hitler. In throwing off bourgeois values, you glorified animal
cruelty along with passion. Were you not disturbed by this
transformation? Did it not make you suspect that your own
revolt was not perhaps quite as healthy and as free as it had
originally seemed to you? German freedom has a queer way
of turning into German servitude, just as German democracy
turns so easily into German despotism. It is time that you
understood the forces in your own past that have made these

changes so commonplace. Surely your intelligence should enable you to free yourselves from this damnable paradox.

If those nightmares are to be banished, you yourself have a part to play in that change: you must admit into the core of your philosophy much that you rejected, because it was non-German. You must ask yourself another question—but a far more important one—*Is it human?* That is a different matter. Beware of your depth; for in the German depths the foulest monsters have been spawned and have flourished in the impenetrable darkness, till they came to light in persecutions and exterminations that have no parallel in the vilest records of the past. Beware of your originality: when you have departed from the human norm, you have not risen above the mediocrity of good and evil, but have sunk below it. Your Nietzsche was an extremely original fellow: he revived the ideal of cruelty and torture, even as he revived the idea of slavery and gave it his intellectual blessing, precisely at the moment that the Russians and the Americans were with great effort overcoming that malign institution. And eventually your Nietzsche gave support to an even more unrestrained originality—that which Himmler practiced in his torture chambers and extermination camps.

*Learn to be commonplace!* my dear Eduard: perhaps the platitudes will save you. You must restore the truth that Schiller rejected in Wallenstein about the "eternal commonplace . . . which will serve tomorrow because it served yesterday." Since you have shown that you don't know how to walk alone without stumbling into the filth, you had better take some older person's hand. That hand is the hand of the human race; its wisdom surpasses the wisdom of any single nation: yes! it even surpasses that of the Germans. Perhaps it is time for your countrymen to remember the prophetic words of Isaiah, who saw even farther than Heine: "Woe unto them that call evil good and good evil; that put darkness for light and light for darkness; that put bitter for sweet and sweet for bitter."

Yes: woe unto them; no matter how often this cheap and easy form of originality is tried, it comes to the same end; and you can see what that end looks like by walking into the center of your own city, once so beautiful. It brings man to destruction and death. This woe that you now see about you was plotted under the shadow of the Frauenkirche, around the tables of the Bratwurstglöcklein, where you and I once had our sausage and beer together. Your task is to undo this evil, which was always visible to you in the threats and promises of the Nazis, but which you hardly suspected as having been rooted also in your own bosom. I know you, dear Eduard, to be a man of courage. You will never be more courageous than when you shatter the mirror in which the German people have worshiped themselves. When you break that mirror your countrymen may, for the first time, be able to see themselves as others see them; that gift for which the Scots poet, Burns, begged. And you will have a compensation for the loss of this mirror. By abandoning the attitude that isolates you from other peoples, you will share their strength, and eventually, when the wounds you have inflicted have healed, you will even share their charity and their brotherhood.

# ENVOY

At the end of the first World War a new religion arose spontaneously in all the countries that had been at war: a religion that expressed a wordless hope that was in all men's hearts, a hope for justice and peace; and the founder of that religion, its one and only symbol, was the Unknown Soldier. His tomb became a shrine: to his namelessness all good men gave their own names. Because the Unknown Soldier had done his duty and suffered and died, so that other sons of men might live, there arose a desire to end forever the institution of war itself, whose dark triumph was to level the victor to the same state as the vanquished. So deep was the hatred for war, so bitter were the memories of war, that democratic governments went to shameful lengths of appeasement and supineness in the face of fascist injustice and violence in order to avoid the ultimate appeal to arms. By trading upon this popular will-to-peace Hitler almost conquered the world. Both sides betrayed the Unknown Soldier. But the Unknown Soldier still remains a symbol of mankind's hope for a better world.

The Unknown German, whom I now address, is a different symbol, but also one of hope. I address him, because he alone will be able to understand the burden of these letters, he alone will be able to restore his country to humanity. Born in the defeat of the German armies, in the wreck and dissolution of the German state, growing up in the midst of ruined cities, often close to starvation, never quite free from want, he will be forced to nourish and hoard his spiritual strength,

311

as no other generation has been forced, if he is to survive at all. So the past that produced these ruins and this misery, will not seem to him so strong and powerful and splendid as it seemed to the contemporaries of Bismarck, of Wilhelm II, of Fritz Ebert, or of Hitler.

When he confronts the deep abysses of hatred and fear and horror that the Nazis have created, this unknown one will ask himself out of what demonic impulses in the German soul were such monsters as the Nazis created; and when he looks honestly at the German past he will find, I think, what I have found; that Nazism is not a weed of sudden growth, but a parasite that has drawn nourishment from the very strength of Germany for the last four hundred years; that its characteristic ideas have not been the exclusive property of madmen, of criminals, of fanatics, of devils, but that they have intertwined themselves around the base and climbed to the very highest branches of German thought; and that it is precisely among those whom the world as well as Germany acknowledges among the great—in a Luther, a Schopenhauer, a Fichte, a Wagner—that the poisons of Nazism are to be found.

Only by a deep re-dedication to life can you redeem your countrymen, my Unknown German. The dark, the barbarous, the unconscious, the primitive, are your constant foes. Germans, more than most other nations, must learn to live by the light of reason and must learn to do nothing that they do not dare to do by daylight, in the full sight of other people's eyes, with the full approval of other men's consciences: for if they trust to their own blind impulses they may again seek to transform the world itself into their extermination camp. Every nation must be constantly on guard against the false sentiments of nationalism, the dangers of self-adulation and self-deception. In that respect, we have all sinned. But you

Germans in particular must doubly beware, because your deepest national roots supply you with a special poison along with the nourishing sap of life.

If you would safeguard yourself from corruption, you must devote yourself for the next hundred years to the non-German, to that which is universal and essentially human. What is vital in your national tradition will not be lost by that effort, any more than what was vital in German poetry was lost by the deep immersion in Shakespeare through which Goethe and Schiller renewed the springs of the drama in Germany. Here is a compass to guide you—directions for your survival:

First, instead of cultivating the national, you will cultivate the regional and the international. You will be a Rhinelander, a Bavarian, a Swabian, a Prussian; and at the other pole, you will be a citizen of the world, making yourself ready, by self-education, for the time when you again will be permitted to travel and even to migrate to other lands, as an equal. You will affirm Friedrich Humboldt and Wilhelm Heinrich Riehl. You will learn from Milton and Locke, from Jefferson and Lincoln, from Mazzini, De Tocqueville, Kropotkin.

Instead of priding yourself on your race and caste, you will blot out these fantasies of Aryan and Germanic purity, and pride yourself on your actual fusing together of many races and strains, on the democratic breaking down of the lines of caste.

Instead of cultivating your apartness and your isolation, you will invite Europe and America and Asia, yes, even Africa, into your own souls, so that you may become more truly human, no longer merely German. *"Sei umschlungen, Millionen!"* Let that cry of Schiller's be yours when you embrace humanity.

Instead of hating the Jews, you will redeem yourself by

love and good works on their behalf. Take upon yourselves as an immediate, most imperative duty the succor and help of those who escaped your extermination camps. Thus you will extirpate the very memory of Hitler. To combat the hardness of heart which made your other sins possible, you will cultivate, as never before, the Christian virtues of love and pity.

Instead of arming yourself for war and seeking death, you will cultivate life and learn from those who celebrate the goods of life: you will seek Bergson rather than Schopenhauer, Emerson rather than Nietzsche, Goethe rather than Spengler, Jesus rather than your gods of battle. In your education, you will cease to produce "reversed cripples" and will create whole men, who will neither submit to iron regimentation nor be tempted to impose it on anyone else.

Finally, instead of asking for the world to accept you as you are, quickly forgetting what you were and forgiving what you did, you will show a capacity for self-transformation which will make such pleas unnecessary. Your own self-accusations, your own remorse and your own repentance, will alone bring about a lightening of your punishment; and without this change of heart you will not discover the road to life.

There lies your task. No one else can perform it for you. There lies your duty and your destiny; and there, at the very end of the road, lies your freedom.